T0311806

Scholars for years have tried to untangle the gnarly Gordian Knot of business profit and human values. In this remarkable book, Georges Enderle wields a powerful axe balanced by human rights and wealth creation in order to cut the knot. His ingenious interpretation of "wealth creation" is one of the book's striking achievements. Other scholars have toyed with mixing wealth creation and values, but none has achieved Enderle's level of sophistication.
Thomas Donaldson, The Mark O. Winkelman Endowed Professor, The Wharton School, University of Pennsylvania

Enderle challenges corporations to put respecting and remedying human rights in the front and center of corporate responsibility along with creating wealth in a comprehensive sense. By providing an expanded definition of wealth to include natural, human and social capital in addition to economic capital, Enderle meticulously explains how corporate responsibility contributes further to the common good by producing both private and public goods. The book gives a comprehensive, nuanced, occasionally surprising and at the end a convincing analysis that the purpose of corporations goes beyond meeting the needs of shareholders and stakeholders. I recommend it to anyone who seeks a comprehensive understanding of corporate responsibility in this pluralistic and globally connected world where humanity's existence is under threat. Business leaders, students and scholars will find nuggets of wisdom throughout the book. It provides not only food for thought for the curious-minded but actional ideas to business leaders who aspire to contribute to a just and sustainable world for both now and future generations.
Anne S. Tsui, Motorola Professor Emerita of International Management, Arizona State University

Finally – the book we have all been waiting for. Professor Enderle has moved the field of business ethics exponentially forward by pushing our thinking beyond wealth creation to imagining commerce as a global interconnected phenomenon that takes into account extensive human and organizational value creation. He then links the globalization of commerce to a rights-based framework that Enderle summarizes as "corporate responsibility for creating wealth and respecting human rights." In the twenty-first century dialogue this book brings together both the globalization of commerce and its ethical challenges in a refreshing innovative manner that will change the conversation in business ethics profoundly.
Patricia Werhane, Professor Emerita, Darden School of Business

Corporate Responsibility for Wealth Creation and Human Rights

Georges Enderle proposes a radically new understanding of corporate responsibility in the global and pluralistic context. This book introduces a framework that integrates the ideas of wealth creation and human rights, which is illustrated by multiple corporate examples, and provides a sharp critique of the maximizing shareholder value ideology. By defining the purpose of business enterprises as creating wealth in a comprehensive sense, encompassing natural, economic, human and social capital while respecting human rights, Enderle draws attention to the fundamental importance of public wealth, without which private wealth cannot be created. This framework further identifies the limitations of the market institution and self-regarding motivations by demonstrating that the creation of public wealth requires collective actors and other-regarding motivations. In line with the UN Guiding Principles on Business and Human Rights, this book provides clear ethical guidance for businesses around the world and a strong voice against human right violations, especially in repressive and authoritarian regimes and populist and discriminatory environments.

Georges Enderle is the John T. Ryan Jr. Professor Emeritus of International Business Ethics at the Mendoza College of Business, University of Notre Dame (Indiana, USA). He is also co-founder of the European Business Ethics Network (EBEN) and former president of the International Society of Business, Economics, and Ethics (ISBEE; 2001–04). Professor Enderle has previously authored or edited 21 books and over 160 articles.

Corporate Responsibility for Wealth Creation and Human Rights

GEORGES ENDERLE
University of Notre Dame

CAMBRIDGE
UNIVERSITY PRESS

Shaftesbury Road, Cambridge CB2 8EA, United Kingdom

One Liberty Plaza, 20th Floor, New York, NY 10006, USA

477 Williamstown Road, Port Melbourne, VIC 3207, Australia

314–321, 3rd Floor, Plot 3, Splendor Forum, Jasola District Centre, New Delhi – 110025, India

103 Penang Road, #05–06/07, Visioncrest Commercial, Singapore 238467

Cambridge University Press is part of Cambridge University Press & Assessment, a department of the University of Cambridge.

We share the University's mission to contribute to society through the pursuit of education, learning and research at the highest international levels of excellence.

www.cambridge.org
Information on this title: www.cambridge.org/9781108823364

DOI: 10.1017/9781108913966

First published 2021
First paperback edition 2023

A catalogue record for this publication is available from the British Library

Library of Congress Cataloging-in-Publication data
Names: Enderle, Georges, author.
Title: Corporate responsibility for wealth creation and human rights / Georges Enderle, University of Notre Dame, Indiana, USA.
Description: 1 Edition. | New York : Cambridge University Press, 2021. | Includes bibliographical references and index.
Identifiers: LCCN 2020022983 (print) | LCCN 2020022984 (ebook) | ISBN 9781108830805 (hardback) | ISBN 9781108823364 (paperback) | ISBN 9781108913966 (epub)
Subjects: LCSH: Social responsibility of business. | Wealth–Moral and ethical aspects. | Globalization–Moral and ethical aspects. | Human rights.
Classification: LCC HD60 .E5583 2020 (print) | LCC HD60 (ebook) | DDC 174/.4–dc23
LC record available at https://lccn.loc.gov/2020022983
LC ebook record available at https://lccn.loc.gov/2020022984

ISBN   978-1-108-83080-5   Hardback
ISBN   978-1-108-82336-4   Paperback

Dedicated to the colleagues and friends in the International Society for Business, Economics, and Ethics (ISBEE)

Contents

Figures, Tables and Boxes

Preface

This book has been in the making for many years. In a way it began in 1970 when I travelled, with two friends, by car from Europe to India, around the subcontinent and back to Europe. It was a life-changing experience to discover people struggling for survival in a developing country. So I decided to complement my studies in philosophy and theology with a Ph.D. in economics on income inequality (Enderle 1982). This led to a Dr. habil. (a second Ph.D.) in business ethics on poverty in Switzerland and the human right to a decent livelihood to be incorporated in the Swiss Constitution (Enderle 1987). Inspired by *A Theology of Liberation* (Gutiérrez 1988) and Amartya Sen's work (Sen 1981, 1999), I discovered how poverty research can open up a wide range of perspectives that are also of great relevance to business and economic ethics in general; for example, a problem-oriented methodology, a focus on human capabilities and awareness of ethical implications in economics (Enderle 1989, 2014a). However, at that time I did not realize the importance of the creation of wealth.

Seven years after my habilitation (completed in 1987), I started doing research and teaching in China. I heard the slogan "to be rich is glorious" – a famous saying attributed to Deng Xiaoping in the mid-1980s (see Enderle 2009, notes 1 and 2). It marked a radical change of attitude toward wealth and prosperity, one that came to constitute a core value of the moral foundation for China's economic reform and open-door policy. It has been embraced by millions and millions of Chinese and proved, overall, to be quite successful. Since 1994, I personally have been fortunate to observe and study the remarkable economic development in China and, particularly in Shanghai, to seek possible lessons applicable to other parts of the globe and to reconsider my own views with regard to poverty and wealth and business' responsibility. I began to understand how important a proper concept of and a determined focus on wealth creation are in order to address the issues of poverty and inequality of income and wealth. Furthermore,

I learned that these vital problems cannot be dealt with in a purely technical and value-free manner. Ethics matters, and human rights provide a common ethical ground for creating wealth in the global and pluralistic context.

I invite the reader to have a fresh look at wealth creation as the purpose of the economy and business enterprises and to consider the thirty internationally recognized human rights (see Chapter 11) as the common ethical ground needed for businesses operating in this global and pluralistic environment. In my view, this vision of "a joint responsibility for both wealth creation and human rights" is attractive and persuasive. It can be designed in clear and measurable terms and is well-founded from both the economic and ethical perspectives. I use numerous positive and negative corporate examples to illustrate the relevance and feasibility of this vision. Of course, the commitment of business people and enterprises is needed, civil society organizations have to watch and fight for its implementation, fair and effective institutions and regulations must support these efforts and much more is required.

In developing this vision and presenting it in this book, I have travelled a long, arduous but interesting route, documented in multiple books, book chapters and articles I published along the way. These works are referenced throughout the book and listed in the Bibliography.

On this journey I got much inspiration, encouraging support, constructive critique and farsighted advice from many friends and colleagues. My special thanks go to Professors Richard De George, Geert Demuijnck, Thomas Donaldson, Amitava Dutt, Patrick Murphy, Carolina Olarte Bácares, Michael Santoro and Anne Tsui, who read and commented on parts of the manuscript. I am also grateful to two anonymous reviewers of Cambridge University Press for critical and helpful comments and suggestions. Finally, I would like to acknowledge Tracey Thomas for critically reading the entire manuscript and making it more fluent and understandable.

In gratitude and hope, I dedicate this book to ISBEE, the International Society of Business, Economics and Ethics.

Acknowledgments

Chapter 19 is derived from the article: Georges Enderle (2018), "Corporate responsibility for less income inequality," *Review of Social Economy* 76 (4), 399–421, DOI: 10.1080/00346764.2018.1525761.

Chapter 20 is derived from the chapter: Georges Enderle (2019), "How can universities promote corporate responsibility in their supply chains? The experience of the University of Notre Dame," in J. B. Ciulla and T. Scharding (eds.) *Ethical Business Leadership in Troubling Times*. Cheltenham: Edward Elgar, 159–88.

1 | *Introduction and Overview*

In this book I argue for a radically[1] new understanding of the ethics of business enterprises or "corporate responsibility" in the global and pluralistic context. This perspective is new in combining three crucial respects. First, business enterprises as primarily economic entities are called to pursue the creation of wealth in a comprehensive sense that is beyond maximizing profit or adding value. Second, business enterprises operate in an increasingly interconnected world. They consist of human beings and affect human beings from the local to the global level. To evaluate their impact, we have worldwide standards stipulated in international agreements: the human rights including civil, political, economic, social and cultural rights and the right to development. With the United Nations Framework (UN 2008a) and the United Nations Guiding Principles on Business and Human Rights (UN 2011), business enterprises – in addition to states – have become accountable in a new way for their impact on human rights. Third, in this interconnected world not only individual business people but also business enterprises as organizations[2]– independent of the duties of states – now carry moral obligations regarding human rights. This means that moral (and not only legal) obligations are attributed to organizations understood as moral actors (but not as moral persons). Based on this theoretical underpinning, moral responsibility can be attributed to corporations in a genuine sense.

In this new approach, the ethics of business enterprises can be summarized as "corporate responsibility for creating wealth and respecting human rights." Creating wealth is conceived in a comprehensive sense with seven features. Moreover, it relates to all internationally recognized human rights. Before explicating this new understanding, I will outline the broader context in which the ethics of business enterprises should be situated today. It is characterized by three key terms: globalization, sustainability and financialization (see Chapter 2). As globalization is a main feature of our situation on the

1

planet Earth today, sustainability proposes to us the direction in which we ought to move and financialization indicates a profound and challenging transformation of the economy with far-reaching consequences for society. All three perspectives underline the need for a new understanding of corporate responsibility that calls for an extensive variety of innovation at multiple levels.

"Corporate responsibility for creating wealth and respecting human rights" will be developed and explained in three parts. In Part I, I take a macro-perspective, applicable nationally and internationally, on the economy that is the primary interface between "business" and "society." This economic approach is an "ethics-related approach" in the sense proposed by Amartya Sen (1987), which is broader than a "value-free" logistical (or "engineering") approach, by including human motivation and the judgment of social achievements. It goes beyond the "creation of wealth" – in line with and beyond Adam Smith – by offering a broad and comprehensive definition of wealth and by revealing many dysfunctional features of the current economy. In Part II, I switch to a normative-ethical perspective by identifying internationally recognized human rights as minimal ethical standards. Given the globalizing economy, universal minimal ethical standards are indispensable for living and working together on Earth. They are conceived as global "public goods," using the precise term developed in the first step. Although human rights are being violated in multiple ways, they are the only worldwide recognized standards and, in addition, provide space for a large diversity of acceptable ethical and cultural values. After arguing for wealth creation in a comprehensive sense and the relevance of human rights as global public goods, in Part III, I draw the implications of this broad view for corporate responsibility that pertains to all types of business enterprises worldwide. As primarily economic organizations, business enterprises are held responsible for creating wealth that includes seven features. And, consisting of and affecting human beings, businesses have to respect all human rights and, when faced with human rights violations, remedy them.

Seven Features of Wealth Creation

Part I presents and explains a comprehensive conception of wealth creation that includes seven features. This stands in stark contrast to

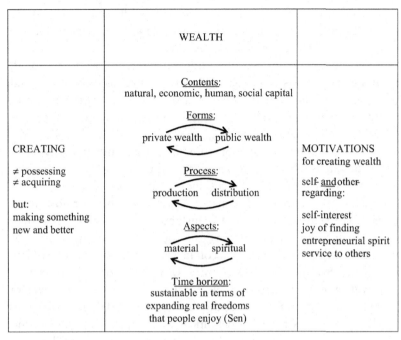

Figure 1.1 Wealth creation – a rich conception

the dysfunctional aspects of national and international economies. Anglo-American capitalism, with its far-reaching impact on the global economy, focuses heavily, if not exclusively, on the accumulation of financial wealth. As well articulated in the Encyclical *On Care for Our Common Home* by Pope Francis (2015), the dictates of maximizing shareholder value recklessly destroy the natural environment. Widespread corruption and bribery impair the economies of many countries. People still suffer from extensive illiteracy and the lack of appropriate training. They get sick and die from unhealthy working conditions, air and water pollution and other deleterious conditions and the lack of decent health care. Trust in the financial services industry and in consumer relations with banks has been seriously undermined and hampered. All these problems indicate the loss of natural capital, economic capital, human capital and social capital. Therefore, the comprehensive conception of wealth creation includes, as a first feature, all four types of capital, which form the substantive contents of wealth (see Chapter 4). Figure 1.1 provides an overview of this rich conception of wealth creation: the middle column shows the first five features, the left column indicates the sixth feature and the right column refers to the seventh feature.

A second feature of wealth proposes different forms of capital, meaning formal as distinct from substantive aspects of capital (Chapter 5). It can be best understood when we look at the wealth of a nation. National wealth is not just an accumulation of private wealth, but also consists, in large part, of public wealth. Thus the wealth of a nation is a combination of private and public wealth. While private wealth is easily perceived and understood, public wealth is harder to discern and is often ignored, although it is essential for producing private wealth. For instance, we may remember how in the Great Recession in 2008–09, the instability of the financial system seriously hurt the global economy and societies around the world. Or we recall the positive impact of a country's fair and effective rule of law on foreigners to invest in this country. Using the economic distinction of private and public goods, public wealth differs from private wealth by the characteristics of non-rivalry and non-excludability. It is note-worthy that this is a formal definition which applies to "good" and "bad" public goods and to wealth and the lack thereof, and therefore needs ethical evaluation (as, for example, climate change does). Wealth in a comprehensive sense includes both private and public wealth, which has far-reaching implications. Markets are powerful for produc-ing private wealth, but fail to generate public wealth, and motivations for public wealth need to be other-regarding, not only self-regarding.

Wealth creation is often conceived as a productive process that is separate from subsequent distribution, according to the saying that one has to bake the cake first before it can be shared. The third feature of wealth creation rejects this separation of production and distribution and claims that the productive and the distributive dimensions of wealth creation are intrinsically interrelated. In fact, the distributive dimension permeates all stages of production from the preconditions to the generation process, the outcome and the use for and allocation within consumption and investment. For too long, the separation between "producing the pie" and "sharing the pie" has marked the ideological struggle between "the right" and "the left," despite its flawed economic underpinning. Therefore, wealth creation is about wealth distribution as much as about wealth production (see Chapter 6).

The fourth feature of wealth creation rejects a materialistic understanding of wealth that is excessively concerned with material possessions and making money, driven by consumerism, acquisitiveness and greed. Such a materialistic view is too narrow, if wealth consists not only of economic capital, but also of human, social and natural capital. It also cannot consider and account for other features of wealth creation to be introduced below: human capital conceived in terms of human capabilities of being healthy and educated persons; creating wealth understood as making something new and better; and other-regarding motivations for creating public wealth. While this proposed concept of wealth undoubtedly has a material aspect, it also includes a spiritual aspect by relating to the human spirit or soul (regardless of religious beliefs) and/or to religion and religious belief (Chapter 7).

Creating sustainable wealth accounts for the long-term time horizon conceptualized in terms of human capabilities or "expanding real freedoms that people enjoy" (Sen 1999) – the fifth feature of wealth creation. Given the multitude of definitions of sustainability, I stick to the "old" proposition from the World Commission on Environment and Development which requires an intergenerational perspective, namely "to meet the needs of the present without compromising the ability of future generations to meet their own needs" (WCED 1987, 7). I further specify this perspective by using the Organisation for Economic Co-operation and Development (OECD's) definition of sustainability of well-being over time in terms of natural, economic, human and social capital (OECD 2013a), which is congruous with the contents of wealth as defined in this book. This perspective of human capability not only substantiates the meaning of human capital; it also helps to measure the impact of natural, economic and social capital on human beings. Thus, creating sustainable wealth becomes a rich and concise purpose of economic life which transcends the growth of (material) resources by focusing on people and sustaining nature (Chapter 8).

The sixth feature specifies what we mean by the "creation" of wealth. Obviously, wealth creation is more than possessing wealth and differs from acquiring wealth. Possessing adds no value and acquiring only means a change of ownership, which may occur by legal or illegal and ethical or unethical means. In the course of history, colonial powers acquired a great deal of wealth, usually with no regard for legal and ethical concerns, which, by and large, amounted to a redistribution rather than a creation of wealth. In the capitalistic system, the "acquisitive spirit," "the accumulation of capital," and the "acquisition of companies" do not entail necessarily the creation of wealth, properly speaking. In a genuine sense, to create is to make something new and better. All three characteristics are essential: (a) It is about making, not only imagining, which is feasible and successful in economic and financial terms. (b) It has to be new, be it a gradual change or an innovation (that is, a radical change in technology, social organization or any other field). And (c) it must be ethical, which improves the well-being of people and sustains nature (Chapter 9).

Finally, concerning the motivations for creating wealth, self-regarding motivations can be powerful for creating private wealth. But they fail in creating public wealth, as sound economic theory tells us. Exclusively self-interested behaviors make collective action (for public wealth) impossible, generate free-rider problems and cannot be coordinated by an "invisible hand." Rather, when economic activities clearly focus on the creation of wealth as a combination of private and public wealth, other-regarding motivations are equally necessary (though not sufficient). They may take a huge variety of forms such as selfless engagement for entrepreneurial success, love for the mother country, solidarity with the poor and the fight for any cause. In each case the other-regarding motivation transcends self-interest, be it for a good or for a bad cause. Still, like public goods or wealth, other-regarding motivations require ethical evaluation. To sum up the seventh feature, wealth creation needs not only self-regarding but also other-regarding motivations (Chapter 10).

In developing the seven features of wealth creation as an "ethics-related" approach to economics, wealth creation turns out to be not only compatible but also relatable to normative-ethical demands. This macro-economic approach pertains to the entire economy, nationally and internationally, including, but not limited, to business. It is not a "value-free" or "engineering" approach which limits itself to the logistics of end-means relations. Rather, it contains numerous connecting features to ethical demands. Four types of capital provide the relevant contents of wealth and two forms of wealth (public and private) require different institutions and motivations. Social achievements involve material and spiritual aspects and are captured in terms of sustainable human capabilities. Two kinds of motivations – other-regarding as well as self-regarding – are necessary for wealth creation, and ethical evaluation is indispensable to identify good vs. bad public wealth, making something not only new but better, and distinguishing good from bad other-regarding motivations.

Human Rights as Public Goods in Wealth Creation

As indicated at the beginning of this chapter, to develop a rich and differentiated concept of wealth creation is the first step in elaborating an ethics of business enterprises or corporate responsibility. In addition to this descriptive-analytical dimension, we investigate, in a second step, the normative-ethical dimension in order to establish, in a third step, a balanced concept of corporate responsibility that "walks on two legs," including a descriptive-analytical as well as a normative-ethical side.

I propose to define the normative-ethical dimension in terms of human rights particularly for three reasons (see Part II, Introduction). In the process of globalization, economies and businesses have expanded far beyond national borders and have increasingly been connected internationally in multiple ways. With this expansion comes a growing need for universal normative standards, not only for countries but for businesses and economies as well. Since the Universal Declaration of Human Rights in 1948 the ethical framework of human rights has developed to a widely accepted, though not undisputed, universal ethical framework. Although violated in countless instances around the world, it has no comparable alternatives. Moreover, in the new millennium, the global concern for business and human rights has strengthened considerably. The United Nations Global Compact (UNGC 2000) calls on business to play an active role to help address worldwide challenges, including human and labor rights. The United Nations Framework (UN 2008a) and Guiding Principles on Business and Human Rights (UN 2011) declare all human rights relevant for business: civil, political, economic, social and cultural rights, including the right to development. And the Sustainable Development Goals (SDGs 2015) are shaped, to a large extent, by human rights demands.

In order to relate human rights to wealth creation in a comprehensive sense, we may begin with clarifying four important components of the underlying human rights conception: (1) the scope, (2) the binding nature, (3) the function and (4) the qualification of human rights as public goods, discussed in Chapters 11–14.

First, in common talks about human rights the scope is often limited to civil and political rights (such as the right to freedom of thought, conscience and religion and the right to freedom of association) or to economic, social and cultural rights (such as the right to health and the right to an adequate standard of living) and, furthermore, often excludes certain groups of people.

Easily overlooked is the powerful idea that people have a right to be treated with dignity in all spheres of life and regardless of their nationality, place of residence, sex, national or ethnic origin, color, religion, language or any other status. It matters therefore to emphasize that the International Bill of Rights and the International Labor Organization's core conventions contain all these rights without discrimination. They apply globally and define the underlying conception of human rights in this book (see Chapter 11).

Second, given the wide range of human rights, one might think this term "human rights" would encompass all ethical norms and values relevant for economies and businesses. However, it commonly constitutes only minimal ethical requirements, distinct from social obligations beyond the minimum and aspirations for ethical ideals (De George 1993, 184–93). In pluralistic societies, nationally and internationally, human rights constitute the necessary common ethical ground for living and working together and are "the minimum reference point for what the Guiding Principles [on Business and Human Rights] describe as internationally recognized rights" (UN 2012a, 10). As minimal requirements, however, they can open and guarantee a wide space for an immense diversity of cultural and ethical values and norms. Grounded in human dignity and specifying its basic contents, they are all interrelated, interdependent and indivisible and thus do not allow for trade-offs between particular rights. This stipulated conception of human rights draws on philosophical reflections and supports – but is not identical to – the legal conception incorporated in the International Bill of Rights and the International Labor Organization's core conventions. It goes without saying that to date this universal ethical conception is not legally enforceable internationally; however, it provides guidance for voluntary action and soft law agreements, which may become legal requirements later on (see Chapter 12).

Third, from an economic perspective the fulfillment of human rights (for example, the rights to health and to an adequate standard of living) has often been considered a cost that might be too expensive to bear. On the other hand, the violation of human rights can be also very damaging. Undoubtedly, it is legitimate to ask the question of what costs human rights fulfillments and violations may incur. But a serious cost analysis has to account for all costs, in financial and non-financial terms, imposed on all affected people and entities. Moreover, not only costs, but also benefits should be accounted for, again in their entirety and in their distributional impact. Though not easy to conduct, one may argue that such comprehensive cost-benefit analyses of human rights would likely show beneficial results. Beyond cost-benefit analysis, human rights may be recognized as external constraints or boundaries which should not be crossed. While such recognition is commendable from the human rights perspective, it still can be interpreted as an engineering approach to economics that stipulates a value-free economic calculus of ends and means within these constraints. In contrast, the ethics-related approach in this book proposes the fulfillment of human rights as ends to be achieved by public policies and corporate strategies whereas violations signify failing policies and strategies. Moreover, human rights are also understood as means to pursue these and other ends. For example, the implemented right to education is instrumental and a strong way for creating an innovative and more productive work force (see Chapter 13).

Fourth, in order to link human rights to wealth creation, we define these rights as ethically demanded public goods or public wealth. As public goods, they are characterized by non-excludability and non-rivalry, needing ethical qualification, that is to be ethically demanded. Applied to human rights, non-excludability means that no human being *should* be excluded from the enjoyment of any human right (that is no discrimination). Non-rivalry implies that the enjoyment of any human right by any person *should not* diminish the enjoyment of any other human right by oneself or any other person. In other words, no trade-offs between human rights for anybody are acceptable. For example, the right to participate in public life should not impair the right to freedom of thought, conscience and religion, nor vice versa; or the freedom of association should not negatively affect the right to non-discrimination, nor vice versa. Beyond the exclusion of any negative impact, one can argue that the enjoyment of one right *may even reinforce* the enjoyment of another right. For instance, the implemented right to an adequate standard of living (including food, clothing and housing) can strengthen the fulfillment of the rights to work and education, and vice versa (see Chapters 14 and 18).

The definition of human rights as ethically demanded public goods, obviously, has far-reaching implications. Their establishment and fulfillment cannot be achieved by market institutions; rather, they need collective actions at multiple levels of society beyond the price mechanism of supply and demand. Moreover, the motivations must be other-regarding because self-regarding motivations would fail to fulfill human rights as public goods.

Implications for Corporate Responsibility

Having outlined – in Parts I and II – the purpose of the economy as creating wealth in a comprehensive sense within the normative-ethical framework of human rights, I then apply – in Part III – this broad conception to the ethics of business enterprises. Since the early 1980s, a variety of terms have been used in English and other languages to express what the ethics of business firms may mean: business ethics (in a narrow sense), corporate ethics, corporate citizenship, corporate social responsibility (CSR), called in Romance languages *éthique de l'entreprise*, *etica degli affari* and *ética de los negocios*, in German *Unternehmensethik* and in Chinese *qiye lunli*, *qiye shehui zeren* and *shangye lunli*. In this book I propose the term "corporate responsibility." Widely used in theory and practice, it points to a key and complex feature of morality and ethics, is easily translatable into other languages and figures prominently in the UN Framework and UN Guiding Principles on Business and Human Rights ("corporate responsibility" as distinct from the "duty of the state").

In Chapter 15, drawing on work of the German philosopher Walter Schulz, I define responsibility as "self-commitment originating from freedom in worldly relationships" (Schulz 1972). It contains a bi-polarity full of tension. On the one hand, the inner pole emphasizes the relevance of inner decisions. On the other hand, self-commitment out of freedom has its point of departure and its point of destination in worldly relationships (that is, the outer pole). Responsibility as a relational concept is always "anchored" in one or more actors (*who* is responsible?), concerns a concrete matter of *for what* one is responsible and relates to an authority or addressee[3] *to whom* one is responsible (for example, stakeholders, tribunal, spouse or one's conscience).

This tripartite concept helps to clearly identify the essential components of responsibility. First of all, responsibility is not a free-standing ethical principle (like "Do not harm!"), but must be related to an actor. As actors, we include – as do the UN Guiding Principles – all business enterprises ranging from gigantic global corporations and large publicly listed companies to limited liability companies, state-owned enterprises, family businesses, medium, small and micro enterprises. The world of business is immense. The enterprises not only pursue an enormous variety of activities; they also show extreme differences in size, structure, legal form and corporate strategies. Hence the question: Does it make sense – and if so, how – to expect enterprises to be ethically responsible actors and to speak of corporate responsibility in an authentic sense?

The question has been debated for decades and will be discussed in Chapter 16. I propose to use James Coleman's sociological definition of actors, that is, to have "control over resources and events, interests in resources and events, and the capability of taking actions to realize those interests through that control" (Coleman 1990, 542). These essential properties call for responsible action and can be attributed to corporate as well as personal actors. In the first case, large, well-structured and powerful business enterprises are conceived as corporate actors that differ from many economic definitions of firms such as production functions, nexuses of contracts, pieces of property or economic mechanisms. Corporate actors can take the forms of communities of people, agents, providers of goods and services or as corporate citizens, that is of collective entities with a primarily (though not exclusively) economic purpose. In contrast, when enterprises lack relatively free-standing formal structures – as micro, small and medium enterprises commonly do – they are not corporate actors, properly speaking, but basically shaped by personal actors such as individual business leaders.

Understanding business enterprises with relatively free-standing formal structures as corporate actors, I ask for their moral status. On the one hand, they are not moral persons who have a conscience and are ends in themselves. On the other hand, they are not amoral actors without the capability of taking actions. Hence we may define them as moral actors in an analogous sense to moral persons: They form collective entities that are distinct but not separated from individual members, having certain spaces of freedom, acting with intention (or at least exhibiting intentional behavior) to achieve their goals and impacting people and nature. As moral actors, they bear "corporate responsibility" and can be held responsible for their conduct in an ethical sense. They qualify as actors at the meso-level of action – as distinct from the macro (or systemic) and the micro (or individual) level. If, however, enterprises (of smaller size) are not corporate actors and hence not moral actors, corporate responsibility pertains to individual persons and groups (that is, at the micro level) who carry this responsibility.

The second component of responsibility concerns its contents or "to be responsible for *what*," discussed in Chapter 17. It draws from the macro-perspective developed as wealth creation and human rights and applies to business enterprises in a specific sense. Responsibility for wealth creation pertains primarily to the core activities of the enterprise, while responsibility for human rights consists of "respecting" human rights and "remedying" violations as defined by the UN Guiding Principles on Business and Human Rights (UN 2011).

All seven features of wealth creation matter for corporate responsibility. Regarding the contents of wealth (that is natural, economic, human and social capital), each enterprise has its special focus and must meet at least a minimal level of each capital. For example, increases of economic capital cannot be compensated for by losses of natural capital beneath the minimum. In other words, trade-offs between changes of capital are acceptable only above these minimums (the definitions of which will be discussed in Chapter 18). As for the forms of wealth, enterprises are supposed to create private wealth. However, benefiting from public wealth in many ways, they also should "give back" and contribute to the creation of public wealth, which can occur in multiple fashions and to various extents. As the generation of wealth is assumed to be an interrelated productive and distributive process, enterprises are accountable not only for their production but also for their interrelated distribution – for example, for income inequality in their organizations. Because wealth creation includes not only material but also spiritual aspects, the culture of enterprises should not be dominated by money making and greed. Rather, through creating natural, economic, human and social capital, wealth creation aims at a noble goal that addresses both material and spiritual needs of employees, customers and other stakeholders. Sustainable enterprises adopt a long-term perspective by focusing on strengthening human capabilities – not merely material resources – and sustaining the natural environment. As creating means "making new and better," enterprises strive for both gradual changes and ground-breaking innovations while considering the ethical implications and respecting the ethical demands, being well aware that innovation by itself can be ethically praiseworthy or repugnant. Finally, the driving motivation of enterprises cannot be exclusively self-regarding because they have to help create public wealth. Other-regarding motivations are required, for public wealth and for human rights.

To further explore the contents of corporate responsibility, we draw on the widely accepted universal ethical framework of human rights and apply, with an ethical underpinning, the UN Framework and UN Guiding Principles on Business and Human Rights. In line with Henry Shue (1996, 35–64), the UN Framework distinguishes three types of obligations to secure human rights: "To protect, to respect and to remedy." To protect human rights – the duty of states – means to demand recognition of the obligation to avoid violations of human rights and to establish "institutional" provisions that prevent, as much as possible, the violation of this obligation through appropriate incentive and punishment systems. To respect human rights – the responsibility of business enterprises – indicates the obligation to avoid violations of human rights. And to remedy – the obligation of both states and enterprises – refers to the obligation to provide the victims of human rights violations access to the remedy of their rights. In other words, "corporate responsibility" is clearly identified with, and limited to, "respect" and "remedy" without including the states' duty to "protect."

What "respect" and "remedy" mean for corporate responsibility is explicated in five foundational principles (FP; see Table 1.1) and eleven operational principles (UN 2012a). These (principles) state that [business enterprises] "should avoid infringing on the human rights of others and should address adverse human rights impacts with which they are involved" (FP #11). The set of human rights includes all human rights, civil, political, economic, social and cultural rights, including the right to development – "understood, at a minimum, as those expressed in the International Bill of Rights, and the principles concerning fundamental rights set out in the International Labour Organization's Declaration on Fundamental Principles and Rights at Work" (FP #12). Foundational Principle #13 explains the responsibility of enterprises for their direct adverse impact on human rights,

Table 1.1 *Foundational principles on business and human rights (UN 2012a)*

#11	Business enterprises should respect human rights. This means that they should avoid infringing on the human rights of others and should address adverse human rights impacts with which they are involved.
#12	The responsibility of business enterprises to respect human rights refers to internationally recognized human rights – understood, at a minimum, as those expressed in the International Bill of Human Rights and the principles concerning fundamental rights set out in the International Labour Organization's Declaration on Fundamental Principles and Rights at Work.
#13	The responsibility to respect human rights requires that business enterprises: (a) Avoid causing or contributing to adverse human rights impacts through their own activities, and address such impacts when they occur; (b) Seek to prevent or mitigate adverse human rights impacts that are directly linked to their operations, products or services by their business relationships, even if they have not contributed to those impacts.
#14	The responsibility of business enterprises to respect human rights applies to all enterprises regardless of their size, sector, operational context, ownership and structure. Nevertheless, the scale and complexity of the means through which enterprises meet that responsibility may vary according to these factors and with the severity of the enterprise's adverse human rights impacts.
#15	In order to meet their responsibility to respect human rights, business enterprises should have in place policies and processes appropriate to their size and circumstances, including: (a) A policy commitment to meet their responsibility to respect human rights; (b) A human rights due diligence process to identify, prevent, mitigate and account for how they address their impacts on human rights; (c) Processes to enable the remediation of any adverse human rights impacts they cause or to which they contribute.

namely, to "(a) [A]void causing or contributing to adverse human rights impacts through their own activities and address such impacts when they occur; (b) [S]eek to prevent or mitigate adverse human rights impacts that are directly linked to their operations, products or services by their business relationships, even if they have not contributed to those impacts." Corporate responsibility "applies to all enterprises regardless of their size, sector, operational context, ownership and structure (FP #14). And "business enterprises should have in place policies and processes appropriate to their size and circumstances" (FP #15).

This brief overview of the UN Guiding Principles on Business and Human Rights may suffice for the time being because they will be discussed more extensively in Chapter 17. Still, it is noteworthy that they include many important ethical implications to be addressed as well. The terms such as "corporate responsibility," "due diligence" and "policy commitment" clearly have an ethical meaning, in addition to their legal and social-psychological significance. However, these implications are barely articulated in the UN Framework and Guiding Principles and most often remain hidden, perhaps in order to avoid philosophical controversies that might divert attention from the urgent need of taking action against gross human rights abuses.

Having explored the actors and contents of corporate responsibility, we now turn to the third component: to which authorities or addressees business enterprises are supposed to be responsible, also discussed in Chapter 17. A first answer is given by free-market economists who claim that business executives as the "agents" are solely responsible to the shareholders of the enterprise (as the "principals") for maximizing shareholder value. This widespread view – particularly in Anglo-Saxon countries – was strongly influenced by Milton Friedman (1970) and Michael Jensen and William Meckling (1976) and is still dominant among business practitioners, professors and students and many people in other fields. However, more recently, it has been sharply criticized by, among others, Joseph Bower and Lynn Paine (2017) in a *Harvard Business Review* article.

In fact, the critique of the sole focus on shareholders has a long history going back to the early twentieth century and was thoroughly developed and expanded by Edward Freeman's seminal contribution (1984) and numerous scholars in philosophy and social sciences (Johnson-Cramer 2018). Proposing a second answer of the question to whom an enterprise is responsible, the stakeholder approach includes the enterprise's relations with all "stakeholders" defined as "any group or individual who can affect or is affected by the achievement of an organization's objectives" (Freeman 1984, 46). That means not only shareholders and owners but also employees, customers, suppliers, communities and other stakeholders are relevant for managerial decisions. Managers have to respond to the interests and claims of the stakeholders and can do it in an "instrumental" way (that is, using these relations for pursuing the organization's own interest) and/ or in a "normative" way (that is, respecting the stakeholders' rights and interests for their own sake). In other words, the responses can be viewed and theorized from the descriptive-analytical perspective of social sciences and/or from the normative-ethical perspective of philosophy, leading to so-called stakeholder theories. Thereby, many questions arise and have not been answered satisfactorily so far. Who are the relevant stakeholders? Are competitors included, as in Japanese approaches and the Caux Round Table Principles, in contrast to western approaches? Are there crucial differences between stakeholders and how are they distinguished, say, for example, between government and civil society organizations or between "primary" and "secondary" stakeholders? Can the stakeholder approach account for all key factors by which strategic management decisions are affected and which they can affect in turn? And how are instrumental and normative approaches connected to each other?

While the stakeholder approach substantially broadens and deepens the understanding of the enterprise's connections with other social actors and its potential responsibilities towards them, it also has clear limitations for conceiving corporate responsibility in a comprehensive sense. A third answer to the question of whom an enterprise is responsible should go beyond individual social actors and include society as a whole. Public goods cannot be created and maintained by individual actors alone, but need collective actors and society as such with its formal and informal institutions. Moreover, adopting an intergenerational perspective of sustainability, corporate responsibility extends to future generations who do not yet exist and cannot be identified now, but matter nevertheless. Furthermore, as the stakeholder approach focuses on the enterprise's relations with stakeholders, the contents of these relationships are not directly addressed. They might be partially influenced by the types of relationship with specific stakeholders and developed through stakeholder engagement and dialogue. But the stakeholder approach itself needs to be complemented by the explicit questions of contents and metrics. It cannot replace the indispensable role of widely agreed upon standards of measurement of corporate responsibility such as the sustainability reporting of the Global Reporting Initiative, the ISO 26000 standards and the UN Guiding Principles on Business and Human Rights.

In sum, all three components of responsibility are essential to fully grasp what corporate responsibility means. If any of them is missing, one cannot understand the ethics of business enterprises in a comprehensive sense. The actors who bear responsibility have to be clearly identified. The contents of responsibility need to be determined in a precise and comprehensive manner. And the authorities or addressees to whom enterprises are responsible should be legitimately established. Chapter 17 maps out these different aspects and provides numerous examples for illustration.

Chapter 18 is dedicated to corporate governance, that is, the locus where corporate responsibility has to be addressed in the first place. It is defined as the responsible direction and control of the business organization in its pursuit of creating wealth in the comprehensive sense and respecting human rights. All seven features of wealth creation are relevant for corporate governance. The narrow focus on financial capital has to be extended to economic, natural, human and social capital. The creation of wealth should include not only private but also public wealth and pay equal attention to the productive and the distributive side of directing and controlling the company. Inspired by a spiritual vision, corporate governance promotes ethical innovation in sustainable ways and is assessed in terms of human capabilities. Moreover, human rights serve as the guiding principles for corporate governance as defined in the UN Framework for Business and Human Rights. When facing difficult trade-offs and ethical dilemmas, the board has to scrutinize the seriousness of the situation, use its well-reasoned judgment and make considerate decisions: it may stick to the company's principles and reject the trade-offs or it may strike a compromise while respecting the minimal requirements.

To conclude Part III of this book, two specific studies explicate important aspects of corporate responsibility. Chapter 19 examines corporate responsibility for reducing income inequality within the boundaries of the organization and with regard to society at large. Instead of examining the entire range of income distribution, the focus is on the lower and upper ends. The "floor" is defined as a living wage, supported by strong economic and ethical arguments and proposed as a minimum income standard that can – and thus should – be implemented by companies. As for the ethically acceptable "ceiling" of executive compensation, its identification and justification are more complicated. However, strong economic and ethical arguments can be made in favor of a drastic reduction of top executive pay. Corporate responsibility for reducing income inequality in society means, first, to "walk the talk" and set an example and, second, to be "a good corporate citizen" by supporting legislation for a living wage and an ethically acceptable ceiling of executive pay.

Chapter 20 investigates corporate responsibility in global supply chains and how universities as powerful economic actors with a clear ethical mission can promote corporate responsibility in collaboration with their licensees and factories manufacturing trademark licensed products. This chapter chronicles the twenty-plus year history of the search of the University of Notre Dame for a responsible policy of "trademark licensing and human rights." Notre Dame engaged two specialized organizations to assess worker participation and corporate responsibility in fourteen factories in Bangladesh, China, El Salvador, Honduras and India. In line with the United Nations Guiding Principles on Business and Human Rights, the chapter concludes with policy suggestions for other like-minded universities and outlines several research opportunities.

To round out the twenty chapters of this book, the epilogue asks again the question of the purpose of business. It has to be aligned with the purpose of the economy and take seriously its people-centered orientation. The answer proposed in this book is creating wealth in the comprehensive sense and respecting human rights. It presents a universal vision for corporate responsibility in the global and pluralistic context and aims to be relevant for any economic, political and cultural system. However, it does not address more specific challenges, which wealth creation and human rights pose in different countries, cultures and industries. Thus this book is only a beginning. It invites further investigations and conversations from multiple geographic and cultural perspectives in order to promote and strengthen the commitment of business enterprises to wealth creation and human rights.

Notes

1 I understand radicalness in the sense of Arthur Rich: "[It] differs from extremism in that it aims even with one-sided partisanship at the whole of

humanity originating from faith, hope, and love, and does not make partial truths into a pseudo-whole" (Rich 2006, 188).

2 In this book the terms "business enterprise" and "business organization" are used synonymously.

3 The addressee is "one to whom something is addressed" (Merriam-Webster Dictionary). The term emphasizes the relational character of responsibility. The addressee is someone to whom one is answerable or accountable, for example, the spouse, a stakeholder, society, one's own conscience or God.

2 | *The Context of Globalization, Sustainability and Financialization*

Conversation about globalization and sustainability today, and even more so about financialization, is often confusing and can provoke multiple reactions – from anger and frustration to helplessness and disorientation or to wishful thinking and unrealistic expectations. Against this emotional backdrop the focus on wealth creation and human rights might produce a sobering effect and can help discern essential features, which shape our societies for many years to come, whether we like it or not. By describing the major traits of globalization, sustainability and financialization, this radically new approach to corporate responsibility will hopefully become more visible and understandable.

Globalization

Globalization can be understood as a kind of international system in the making. It is "not simply a trend or a fad but is, rather, an international system ... that has now replaced the old Cold War system, and ... has its own rules and logic that today directly or indirectly influence the politics, environment, geopolitics and economics of virtually every country in the world" (Friedman 2000, ix). It is characterized by an increasing interconnectedness of the world, due to the revolution of information technology and an immense reduction in the cost of transportation and communication. This dynamic system in the making is about "global transformations" in the plural, including political, cultural and environmental globalization, migration and the expanding reach of organized violence (see Held et al. 1999; Held & McGrew 2000, 2002). Moreover, one should add religion's growing influence in international politics (see Thomas 2010, chapter 7).

In business and economic terms, the increasing interconnectedness of the world means expanding markets and division of labor, reminiscent of the emergence of the Industrial Revolution in Europe, but, of course, at a definitively global scale. Trade, investment and the migration of people have dramatically increased, which forces all countries and businesses alike to account for the radical changes of the international system in the making.

Here is not the place to recall the empirical evidence of these groundbreaking developments in the last thirty plus years. The multiple dimensions of globalization, which were observed, analyzed and criticized at the turn of the millennium – expressed at and around the meeting of the World Trade Organization (WTO) in November 1999 in Seattle and in the wake of the terrorist attacks on September 11, 2001 in New York – have become even more complex and challenging in the years since. The build-up of the international production system, the expanding roles of markets and competition through liberalization, deregulation and privatization, the growing inequalities between winners and losers of these transformations and the powerful driving force of transnational enterprises characterize some important features of economic globalization.[1] Chapters 19 and 20 will discuss, in some depth, two major challenges: income inequality and corporate responsibility in the supply chains, respectively.

Although globalization is a key characteristic of our world today, it would be wrong to characterize all international relations as global. In fact, there is an enormous variety of international relations that cannot simply be subsumed under the category of "globalization." Hence, a more sophisticated understanding of international relations is required. Although the decline of the nation-state has been rung in (for example, by Ohmae 1995) and a new, globally oriented post-Westphalian world order seems to be emerging (see, for example, Habermas 2001), the nation-state has proved to be quite resilient and has remained or become again a central and, in many respects, the decisive, actor in international relations. In fact, the recent rise of nationalism powerfully illustrates this trend, often in conjunction with increasing autocracy (see Foreign Affairs 2019). There is no doubt that "global centrifugal forces" (Hösle 2019) are at work. All the more is it important to emphasize patriotism as "the exact opposite of nationalism" (Emmanuel Macron in Baker 2019).

Global challenges such as climate change, international terrorism, cyber security and the COVID-19 pandemic undoubtedly require collective action at the global level. But many challenges are less global than they seem to be at the first glance; we may think of health epidemics like SARS or the instability threat to the financial system. Although the old times of colonial powers are gone, we can observe new forms of empires in political, economic, technological, business and other terms. Those in the driver's seat who determine the rules of the game may ignore, disregard or take for granted the power imbalances, while those affected by them usually feel the impacts, but have no say in changing them. Moreover, despite globalization, there are still pockets of countries, areas, and spheres of life that are secluded from and "foreign" to outsiders. Ethnological studies have often emphasized the striking differences of native cultures that should be recognized in their own right. Little or no interaction appears to occur between them and the rest of the world.

These few examples may illustrate the fact that there is indeed a wide variety of international relations. They have to be taken seriously in a differentiated way, if one wants ethics to address more concrete challenges and be relevant in international affairs. This holds true not only in general terms, but also in order to contextualize the topic of this book "corporate responsibility for wealth creation and human rights." Therefore, I suggest a typology of international relations, the criterion for which is the permeability of the borders between the national and the international realms. According to the degree of permeability, four types are distinguished, which intersect with the individual (micro-), organizational (meso-) and systemic (macro-) levels of analysis and form the "extended conception" of business and economic ethics developed in Enderle (2003a) (see Figure 2.1).[2]

To illustrate the varying significance of borders, one may recall examples such as the dramatic changes of relations between East and West Germany before and after the fall of the Berlin Wall, the far-reaching permeability of borders between the countries of the European Union, the reinforcement of the US-Mexico border and the erection of border barriers in conflict zones such as the occupied Palestinian territories. Border situations vary a great deal across the globe. They are visualized by photographers such as Valerio Vincenzo (in Kuper 2013) and Kai Wiedenhöfer (2013) and discussed by journalists such as Simon Kuper (2013), Gary Knight (2013) and Raja Shehadeh (2013). In addition to borders in geographic, historic, economic and political terms, they can be defined in technological, socio-cultural, environmental and other terms. Needless to say, this diversity of perspectives renders the understanding of borders far more complex

MICRO – LEVEL	Foreign Country Type	Empire Type	Interconnection Type	Globalization Type
MESO - LEVEL				
MACRO - LEVEL				

| NATIONAL | INTERNATIONAL |

Figure 2.1 The extended conception of business and economic ethics

and much richer. In this chapter, however, the systematic considerations are limited to some key characteristics of border permeability
in general.

Borders can be permeable in various degrees. At one extreme is
hermetic seclusion, which characterized the Ming Dynasty in China
in the late sixteenth century or the former communist Albania *vis-a`-vis*
its neighbors. At the other extreme of the spectrum is the complete
abolition of all borders and total openness as proposed by some
proponents of globalization. In-between these extremes are multiple
forms of international relationships, which encompass all cross-
national variants, including both imminent conflicts and opportunities
for collaboration between various actors. These variants can be classi-
fied into four types of international relations: foreign country type,
empire type, interconnection type and globalization type. Although
these types can be found at all three levels, the explanations below
refer mainly to the macro- and meso-levels.

(A) The *foreign country* type is exemplified by the relationship of a
    small economy or small company with a foreign country, for
    example, Switzerland or Schläpfer *Embroideries* with Nigeria.
    International relations differ significantly from domestic relations
    and have no relevant repercussions on them. The international
    relations are added to the national framework and can be

relatively easily detached from it. Each country is different. Foreigners have to adapt themselves to the host countries, and national borders are relatively impermeable in both directions.

(B) Examples of the *empire* type are seen in the relationship between Great Britain and India during British colonialism and the United Fruit Company in Central America. This type characterizes international relations as a pure cross-national expansion of domestic relations without significant modification. From the host country's perspective, the asymmetric power relationship often involves misunderstanding, exploitation and repression. Repercussions on the home country are negligible, since national borders are much more permeable from the home to the host country than in the opposite direction.

(C) The *interconnection* type can be illustrated by the relationship between Italy and the European Union. International relations differ significantly from domestic relations, but are intrinsically interconnected with the latter. What is beyond national borders impacts on domestic relations and domestic relations impact on international relations. Interdependence blurs the notion of a national interest that disregards the interests of other nations and supranational entities. Although they are still important, national borders are pervious to a significant extent in both directions.

(D) In the *globalization* type, exemplified by global warming, international relations are so important that national borders become almost irrelevant. Citizens turn out to be cosmopolitan; multinational firms change into global entities and nation-states fade away. In principle, this type can comprehend the whole Earth, although until now it has not been fully realized.

This extended three-level conception of business ethics provides a useful mapping to identify different levels of decision-making and acting in various national and international environments. How can it contribute to clarifying the understanding and relevance of wealth creation and human rights?

Significance for Wealth Creation

The seven features of wealth creation outlined in the first chapter gain more profile by relating them to the four types of international relations. Several examples (out of the $4 \times 7 = 28$ possible combinations) may illustrate the usefulness of this conceptual mapping. Natural capital as part of the comprehensive definition of wealth appears in a large variety of ways. The foreign country type (A) may indicate locally limited, clean or polluted groundwater, which exists independently of other countries. An example of the empire type (B) are natural resources such as oil, gas and minerals exploited by dominant transnational corporations (Cameron & Stanley 2016). Sharing the river Rhine as common border and space between France and Germany exemplifies the interconnection type (C). And, standing for the globalization type (D), the global climate does not know any national borders so that no country can exclude itself from it.

The relevance of the typology of international relations becomes particularly clear when considering public goods and public bads, public wealth and the lack thereof. Public wealth in the foreign country type (A) is a matter for the foreign country and neither affects nor concerns other countries. The empire type (B), however, can exert a huge impact on the creation or destruction of public wealth. In the interconnection type (C), public wealth (and the lack thereof) in one country depends on the public wealth (and the lack thereof) of another country. As for the globalization type (D), nobody on the planet Earth can be excluded from the benefit of public wealth and from the harm the lack thereof generates.

Because the productive and the distributive dimensions of wealth creation are intrinsically interrelated, each type of international relations accounts not only for production and growth but also for distribution and inequality. Regarding the foreign country type (A), inequality – within the country and related to other countries – may not play an important role from the perspective of the outsider. In the empire type (B), inequality is deeply shaped by powerful countries and corporations. The interconnection type (C) allows for a certain balance between and within interdependent countries; an example is the Cohesion Fund of the European Union that aims to reduce economic and *social* disparities and to promote sustainable development.[3] Since virtually no borders exist in the globalizing type (D), the challenges of inequality are becoming even more visible and pressing.

Creativity and innovation are also strongly influenced by the type of international relations. The first type (A) brings little stimulation for new ideas and practices to the foreign country. As for the empire type

(B), innovation may spread through the dominated countries, but its impact is not necessarily good and can be devastating. The interconnection type (C) can generate mutually beneficial outcomes when, for example, two countries complement each other in research and development as well as market opportunities (see the expectations of Macron's visit to China in January 2018; *Financial Times* 2018). The globalization type (D) offers great opportunities for innovation at a global scale; but, irresponsibly managed, it also can lead to confusion and chaos.

Significance for Human Rights

Considering the four types of international relations explained above, one may ask which types are more or less conducive to securing human rights. Given the small and unilateral degree of permeability of borders respectively, the foreign country type (A) and the empire type (B) hardly allow promotion of the advancement of human rights. As many historic examples of isolated countries and multiple forms of colonialism have revealed, these types have prevented rather than promoted the emergence of human rights by spreading ethical relativism and ethical imperialism. More conducive to securing human rights have been the interconnection type (C) and the globalization type (D) of international relations. Both types open national borders substantially, to the point that, in the latter case, they are practically irrelevant. While the interconnection type presupposes a relatively robust system of nation-states with some fairly established international institutions, the globalization type is still in need of a set of strong global institutions.

Both types can lead to better ways of securing human rights because they strongly expose countries to other countries' and peoples' attitudes and behaviors. In the interconnection type the flows of goods, ideas, people and other items in one direction are reciprocated by flows of goods, ideas, people and other items in the opposite direction. The way one affects others is strongly influenced by the way one is affected by others. This mutual dependence calls for an ethics of reciprocity or, simply speaking, for the Golden Rule between collective entities (which, originally, is a moral principle for interpersonal relationships). In expanding this relation between interconnection and reciprocity further, one can understand that human rights have become necessary basic ethical standards within the European Union.

The globalization type assumes that the inflows into the country are so overwhelming that national borders are insignificant and meaningless. Sooner or later, the country has to face these threats willy-nilly from outside and try to turn them into opportunities. With good reason one can say that "all human beings on earth are in the same boat." Regardless of nationality, ethnicity, sex, race and religion, we are all "naked" human beings. This insight calls for a universal ethics in terms of human rights, given the fact that there are no feasible alternatives.

It is noteworthy to recall that these four types of international relations exist simultaneously, to some extent, and influence each other. While the third and the fourth types are growing in importance under the impact of globalization, the first and the second types remain powerful, causing multiple conflicts between all four types. Moreover, the interconnection type and the globalization type are important correctives to each other, the former emphasizing the rootedness in the nation-state and the reciprocity between partners and the latter transcending the nation-state and affirming the universal common ethical ground.

Sustainability

As globalization with its multiple layers is a main feature of our situation on the planet Earth today, sustainability proposes to us the direction in which we ought to move. However, the term "sustainability" has proliferated in many and confusing ways. In business circles, a sustainable activity or company often means that, "functioning roughly as it does, it can continue indefinitely" (Audi 2009, 47). Similarly, most CEOs equate corporate sustainability with the company's continuity over time (Rego et al. 2017, 133–36). Moreover, not infrequently, sustainability is taken as synonymous with eco-efficiency, which denotes both economic and ecological efficiency. However, as the World Business Council for Sustainable Development warns, "eco-efficiency should not be confused with sustainable development, which is a goal for society as a whole." Indeed, "it is even possible to have a world in which every company is becoming ever more eco-efficient and yet the planet's resource base is deteriorating due to population growth and the sheer increase in business and industry" (Schmidheiny & Zorraquín 1996, 17).

In this book I stick to the famous definition of the World Commission on Environment and Development in its report *Our Common Future* published in 1987. Sustainable development means "to meet the needs of the present without compromising the ability of the future generations to meet their own needs" (WCED 1987, 8).

This definition adopts a long-term, intergenerational perspective and has been widely embraced not only by scientists and policy makers but also by business and civil society. It overcomes the separation of environmental and development concerns, which had characterized the public discussion before this groundbreaking report. It also provided the conceptual basis for the UN Conference on the Environment and Development 1992 in Rio de Janeiro, in its Agenda 21, to call upon all countries, poor and rich, to commit themselves to sustainable development. Sustainability in this comprehensive sense "recognizes and incorporates the social, economic and ecological objectives of multi-generations" (Prizzia 2007, 20). This three-fold conception has also shaped the so-called "Sustainability Reporting Guidelines" launched in 1997. They enable all organizations to measure and report their performance in three key areas: economic, environmental and social, recently supplemented by governance as a fourth key area (www.globalreporting.org).

Again, at the UN Conference on Sustainable Development in 2012, the three-fold conception of sustainable development played a fundamental role and shaped the Rio+20 outcome document *The Future We Want* (UN 2012b). In "our common vision" the signatories renew their commitment "to ensuring the promotion of an economically, socially and environmentally sustainable future for our planet and for present and future generations" (§ 1) and acknowledge "the need to further mainstream sustainable development at all levels, integrating economic, social and environmental aspects and recognizing their interlinkages, so as to achieve sustainable development in all its dimensions" (§ 3).

On September 25, 2015, the UN General Assembly adopted the Resolution *Transforming Our World: The 2030 Agenda for Sustainable Development* (UN 2015). It promulgates 17 Sustainable Development Goals (SDGs) and 169 targets, which succeeded the Millennium Development Goals of 2000 and were elaborated in multiple consultations around the world.

They seek to realize the human rights of all and to achieve gender equality and the empowerment of all women and girls. They are integrated and indivisible and balance the three dimensions of sustainable development: the economic, social and environmental. The Goals and targets will stimulate action over the next 15 years in areas of critical importance for humanity and the planet. (UN 2015 from the Preamble)[4]

It is easy to see that the SDGs substantiate comprehensive wealth creation and human rights in multiple ways. The importance of natural capital is highlighted in Goal 6 (clean water and sanitation), Goal 7 (renewable energy), Goal 13 (climate action), Goal 14 (life below water) and Goal 15 (life on land). Economic capital relates to Goal 1 (no poverty), Goal 8 (good jobs and economic growth), Goal 9 (innovation and infrastructure), Goal 10 (reduced inequality), Goal 11 (sustainable cities and communities) and Goal 12 (responsible consumption). Human capital in terms of healthy and educated people is emphasized in Goal 2 (no hunger), Goal 3 (good health), Goal 4 (quality education) and Goal 5 (gender equality). Social capital pertains to Goal 11 (sustainable cities and communities), Goal 16 (peace and justice) and Goal 17 (partnerships for the goals). Moreover, all goals not only consist of private goods, but are also made up of public goods. Needless to say that the goals relate to each other and are interdependent. Regarding the time horizon of their implementation, fifteen years (until 2030) are given for the implementation of this ambitious agenda.

The UN Resolution clearly relates the 17 goals and 169 targets to human rights, stating that "they seek to realize the human rights of all." While the goals are rather general, the targets are more specific and indicate in many cases how they concern particular groups of people (women and girls, minorities, disabled persons, etc.) and involve specific human rights such as civil, political, economic, social and cultural rights or the right to development. It is noteworthy that the document defines the rights as goals to be achieved, not only as constraints to be respected (see Chapter 13).

Financialization

While the terms of "globalization" and "sustainability" are fairly well established and defined, the term of "financialization" is not widely known. It is absent in most encyclopedic works on economics, money and finance, and, when used, it can take on very different meanings. Kevin Phillips describes the financialization of the United States (1980–2000) as a process that substituted the securities sector for the banking sector as the linchpin of the overall financial sector. This allowed finance to make a mega-leap in economic importance (Phillips 2002, 138–47), leading to extremes of income and wealth polarization, a culture of money worship, and overt philosophic embrace of speculation and wide-open markets (Phillips 2009, 21).

In *Financialization and the World Economy* Gerald Epstein defines the term as "the increasing role of financial motives, financial markets, financial actors and financial institutions in the operation of the domestic and international economies" (Epstein 2005, 3). Greta Krippner presents systematic empirical evidence for the financialization of the US economy in the post-1970s period (Krippner 2005). She looks at the activities of both financial and non-financial firms and uses two distinct measures to gauge financialization: (1) "portfolio income" (comprising income from interest payments, dividends and capital gains on investment) relative to revenue generated by productive activities on the side of non-financial firms and (2) the profits generated in financial and non-financial sectors of the economy. The data show a considerable degree of financialization with regard to the ratio of portfolio income to corporate cash flow and to the ratio of financial to non-financial profit.

While these and other studies (Palley 2007; Orhangazi 2008) focus on macro- and micro-economic developments from a progressive angle, Paul Dembinski offers quite a different view that can be described as both holistic and radical: financialization as a profound social transformation. Finance is understood as a kind of rationality that is incorporated in a pattern of behavior and becomes an organizing principle, leading to far-reaching psychological, social, economic and political changes (Dembinski 2009, 5–6). As stated in the Manifesto of the Observatoire de la Finance (of which Dembinski is director), financialization has led to the almost total triumph of transactions over relationships; the ethos of efficiency has become the ultimate criterion of judgment and, when dissociated from moral considerations, it has led to the increasingly brutal expression of greed (Dembinski 2009, 168). Therefore, the manifesto calls to "reverse the financialization process and ensure that finance once again operates in the interests of human dignity and progress" by providing the basic services of channeling savings and giving the finances for productive investment (Observatoire de la Finance 2011). It is noteworthy that the manifesto (in its first version) was proclaimed in April 2008 before the outbreak of the global financial crisis. It is also interesting that financialization is presented as a main characteristic of the world of business today in the Vatican document *Vocation of the Business Leader. A Reflection* (Vocation 2018, §§ 17, 22, 23), defined as "the shift in the capitalist economy from production to finance. The revenue and profits of the financial sector have become an increasingly large segment of the worldwide economy. Its institutions, instruments and motives are having a significant influence on the operations and understanding of business" (ibid., § 22). Here financialization is assessed in a cautious way, distinct from Dembinski's radical view.

It does not come as a surprise that in the wake of the financial crisis and the European sovereign debt crisis, the financial services industry has been caught in sharp criticism and the accusations of financialization have become even stronger. Christine Lagarde, managing director of the International Monetary Fund (IMF), called upon the financial services industry to align financial incentives with societal objectives (Lagarde 2015). And Professor Luigi Zingales self-critically scrutinized in his presidential address to the American Finance Association in 2014 how finance, without proper rules, can easily degenerate into a rent-seeking activity and what finance academics can do, from a research and from an education point of view, to promote good finance and minimize the bad (Zingales 2015).

These few remarks on financialization are only meant to point to the undeniable fact that financialization, in some form, has taken place and become a major challenge, along with globalization and sustainability. Obviously, it stands in stark contrast to the comprehensive conception of wealth creation advanced in this book. It does not properly account for economic capital, let alone for natural, human and social capital. The stability of the financial system, an indispensable public good for the functioning of the economy, is jeopardized and undermined. The innovation of a host of highly complex financial products, hardly understandable even for financial specialists, may help to make a lot of money in the short run, yet fails to create, or even destroys, wealth. Financialization in business organizations, as a consequence of a management imperative to maximize shareholder value, "can cause insecurity, work intensification, suppression of voice … [and] prompt distress and anger … amongst workers" (Cushen 2013, 314). It has even led to sixty-nine employee suicides at a French telecommunication company (Chabrak et al. 2016).

This is a drastic example of how financialization can violate human rights. But there are many more cases of how financialization impacts on human rights through extreme inequality of income and wealth, through paying starving wages, through the destruction of jobs, the loss of homes and the shutdown of good businesses. When transactions triumph over relationships, the dignity of people gets lost in indifference and contempt.

* * * * *

After depicting the contemporary context of globalization, sustainability and financialization, we now turn to the main theme of the book and develop, first, the conception of wealth creation as the purpose of business and the economy.

Notes

1 From the immense literature on globalization, only a few publications can be added here: Hesse 1993; Mazur 2000; Stiglitz 2002, 2006; Virt 2002; Arruda & Enderle 2004; Bhagwati 2004; Enderle 2005; Radin 2018, *Journal of Globalization and Development* (since 2010).

2 The three-level conception of business and economic ethics has evolved under the influence of globalization. Early testimonies of this comprehensive understanding are articles by Goodpaster (1992/2001) and Enderle (1996, 2003a). Over time, this framework has been widely adopted, by, among others, Ulrich (2008) and in the *Global Survey of Business Ethics* edited by Rossouw and Stückelberger (2011). A three-level approach is also used by Allenby and Sarewitz (2011) for analyzing technology (see Chapter 9). Regarding the typology of international relations, see Enderle (2015a).

3 The *Cohesion Fund* is aimed at EU member states whose Gross National Income (GNI) per inhabitant is less than 90 percent of the EU average. See http://ec.europa.eu/regional_policy/en/ funding/cohesion-fund.

4 An extended preparatory discussion can be found in *Journal of Global Ethics*, 11 (1) (April 2015): "Forum: The Sustainable Development Goals."

PART I

Wealth Creation

The Purpose of Business and the Economy

3 | *Semantics and the Wealth of Nations*

A Brief Semantic Exploration

Wealth can have many different meanings. In colloquial language it can mean a huge amount of money or a plenitude of material things. Merriam Webster's Collegiate Dictionary (2003) defines wealth as an abundance of valuable material possessions or resources, abundant supply, property that has a monetary value or an exchange value, or material objects that have economic utility, especially the stock of useful goods having economic value in existence at any one time (as in "national wealth"). Because wealth often has a connotation of extreme riches, one tends to avoid this ostentatious word and prefers to speak of "prosperity." But wealth can also have a figurative sense, as in the wealth of data (available, for instance, at the World Bank), the wealth of new ideas, the wealth of good health or "the immeasurable riches [πλοῦτος] of his grace" (as Paul writes of God to the Ephesians in chapter 2:7).

As Robert Heilbroner states (1987, 880), "wealth is a fundamental concept in economics indeed, perhaps the conceptual starting point for the discipline. Despite its centrality, however, the concept of wealth has never been a matter of general consensus." As for the term itself, it figures prominently in Adam Smith's book *An Inquiry into the Nature and Causes of the Wealth of Nations* (1776), but is conspicuously absent from Gunnar Myrdal's book *Asian Drama: An Inquiry into the Poverty of Nations* (1968). It is complemented with its opposite in David Landes's book *The Wealth and Poverty of Nations: Why Some Are So Rich and Some So Poor* (1999), following Malthus's quote in his letter of January 26, 1817 to Ricardo: ". . . the causes of the wealth and poverty of nations – the grand object of all enquiries in Political Economy" (Keynes 1933/1972, 97–98; Landes 1999, vii).

It is noteworthy to see how Smith's "wealth" is translated into other languages: in German as *Wohlstand* – prosperity (not as: *Reichtum* –

riches, *Wohlfahrt* – welfare, *Wohlergehen* – well-being, *Vermögen* – wealth); in French as *richesses* – riches (not as: *prospérité* – prosperity, *opulence* – abundance , *aisance* – well-to-do-ness); in Spanish as *riqueza* – riches (not as: *bienestar* – well-being, *prosperidad* – prosperity), and in Chinese as *cái fù* – wealth (not as: *fán róng* – prosperity).

This short semantic exploration shows that wealth signifies an abundance of material things and does not equate with money. While emphasizing materiality, it is not limited to it but can transcend it. Moreover, wealth can be attributed to different subjects: to individuals, families, communities, business and other organizations, economies, nations, world regions and the whole planet Earth. Accordingly, the meaning of wealth may vary to some extent and highlight different aspects of wealth. Wealthy individuals may own vast amounts of securities or real estate. Transnational corporations may have hundreds of subsidiaries in multiple countries. The planet Earth is full of natural resources. And a rich country is not only the sum of wealthy individuals and organizations, but also made of strong institutions, reliable infrastructures, vibrant cultures and other so-called public goods. However, it is noticeable that wealth often is only related to persons, not countries. For example, the *Oxford Dictionary of Economics* (Black et al. 2009) has no entry on the wealth of nations and treats wealth only from the individual's perspective.

What Makes a Country Rich? Focusing on the Wealth of Nations

In order to discuss the concept of wealth, we first might concentrate on what is meant by the wealth of a single nation or country (as we use these two terms interchangeably). At first glance, this approach may seem outmoded and inappropriate because of the "decline of the nation-state" in present times, the increasing number of pressing international challenges and the extraordinary power of many transnational corporations. However, with the recent resurgence of the nation-state, the focus on the wealth of a single nation provides some advantages for a better understanding of wealth when compared to other approaches. Despite the advances of globalization with its growing interconnectedness, the nation-state is still an indispensable entity that incorporates many traditions, institutions and practices that are specific to the nation and distinct from individuals, organizations and supranational entities. Also, the perspective of the nation-state can provide useful lessons for addressing international challenges because essential aspects of communal life in the national context might be important, with the necessary changes, in the international context as well. In addition, the global financial crisis spreading from the United States around the world and the euro crisis in Europe have demonstrated quite clearly that national institutions, policies and behaviors matter a great deal in spite of the far-reaching financial and other interdependencies.

Some historic examples in the twentieth century can illustrate the importance of the nation (or territory in the case of Taiwan) as a unit for analyzing the creation of wealth. In his fascinating and powerful historical account "why some [nations] are so rich and some so poor," Landes scrutinizes the winners and losers in the process of wealth creation over the last fifty years. On the winners' side, in addition to "the thirty wonderful years from 1945 to 1975" of France and the "economic miracle" in Germany, he highlights the East Asian success stories of Japan, the four "Little Tigers" (South Korea, Taiwan, Singapore and Hong Kong) and the regional followers such as Malaysia, Thailand and Indonesia, referring, among others, to the World Bank's study *The East Asian Miracle* (1993), and adding China in his "Epilogue 1999" (Landes 1999: 524–31). The losers are the Middle East, Latin America, the countries of the Communist-Socialist bloc and sub-Saharan Africa.

Indeed, the economic miracles in East Asia, first in the eight economies mentioned above and then in the People's Republic of China (PRC) since 1978, have unfolded primarily in the national context, supported by strong governments. They offer valuable lessons for a better understanding of economic development and the role ethics can play in this process. In the mid-1990s I discussed the World Bank report (1993) from an ethical perspective and highlighted the importance of: (1) a morality of inclusion, (2) the understanding of the economy as an interconnected process of production and distribution, (3) a government-led relationship between government and private business and (4) a group-oriented conception of the business organization (Enderle 1995, 95–105). More recently, on the thirtieth anniversary of PRC's economic reform and opening-up of the country, I examined its economic growth as a process of "wealth creation" (Enderle 2010a, 2013c). Using the comprehensive notion of wealth (explained in Part I of this book), the Chinese experiences provide some important lessons for developing countries: (1) Genuine wealth creation is much more than economic growth measured in Gross Domestic Product (GDP), encompassing not only economic but also natural, human and social capital. (2) The "entrepreneurial decade" of the 1980s demonstrated the liberating and creative role that relatively free business can play in creating more wealth and in overcoming poverty for large segments of the population. (3) Understanding the dialectic between economic reform and an opening-up of the country is crucial to address the challenges of globalization. (4) Successful economic development can only be understood as a combined effort of creating private and public wealth. (5) Serious attention has to be paid to the interconnection between the productive and the distributive dimensions of the wealth creation process. And (6) wealth creation is not merely a material process, but also includes a spiritual aspect.[1]

In addition to the historical perspective, the question of the wealth of a nation has gained considerable attention from the analytical perspective as well. Increasing concerns have been raised about the adequacy of current measures of economic performance, especially those based on GDP figures. Furthermore, there are broader concerns about the relevance of these figures as measures of societal well-being as well as measures of economic, environmental and social sustainability. In order to address these concerns, the report on the measurement of economic performance and social progress by Joseph E. Stiglitz, Amartya Sen and Jean-Paul Fitoussi (2009) proposes far-reaching changes (see a summary on pp. 11–18). A few of them are briefly mentioned here: Measuring production – a variable which among other things determines the level of employment – should also capture quality changes, which is vital to measuring real income and consumption, some of the key determinants of people's material well-being. The household perspective should be emphasized, and income measures should be broadened to non-market activities (for example, services provided in-kind and/or within families). As for *wealth*, the report summarizes:

Income and consumption are crucial for assessing living standards, but in the end they can only be gauged in conjunction with information on wealth. A household that spends its wealth on consumption goods increases its current well-being but at the expense of its future well-being. The consequences of such behavior would be captured in a household's balance sheet, and the same holds for other sectors of the economy, and for the economy as a whole. To construct balance sheets, we need comprehensive accounts of assets and liabilities. Balance sheets for countries are not novel in concept, but their availability is still limited and their construction should be promoted. *Measures of wealth are central to measuring sustainability. What is carried over into the future necessarily has to be expressed in stocks – of physical, natural, human and social capital.* (Report 2009, 13; emphasis added)

Hence, the wealth of a nation – a stock at a certain point in time – is expressed in a comprehensive national balance sheet with all assets and liabilities, which determines the sustainability of the nation's future development.

There is a growing body of literature on constructing such comprehensive balance sheets (Hamilton & Clemens 1999; Dasgupta & Mäler 2000, 2004; Arrow et al. 2003; UN et al. 2003; UNECE et al. 2008). The Stiglitz-Sen-Fitoussi Report provides an excellent, fairly comprehensive discussion. Of particular significance for our focus are three World Bank studies: *Where Is the Wealth of Nations? Measuring Capital for the 21st Century* (World Bank 2006), *The Changing Wealth of Nations: Measuring Sustainable Development in the New Millennium* (World Bank 2011) and *The Changing Wealth of Nations 2018: Building a Sustainable Future* (Lange et al. 2018).

How do these studies conceptualize and measure the wealth of nations? While the first publication distinguishes four categories of assets (natural capital, produced capital, intangible capital and total wealth), the second publication builds on this distinction and adds net foreign assets. The five categories of assets are as follows (World Bank 2011, 3–5, Appendix C):

(1) *Total wealth that comprehends all net financial and non-financial assets.* The measure of total (or comprehensive) wealth is built upon the intuitive notion that current wealth must constrain future consumption. (The report presents the theory underpinning this assumption and the methods used to estimate total wealth in Chapter 5).

(2) *Produced capital* that comprises machinery, structures and equipment, and also includes urban land.

(3) *Natural capital* that comprises agricultural land, protected areas, forests, minerals and energy.

(4) *Net foreign assets* are calculated as total foreign assets minus total foreign liabilities; that is the sum of foreign direct investment (FDI) assets, portfolio equity assets, debt assets, derivative assets and foreign exchange reserves, minus the sum of FDI liabilities, portfolio equity liabilities, debt liabilities and derivative liabilities.

(5) *Intangible capital* is measured as a residual, the difference between total wealth and net foreign assets, produced and natural capital. It implicitly includes human, social and institutional capital, which comprises factors such as the rule of law, governance, levels of education, confidence in institutions and absence of violence in society; in other words, kinds of "public goods" that will be discussed later on.

In order to give a more palpable idea of the notion of national wealth with its different components, one may look at the estimates of a few countries. Two methods are used for the estimations (World Bank 2011, appendix A). For the value of produced capital stocks, the perpetual inventory method (PIM) is applied that estimates the capital as the sum of the additions, minus the subtractions, made over time to an initial stock. For the value of natural capital and total wealth, the net present value (NPV) is used to gauge the capital as net present value that the capital is able to produce over time. Obviously, these estimates are of quite a rough nature, particularly with regard to NPV, depending on the assumptions about the (uncertain) future value flow and the (uncertain) choice of the discount rate.

Table 3.1 shows the estimates of five countries, expressed in 2005 US dollars per capita. The poorest country is Burundi, the richest Norway.[2] Given the size of their populations, India and China clearly belong to the group of lower-middle-income developing countries (with an average of 17,112 USD). Among the high-income OECD countries (with an average of 581,424 USD) the United States and Norway rank in the top group.

Several features are of particular interest. First, total wealth and its components figure not only for the entire countries, but also for the average person (that is, per capita). Second, conspicuous is the extreme inequality of wealth between countries; total wealth per capita in Norway is almost 400 times greater than in Burundi. This means the prospect for sustainable life for Norwegians is tremendously better than for Burundians. Third, the size of the country also matters greatly.

Table 3.1 *Wealth estimates in 2005 of selected countries (in 2005 USD per capita)*

Country	Population	Natural capital	Produced capital + urban land	Net foreign assets	Intangible capital	Total wealth
Burundi	7,547,515	2,697	166	−145	−527	2,191
India	1,094,583,000	2,704	1,980	−107	5,961	10,539
China	1,304,500,000	4,013	6,017	284	8,921	19,234
United States	296,410,404	13,822	100,075	−6,947	627,246	734,195
Norway	4,623,300	110,162	183,078	36,436	532,121	861,797

Source: World Bank (2011, 173–83)

In 2005 China's total wealth was already very large with about 25 trillion USD (yet behind the five wealthiest countries: United States, Germany, United Kingdom, France and Italy), and in 2010 its economy (as GDP) became the second biggest in the world (after the United States). Nonetheless, with its huge population, it still remains a developing country. Fourth, considering the composition of total wealth, the most important component in rich countries is intangible wealth that includes human, social and institutional capital. Fifth, it follows that, in order to move out of poverty, developing countries have to place great emphasis on increasing their intangible capital.

The third and most recent World Bank publication on the changing wealth of nations (Lange et al. 2018) dropped the category of intangible capital and substantially improved the estimates of human capital and natural capital. It is noticeable that social capital and institutional capital are not included in total wealth anymore. The poorest country is now Gabon and the richest country is Norway.[3] Table 3.2 shows the estimates of five countries, expressed in constant 2014 USD per capita.

Comparing Tables 3.1 with 3.2 (that is, values of 2005 with values of 2014), several changes are remarkable. First, the difference of wealth per capita between the poorest country (Burundi, Gambia) and Norway decreased from almost 400 times to 321 times. Second, the difference of wealth per capita between India and China increased more than 10 times (from USD 8,695 to USD 89,961). Third, the increase of wealth per capita varies a great deal across countries: it is 72 percent in India, 562 percent in China, 34 percent in the USA and 194 percent in Norway.

As these studies show, a comprehensive and well-founded notion of national wealth is of paramount importance not only for comparative but also for policy purposes. At stake is the fundamental question about the kind of development a country should pursue. Given the limited space of this chapter, we may only compare the conception of development according to these World Bank studies with that of the United Nations Development Programme (UNDP) for "human development." They are different and mark a certain tension, but they also contain common elements. The World Bank defines development as "a process of building and managing a portfolio of assets in a sustainable way":

Table 3.2 *Wealth estimates in 2014 of selected countries (in constant 2014 USD per capita)*

Country	Population	Natural capital	Produced capital + urban land	Human capital	Net foreign assets	Total wealth
Gambia	1,928,201	1,413	1,545	2,745	–496	5,208
India	1,295,291,543	4,739	5,161	8,755	–444	18,211
China	1,264,270,000	15,133	28,566	63,369	1,104	108,172
United States	318,907,401	23,624	216,186	766,470	–23,000	983,280
Norway	5,173,232	103,184	423,905	1,004,649	140,018	1,671,756

Source: Lange et al. (2018, 225–33)

The challenge of development is to manage not only the total volume of assets – how much to save versus how much to consume – but also the composition of the asset portfolio, that is, how much to invest in different types of capital, including the institutions and governance that constitute social capital. (World Bank 2011, 4)

In contrast, the UNDP coined the term "human development" in its first annual *Human Development Report 1990* and defined it as a process of "enlarging people's choices" (UNDP 1990, 10). In its twentieth anniversary edition, the *Human Development Report 2010* with its subtitle "The real wealth of nations: Pathways to human development," proclaims that "people are the real wealth of nations" (UNDP 2010, 1), reaffirming its longstanding focus:

Human development is the expansion of people's freedoms to live long, healthy and creative lives; to advance other goals they have reason to value; and to engage actively in shaping development equitably and sustainably on a shared planet. People are both the beneficiaries and the drivers of human development, as individuals and as groups. (UNDP 2010, 2)

It seems that, by equating real wealth with people, the Human Development Report adopts a holistic approach that points to the final goal human development should strive for. On the other hand, the World Bank seems to take an economic approach, speaking of a "portfolio of assets" to be built and managed in a sustainable way and focusing on the means to achieve the well-being of people.

These opposing views are not necessarily contradictory, but they emphasize different perspectives and yet have several features in common. "Total wealth" of a nation is not only material wealth, as natural and produced capital and net foreign assets are. Total wealth also includes human and social capital – parts of an intangible capital – that means healthy and educated people and trustworthy relations. People, as intangible capital, are considered "assets" to be built and managed, or, to be used as instruments. However, this instrumental use, as means, does not necessarily imply that healthy and educated people and trustworthy relations are *only* means; they can also have intrinsic value. In other words, the World Bank definition is broader than material wealth and includes an immaterial dimension without defining the well-being of people explicitly.

Regarding the human development view, the claim that people are the real wealth of nations seems to imply that material wealth is not "real" or good in itself, rather nothing else than a means. This may remind us of Aristotle's famous saying – quoted by Sen in *Development as Freedom* (Sen 1999, 14) – that "wealth is evidently not the good we are seeking; for it is merely useful and for the sake of something else" (Aristotle 1980, 7). However, this sharp separation between people and material assets can be questioned from an anthropological perspective. If the person constitutes an intimate unity of body and soul which are mutually dependent (that is, in contrast to Aristotle's philosophy), materiality is part of the person and matters for her well-being intimately so that it hardly can be qualified as "nonreal." But, by interpreting the report's subtitle differently, the provocative claim can be toned down: "the real wealth of nations" is not only the goal (that is, the people) but also "the pathway [that is, the means] to human development."

At this point we conclude our considerations on why we may focus first on the wealth of nations. This methodological way, enriched with several examples and different conceptual approaches, can provide a richer understanding of wealth than if it were based on the usual notion of wealth related to individuals and organizations. Wealth includes natural, produced, financial, human and social capital (some of them defined as intangible capital or institutional/social capital). It has a strong material component and also involves, to some extent, people with their educational endowments and trust relationships. These are some essential features of the wealth of nations. They also apply to entities beyond the nation-states, that is to regions, continents and the planet Earth. It goes without saying that the focus on the nation as unit of analysis in this chapter should not mislead to underestimating the growing importance of other entities in the regional, continental and global contexts in an increasingly connected world.

Notes

1 A recent report of the World Bank, *Riding the Wave: An East Asia Miracle for the 21st Century* (2017), shows how a rapid and broadly shared growth can lift millions out of poverty, and a solid middle class has emerged in most countries. But it also recalls that these successes do not guarantee that inclusive growth – growth that reduces poverty and delivers upward mobility and economic security for all – is assured.

2 In 2005 Iceland and Luxembourg indicated bigger total wealth per capita, that is USD 902,960 and USD 917,530, respectively. Iceland had by far the biggest intangible net foreign assets (USD 799,123) – that was before

the financial crisis – and Luxembourg had by far the biggest net foreign assets (USD 99,499). These results may suggest that the concept of intangible capital needed some revision that actually was undertaken by the 2018 World Bank publication (Lange et al. 2018).

3 As the first author explained in an email exchange with G. Enderle, the old way of measuring wealth was unsatisfactory for a number of reasons: (1) The estimate of total wealth assumed the same rate of return in all countries, which is simply not accurate. It is better to estimate all components of wealth and total them. One can then calculate the implicit return for countries. (2) The concept of intangible capital was very unsatisfactory because it was only a residual of the things one could measure. However, most of the residual was human capital, which could not be measured directly. (3) It is very difficult to get support from colleagues for an indicator (per capita wealth and its growth over time), when the largest component is a residual. Institutional/social capital are considered not separable assets. They influence the ranking of institutions/governance of countries and will be accounted for in a following study.

4 | Wealth Includes Natural, Economic, Human and Social Capital

The exploration of the question of wealth in Chapter 3 aimed at a first understanding of conceptual and methodological issues; this was accomplished by drawing on recent literature and illuminating them with semantic considerations and historical examples. The focus on the wealth of nations has brought about a fairly rich and comprehensive concept of wealth that transcends by far the vulgar notion of wealth as the equivalence of money.

In this and the next six chapters we undertake a more systematic investigation of wealth and its creation and elaborate on seven features which define the conception of wealth creation proposed in this book (see Figure 1.1). First, in terms of substantive contents, four types of capital are included: natural, economic (that is, produced and financial), human and social capital (see Box 4.1).

Second, in terms of forms – that means formal aspects – of capital, both private and public wealth are relevant. Third, in terms of process, the generation of wealth involves both a productive and a distributive dimension, which are dependent upon each other. Fourth, this process is not merely a material process but has a spiritual aspect as well. Fifth, the time horizon of this process encompasses not only present but also future generations, which is to say, wealth creation is "sustainable" and substantiated in terms of "human capabilities" (Amartya Sen). Sixth, more specifically, the generation of wealth is understood as a creative process that makes things new and better. And seventh, wealth creation needs both self-regarding and other-regarding motivations.

Wealth Includes Natural, Economic, Human and Social Capital

As briefly discussed in the previous chapter, the recent literature on national accounting identifies and elaborates five types of wealth: natural, produced, financial, human and social capital.[1] Although the definitions of each type vary to some extent, this typology can serve as

Figure 4.1 The OECD well-being conceptual framework.
Source: OECD (2011) *How's Life? Measuring Well-Being*, OECD Publishing, Paris,
http://dx.doi.org/10.1787/9789264121164.en

a starting basis of our investigation, following the capital approach to
sustainable development explained in UNECE et al. (2008). Thereby,
in line with the OECD (2013a) definition, produced and financial
capital are aggregated and conceived as economic capital. So
I propose to define the wealth of a society – for example, of a country –
as the total amount of economically relevant private and public assets
including natural, economic, human and social capital. Needless to
say, this comprehensive notion of capital extends far beyond the usual
concepts employed in "capitalism" and Karl Marx's *Das Kapital*.

All four types are considered indispensable to capture a broad and
realistic understanding of wealth. If any of these types is missed or ignored,
the truncated conception of wealth leads to serious misunderstandings and
policy flaws. It is noteworthy that this proposed conception of wealth
comprehending four types of capital is congruous with the OECD well-
being framework, according to which sustainability of well-being over
time requires preserving all four types of capital (see Figure 4.1).

However, insisting on these four essential components of wealth does
not imply that no other type of wealth could be added in the future.

Box 4.1 Four types of capital of wealth creation

Natural capital comprises:

- nonrenewable natural assets: oil, gas, copper and all the other minerals;
- conditionally renewable natural assets: fish and trees reproducing themselves;
- natural liabilities: carbon dioxide (CO_2) and other chemicals.

Economic capital consists of:

- physical capital: machinery, equipment and structures as well as urban land
- financial capital: any asset for which a counterpart liability exists somewhere on the part of another institutional unit ... [as well as] gold reserves ... though they have no corresponding liability.

Human capital includes:

- the knowledge, skills, competencies and attributes embodied in individuals that facilitate the creation of personal, social and economic well-being ("educated people");
- a state of complete physical, social and mental well-being, and not merely the absence of disease or infirmity ("healthy people").

Social capital means:

- connections among individuals – social networks and the norm of reciprocity and trustworthiness that arise from them.

One may think of "cultural wealth" and "ethical wealth," notions used in the literature (for example, Donaldson 2001; Pagel & Mace 2004; Bandelj & Wherry 2011; Jennings & Velasquez 2015). However, because these are very difficult to conceptualize and operationalize, they will not be pursued here further.

Before elaborating on the four types of wealth, it should be emphasized that the concept of wealth used in this book comprehends both stocks and flows, embracing not only economically relevant stocks of capital at a certain point in time but also changes of capital stocks over a certain period of time. In this way, one takes into account, for example, both wealth and income, and both stocks of natural resources and changes thereof. A stock is the result of positive and

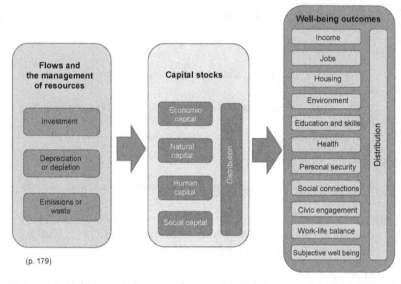

(p. 179)

Figure 4.2 Linking capital stocks, flows and well-being outcomes in the OECD well-being framework

negative flows over the previous period of time, and, even more importantly, it indicates the potential flow in the subsequent period of time: as an asset, the stock opens opportunities for the future; as a liability, it burdens the prospect. Hence the relevance of stocks for sustainable development, as stated in the Stiglitz-Sen-Fitoussi report (Report 2009, 13) mentioned in Chapter 3: "Measures of wealth are central to measuring sustainability. What is carried over into the future necessarily has to be expressed in stocks – of physical, natural, human and social capital." Figure 4.2 shows how the OECD well-being framework links capital stocks, flows and well-being outcomes and explicitly accounts for their distributions.[2]

Natural capital, the first type of wealth, comprises nonrenewable and conditionally renewable natural assets and natural liabilities.[3] Nonrenewable natural assets such as oil, gas, copper and all the other minerals can only be used once, being intrinsically depletable. Conditionally renewable natural assets like fish and trees reproduce themselves, being nature-made stocks and generating natural harvest over time, under the condition that the massive stocks needed for reproduction are not overharvested. Among the natural liabilities, carbon dioxide (CO_2) has become the most important, causing climate change according to a wide scientific consensus. Carbon actually is a basic ingredient of life. It accumulates up in the atmosphere, trapping in heat. But with massive economic growth worldwide, it has become a problem since the accumulated amount of carbon passed the critical threshold to increase the global temperature significantly.

Both natural assets and liabilities are essential to determine natural capital. However, much more is needed to make it fruitful for people. In his groundbreaking book *The Plundered Planet* (2010) Paul Collier distinguishes four crucial phases of the decision chain: (1) discovering natural assets, (2) capturing natural assets, (3) selling natural assets and (4) "investing in investing." His goal is to explain (as the subtitle indicates) "why we must – and how we can – manage nature for global prosperity."

A more comprehensive definition of natural capital is proposed in the report of UNECE et al. (2008), drawing on the work of the System of Environmental-Economic Accounting (SEEA 2003) and the United Nations Millennium Ecosystem Assessment (UN 2005). According to the SEEA:

> Natural capital is generally considered to comprise three principal categories: natural resource stocks, land and ecosystems. All are considered essential to the long-term sustainability of development for their provision of 'functions' to the economy, as well as to mankind outside the economy and other living beings. (Quoted in UNECE et al. 2008, 49)

Thus natural capital covers nonrenewable and conditionally renewable natural resources. In addition, it covers ecosystems and other natural systems that provide various essential services to mankind. Following the Millennium Ecosystem Assessment, ecosystems may be divided into provisioning, regulating and cultural services: the first including material resources like minerals, timber, fish and water; the second covering services like absorption of unwanted wastes from production and consumption and regulation of the global climate; and the third sometimes called amenity functions such as aesthetic, spiritual, educational and recreational services. In various forms and degrees, all ecosystem services contribute to human well-being in terms of security, basic material for a good life, health and good social relations. As constituents of well-being, this classification includes even "freedom of choice and action [that is] the opportunity to be able to achieve what an individual values doing and being" (quoted in UNECE et al. 2008,

50). This is the key concept of the capability approach that will be discussed in Chapter 8.

To conclude, the report raises the question of how to value natural capital. It succinctly summarizes the situation as follows:

> The problems ... are as varied as the resources themselves. For most traditional natural resources (minerals, fossil fuels, timber, etc.), market prices exist, though they seldom reflect negative externalities resulting from exploitation of the resources. For instance, timber extraction often comes at the expense of biodiversity preservation, soil protection and other environmental services provided by the same trees that give us timber. To arrive at an approximation of the accounting price of forest capital, market prices will have to be corrected for these kinds of negative externalities.
>
> Since ecosystem services are not usually priced in the market, special methods must be employed to make these corrections. In a fair number of cases it is difficult to find reliable and objective accounting prices. Overall it is fair to say that *monetary accounting for natural capital is not yet operational* in the same way as for produced and financial capital. In view of these difficulties, *physical measures of natural capital* must be sought as part of any suite of capital-based sustainable development indicators. (UNECE et al. 2008, 51; emphases added)

In spite of these difficulties, the World Bank study of 2011 attempts to estimate some changes in natural capital. It concentrates on the following components for the period of 1995–2005: land (cereals, fruits, vegetables, sugar, other crops, pasture and protected areas), forest (timber and nontimber), and subsoil assets (oil, gas, coal and minerals) (pp. 51–71). It also admits that some important sources of environmental degradation such as underground water depletion, unsustainable fisheries and soil degradation are not included (p. 150). By decomposing price and quantity effects, the estimates show that positive changes in natural capital occurred particularly in the Middle East and North Africa, while negative changes affected especially sub-Saharan Africa. Moreover, the study dedicates another chapter to "wealth accounting in the greenhouse" (pp. 75–91). It outlines the economics of climate change, highlighting the social cost of carbon as a key element. It examines how property rights to the global commons influence how we should do the wealth accounting and concludes with estimating the value of CO_2 stocks and flows in 2005 for a number of countries.

The World Bank study of 2018 builds on the study of 2011 and covers the period of 1995–2014. Natural capital includes the renewable resources of agricultural land, forests (timber and nontimber) and protected areas (for preservation and protection of ecosystems) and the nonrenewable resources of energy (oil, gas and coal) and mineral resources (pp. 8–14, 85–95, 212–19). The study also discusses "the carbon wealth of nations: from rents to risks" (pp. 97–113), the impact of air pollution on human health and wealth (pp. 171–88) and "subsidies [that] reduce marine fisheries wealth" (pp. 189–97). Moreover, to fill the gap in "missing" natural capital, it develops biophysical quantification of ecosystem services (pp. 199–210).

In addition to these problems of valuing natural capital, there is the inescapable ethical question as to whom the property rights of natural assets and liabilities should be allocated. As Collier writes, *"natural assets have no natural owners"* (Collier 2010, 17; emphasis in the original). Who owns the fish in the open sea and the subsoil resources in the Arctic? What right to ownership of natural assets do future generations have? Who is willing to own natural liabilities like carbon emissions? It is not difficult to foresee fierce competition for the assets on the one hand and equally strong refusal of the liabilities on the other. This question will arise again in the discussion about *public goods and public "bads"* in Chapter 5.

The second type of wealth is *economic capital* consisting of physical and financial capital. While the World Bank study of 2011 includes as physical capital "machinery, equipment and structures" as well as urban land as a fixed proportion of the value of physical capital, the report by UNECE et al. (2008) uses the following fairly precise definition:

Produced capital includes fixed assets that are used repeatedly or continuously in production processes for more than one year. Fixed assets can be tangible – such as machinery, buildings, roads, harbours and airports – and intangible – such as computer software, original works of artistic value (recordings, manuscripts) and other specialized knowledge used in production. Inventories of raw materials, semi-finished and finished goods held for future sale are also included in produced capital, as are valuables such as precious stones, antiques and paintings. (UNECE et al. 2008, 49)

The Stiglitz-Sen-Fitoussi report urges a broadened definition of production measures by also capturing quality changes. They do not seem to be included in the definition above, but will be taken up in the discussion of the *creation* of wealth in Chapter 9.

Valuing produced capital is by far less complicated than valuing natural capital because the former is recorded in the balance sheets of national accounts. The report by UNECE et al. (2008, 49) points to "the common assumption that observed market prices for produced and financial capital are fair reflections of their well-being effects. In other words, market prices come close to the theoretical ideal of accounting prices for produced and financial capital. In practice, however, the reported numbers are not always certain."

Financial capital as part of economic capital is formally defined "to include any asset for which a counterpart liability exists somewhere on the part of another institutional unit ... [as well as] gold reserves ... though they have no corresponding liability" (UNECE et al. 2008, 48). This means assets and liabilities within the unit cancel each other out. For example, if a brother owes his sister $100, it comprises part of the sister's wealth but not that of the family as a whole. Similarly, the financial capital of a country is the net foreign financial assets, canceling out the domestic assets and liabilities. Financial capital includes currency and other forms of bank deposits, stocks and bonds, derivatives, accounts receivable, pension funds and insurance reserves.

Human capital, the third type of wealth, can be defined in various ways. J. R. Behrman and B. J. Taubman (1994, 493) emphasize the economic aspect: human capital is "the stock of economically productive human capabilities." So does S. Rosen (1987, 681) who refers "to the productive capacities of human beings as income producing agents in the economy." They follow Gary Becker's standard reference *Human Capital* (Becker 1964) in which on-the-job training (general and specific), schooling and other knowledge (such as information about employment opportunities) are conceived as components of human capital with consequences for earnings and economic productivity.

Others place more weight on the well-being aspect: human capital is "the knowledge, skills, competencies and attributes embodied in individuals that facilitate the creation of personal, social and economic well-being" (OECD 2001, 18). It is individually possessed (that is, "embodied" and thus inalienable), includes cognitive and non-cognitive skills, is formal and informal learning, lifelong and multifaceted, and comprises qualities ranging from literacy to teamwork and perseverance. Human capital brings about not only private economic benefits (which was at the core of the original human capital theory). It is also a key factor for economic growth and yields a wide range of non-market benefits (such as better health, lower crime and delinquency rates and the promotion of education to the next generation; UNECE et al. 2008, 51–52).

I propose to adopt this OECD definition of human capital and to supplement it with the notion of *health,* which the World Health Organization defines in its constitution of 1948 as "a state of complete physical, social and mental well-being and not merely the absence of disease or infirmity" (WHO 1948/ 2006). In the 1980s, within the context of health promotion, the WHO revised this aspirational definition by emphasizing health in dynamic terms of resiliency or as "a resource for living." Health means "the extent to which an individual or group is able to realize aspirations and satisfy needs and to change or cope with the environment. Health is a resource for everyday life, not the objective of living; it is a positive concept, emphasizing social and personal resources, as well as physical capacities" (WHO 1984) This revised definition is akin to Sen's notion of human capabilities (see Chapter 8) and basically means "healthy people."

Human capital composed of education and health is of great relevance for the creation of wealth. As an example, Sen points to the positive unintended consequences of Maoist policy for China after Mao's death. Land reform, expansion of literacy, enlargement of public health care and other social policies executed in pre-reform China had a very favorable effect on economic growth in post-reform China Sen 1999, 259–60).

Generally speaking, education and health as components of human capital are personal characteristics and hence not separable from individuals as produced capital is. They can be valued either directly or indirectly. A direct reason for valuing a good education and good health is the enrichment of human life; an indirect reason lies in the fact that they can contribute to more efficient production and command a price in the market. This latter, indirect role of human capital certainly underpins the human capital theory in the narrow sense as well as in the Chinese example. It is noteworthy, however, that this human capital approach contrasts with the human capability approach which also incorporates the *direct* relevance of being well-educated and healthy (so-called functionings) for the well-being and freedom of people (see Sen 1999, 292–97). Suffice it to say at this point that the human capability approach will be further discussed in Chapter 8.

Finally, *social capital*, the fourth type of wealth, is a relatively new notion that has attracted a considerable amount of research and attention in recent years. However, there is a multitude of facets and definitions (see Dasgupta & Mäler 2000; Bartkus & Davis 2009; Svendsen & Haase Svendsen 2012; Ayios et al. 2014; Kwon & Adler 2014), strong promoters such as Pierre Bourdieu (1986), James Coleman (1990, 2000), Robert Putnam (1983, 1995, 2000) and Elinor Ostrom (2000, 2009), and abundant criticism by economists such as Kenneth Arrow and Robert Solow (in Dasgupta & Mäler 2000). After reviewing over ninety books and articles, Kwon and Adler conclude: "The basic thesis – that the social ties can be efficacious in providing information, influence, and solidarity – is no longer in dispute" (Kwon & Adler 2014, 419). Also, the report of UNECE et al. (2008) observes "a growing consensus around the idea that it is social networks and their associated norms that generate benefits" and supports the most commonly adopted definition of social capital proposed by the OECD (2001):

Networks, together with shared norms, values and understandings which facilitate cooperation within and among groups. (UNECE et al. 2008, 53)

Social capital can be understood with a simple model of sources, assets and outcomes. The sources are individuals, groups and institutions. The assets are the networks and associated norms such as shared understanding and informal rules that influence behavior. They link individuals, groups and institutions in many different modes and forums, including face-to-face meetings, legislation and technology-assisted transmission of information. The outcomes from social capital are the positive and negative effects: identity and sense of belonging, increased knowledge and understanding, community resilience, lowering transaction costs, conflict resolution, social exclusion or intolerance of difference, reduced family functioning and corruption (UNECE et al. 2008, 51).

In his essay "Social capital and economic performance: Analytics," Partha Dasgupta argues that social capital is most usefully viewed as a system of interpersonal networks. It is an aspect of human capital (in the economic sense mentioned above), provided that network formation gives rise to localized externalities. However, if network externalities are more in the nature of public goods, social capital is a component of total factor productivity. There is no single object called social capital, but a multitude of bits that together can be called social capital, which is distinct from trust, culture, and institutions (Dasgupta 2003; based on his chapter in Dasgupta & Serageldin 2000).

In this book, I concentrate on economically relevant social capital and use Robert Putnam's definition, which refers to "connections among individuals – social networks and the norm of reciprocity and trustworthiness that arise from them" (Putnam 2000, 19). Social capital can be either a private or a public good and can have "a dark side" (meaning restricting freedom and encouraging intolerance) which is examined from an ethical perspective by Ayios et al. (2014). Thus, the definition of social capital used in this book differs from the concept of social cohesion discussed in Enderle (2018d).

Notes

1 Similarly, the International Integrated Reporting Committee distinguishes six types of capital: financial, manufactured, intellectual, human, social and relationship, and natural (IIRC 2013, particularly 12–13; see also Adams 2015, Dumas et al. 2016).

2 According to OECD (2013a, 190), "[c]onsistent with Stiglitz et al. (2009) and the TFSD, . . . a dashboard of physical and monetary measures is most appropriate for monitoring the capital stocks that sustain well-being over time." TFSD is the Task Force for Measuring Sustainable Development (OECD 2013, 211).

3 The important concept of natural capital has been emphasized by The Natural Capital Declaration (2012), a commitment of the finance sector for Rio+20 and beyond. It defines natural capital as Earth's natural assets (soil, air, water, flora and fauna) and the ecosystem services resulting from them, which make human life possible. The signatories of the declaration wish to demonstrate their commitment to the eventual integration of natural capital considerations into private sector reporting, accounting and decision making, with standardization of measurement and disclosure of natural capital use by the private sector (www.naturalcapitaldeclaration.org).

5 | Wealth Is a Combination of Private and Public Wealth

When we undertake to define "the wealth of a nation," it is difficult to deny that wealth should encompass both private and public goods. These two types of goods can be fundamentally defined as those that can be attributed to, enjoyed and controlled by individual actors (persons, groups or organizations), and those from which no actor inside the country can be excluded. In mainstream neoclassical economic theory, "public goods" – and thus public wealth – are defined with the characteristics of non-excludability and non-rivalry (see a good summary in Windsor 2018a). A classic example is national defense (in a democratic setting). When it is established, no one can be excluded from it. Moreover, one person can benefit from it without reducing the benefit of it for another person; in other words, the "consumption" or "enjoyment" of one person does not rival the "consumption" or "enjoyment" of another person. Or take another example: the use of a software program or the enjoyment of a music CD. Without exclusive copyright protection, the program and the CD can be used (that is, "copied") by anyone without diminishing the quality (while reducing the profit of the producing firm with that intellectual property right). In contrast, private goods are characterized by the attributes of excludability and rivalry.

These two formal criteria of public goods and public wealth – as distinct from the substantive criteria of natural, economic, human and social capital – apply also to negative public goods, which can be called "public bads."[1] When a region is struck by an epidemic disease (like Ebola), no one can (in principle) be excluded, and the risk of infection for one inhabitant of that ravaged region does not reduce the risk of infection of other inhabitants. On the contrary, it might even reinforce the risk for other persons.

It is important to understand that the wealth of a society, ranging from the local up to the global level, must be conceived as a combination of private and public wealth – not just as an aggregation of

---

Box 5.1 Public goods and public bads

Public goods and public bads are formally defined by the characteristics of non-excludability and non-rivalry.

Examples of public goods: a fair and effective rule of law, a relatively corruption-free business environment, the stability of the financial system.

Examples of public bads: climate change (global warming), air and water pollution, discrimination by gender, race and ethnicity, conflict-stricken areas.

---

private wealth. This means that the creation of private goods depends on the availability of public goods and, in turn, the creation of public goods is dependent on the availability of private goods.

To illustrate this thesis, I would like to mention an example from China's recent history. When, in 1978, after the death of Mao Zedong, Deng Xiaoping launched the economic reform and opening-up of the country, the Chinese people were called upon "to jump into the sea" (xià hǎi); that is, to leave the security of state-owned enterprises behind and run the risk of opening and operating their own businesses. In the following decades the introduction of the market economy has proven, by and large, to be very successful (which, of course, does not deny the downsides of this economic development). A decisive factor of success was the so-called "Deng Xiaoping effect" (Huang 2008, 34–38). Although no well-established rule of law to protect private entrepreneurs existed at that time, the Chinese trusted that Deng Xiaoping would not deceive them, but rather that he would acknowledge and support their efforts. Thus we may conclude that the existing public good of trust in Deng Xiaoping was a crucial factor of success for private entrepreneurial initiatives in China's economic reform.[2]

On the other hand, it also holds true that the creation of public goods depends on the creation of private goods. It suffices to recall multifaceted private contributions to the creation of public wealth, which are provided through business, education, research and development, arts and health care, in the form of taxes and in many other areas (see Box 5.1).

Table 5.1 *Distinction between private and public goods*

		Rivalry	
		Yes	No
Excludability	Yes	private good	(club goods)
	No	(common resources)	public good

The distinction between private and public goods can be traced back to Paul Samuelson (see Table 5.1). In 1954 and 1955, influenced by Richard Musgrave, Samuelson published two short articles on the theory of public expenditure (Samuelson 1954, 1955) which were of groundbreaking importance for the development of the modern theory of public economics and contained fundamental implications for market failure (Enderle 2000). Inge Kaul, Isabelle Grunberg and Marc Stern expanded the reach of public goods to "global public goods" for international cooperation in the twenty-first century (Kaul et al. 1999a, 1999b, 1999c; Kaul 2003; see Chapter 14).[3]

A third type of goods, developed in the theory of public finance by Richard Musgrave (1957, 1958), are "merit goods." While divergent interpretations exist, some basic features are common (Musgrave 1987). A merit good is not defined by characteristics of the good itself (such as rivalry or excludability), but by the type of consumer preference from which it is derived. Therefore, it should not be confused with a public good. Instead of individual preferences commonly assumed as the basis of the demand for private and public goods, community values (or preferences) restrain individual choice. They determine the goods the community or the government should supply, such as education, vaccination, redistribution or primary distribution of income and wealth. Because community values may diverge from individual preferences, merit goods might be imposed against certain individual preferences (which raises the question of paternalism). Although important in public finance, this type of good will not be discussed here further, given the focus of this chapter and merit goods' specific characteristics.

The crucial distinction between private and public goods, emphasized here, also applies to private and public wealth. While goods in economic terms are "flows," wealth consists of "stocks." However, to

---

Box 5.2 What is the "wealth of a nation"? A combination of private and public wealth

Mutual dependence of producing private and public goods:

- The production of *private* goods depends on public goods and can suffer from public bads. Individuals and companies need public goods in order to be productive.
- The production of *public* goods depends on the contributions by individuals and companies through taxes, philanthropy, expertise in science and technology, arts and the humanities and in many other fields.

Example: "Deng Xiaoping effect" in the 1980s in China (Huang 2008) Two fundamental implications:

- Wealth creation needs both market institutions and collective actors.
- Wealth creation needs both self-regarding and other-regarding motivations.

---

capture the economic performance adequately, flows and stocks have to be accounted for (see Stiglitz et al. 2009 in Chapter 3). Therefore, the concept of wealth in this book includes both flows and stocks. It is a combination of private and public wealth that can be summarized as follows (see Box 5.2). First, wealth as a combination includes both private and public wealth, thus excluding both a strictly individualistic as well as a strictly collectivistic notion of wealth. Second, private and public wealth can be combined by way of addition or multiplication, depending on the more specific forms and respective extents of private and public wealth. Third, notwithstanding the immense variety of possible combinations, the mutual dependence of private and public wealth needs to be stressed. The production of private goods depends on public goods and can suffer from public bads. Individuals and companies need public goods in order to be productive. In turn, the production of public goods depends on the contributions by individuals and companies through taxes, philanthropy and expertise in science and technology, arts and the humanities and in many other fields. Thus, this interdependence of private and public wealth should be neither ignored nor underestimated.

Of course, there exists an immense variety of goods, which lie between pure private and pure public goods, depending on the degrees of rivalry and excludability. A prominent example can be found in Paul Romer's concept of technology. In his theory of "endogenous technological change," he states right at the beginning: "The distinguishing feature of the technology as an input is that it is neither a conventional good nor a public good; it is a non-rival, partially excludable good" (Romer 1990, S71). While he maintains the feature of non-rivalry (characterizing public goods), he introduces different degrees of excludability (departing from the notion of public goods).[4] Take, for example, non-rival goods such as basic research and development (R&D), operations manuals for Walmart stores, a computer code for a software application and an encoded satellite television broadcast. There are multiple ways of increasing the degree of excludability up to 100 percent by secrecy, patents, trademarks, secret ingredients, access codes, proprietary standards, continual innovation and other means (see Warsh 2006, 285–87). And by increasing excludability, the goods become (more) commercially valuable. Nonetheless, the fundamental distinction between private and public wealth remains crucial.

The understanding of wealth as a combination of private and public wealth has far-reaching implications for the types of institutions and motivations required for creating wealth. The discussion of public goods in economic literature has highlighted the strengths and limitations of the market institution. Based on individual preferences and the price system coordinating supply and demand, the market has proved a powerful means for producing private goods in an efficient manner. Prices convey information, provide incentives, guide choices and allocate resources. In theory, the price is "right," if supply meets demand, and more (or less) goods are produced. The basic assumption is that there is a price, which properly reflects supply and demand and clears the market, given there are no large firms, no externalities, perfect information, no distortions due to social institutions etc.

In contrast, no price can be assigned to public goods, which would coordinate supply and demand. Because their consumption is non-rival and non-excludable, the price system does not work. Public goods can be consumed without paying a price (which is the so-called free-rider problem), and public bads cannot be reduced or avoided by charging a higher price (apart from taxes etc.). Thus, by definition, the market institution fails to produce public goods.

Not surprisingly, many attempts have been undertaken to mitigate this sobering result. One might refer to the approximation by shadow pricing.[5] Another way, indicated above, has been by restraining the assumption of individual preferences and introducing community preferences (see Chapter 10). Nevertheless, the fundamental difference between private and public goods remains, and the basic limitation of the market institution has to be accepted.

Because the market institution, in principle, fails to produce public goods, we may ask whether there are other institutional arrangements that can achieve this goal. Major collective actors are the states and the governments at different levels. Depending on the kind and reach of public goods, these actors might be in a position to address this public challenge. But often, particularly in the international arena, they do not exist or may fail because of weakness. In the wake of Garret Hardin's challenging article on "the tragedy of the commons" (Hardin 1968), groundbreaking research on the evolution of institutions for collective action has been conducted, displaying a rich institutional diversity of self-organization and self-government. Elinor Ostrom's work (Ostrom 1990, 2005) is of particular merit. Although her focus is on problems of common pool resources (not public goods in the strict sense, see note 3; Ostrom et al. 1977), her insights certainly also help to better explain successful and failed institutions for producing public goods.[6]

Furthermore, not only does the market institution fail to produce public goods, but it also can be understood as a public good itself in the broader sense mentioned above. It meets the criteria of non-rivalry and non-excludability. In a perfect market, the participation by one actor does not diminish the participation of another, and no actor can be excluded, provided the market participant has the necessary endowment. Thus the functioning of the market is truly a public good and the dis-functioning thereof a public bad. An interesting historical example of this "dialectic" can be found in Adam Smith's work and the creation of wealth in eighteenth-century Scotland: on the one hand, he advocated free international trade to efficiently produce private goods, and, on the other hand, he silently accepted the property regime of his time (technically speaking, a public good) that thrived on the international slave trade from Africa and tobacco production in North America.[7]

This example shows the formal definition of private and public goods mentioned above. Like private goods, public goods can be "good" or "bad." The institution of slavery – well established in the international slave trade – was a "public bad" as we would define it today. In the trade triangle between Europe, Africa and America it impacted everybody, though in different ways; hence it was non-excludable. And the use of the institution of slavery by, say, cotton plantation owners in America did not diminish the benefits of cloth factories in Britain; therefore, they did not rival. On the contrary, generally speaking, they benefited from each other, at the expense of the slaves. In other words, the international trade based on slavery as a "public good" (assumed by Adam Smith) benefitted both the plantation owners and the manufacturers.

Because the definition of "private" and "public" goods is a formal one, it does not involve an ethical evaluation of the goods. As for private goods, such an evaluation might be based on individual preferences and left to individual choices. As for public goods, the ethical evaluation cannot be left to individual choices, but requires collective choices, which tend to be more difficult to make (see James 2018). However, in many situations an ethical evaluation is unavoidable: Is slavery a public good in a positive sense or in a negative sense? Similarly, we wonder how to evaluate global public goods such as climate change? Is it a "public good" or a "public bad"? It is fair to say that wealth as a combination of private and public wealth cannot but demand ethical evaluation. The question of ethical evaluation has already been raised in Chapter 4 by pointing to the property rights of non-human-made natural assets and will be addressed in terms of human rights in Part II of this book.

A further far-reaching implication of wealth conceived as a combination of private and public wealth concerns different types of motivations (see Chapter 10). In order to produce private goods, the motivation of self-interest undoubtedly plays an important, though not an exclusive role. One might recall Smith's famous saying that it "is not of the benevolence of the butcher, the brewer, or the baker that we expect our dinner, but from their regard to their own interest" (Smith 1776/1981, 26–27). However, as Amartya Sen (1993, 7–8) points out, this saying focuses only on exchange (not production and distribution) and does not express the whole motivational structure of Smith's theory. After all, Smith published not only the book on the wealth of nations but also *The Theory of Moral Sentiments* (Smith 1759/1976).

When it comes to producing public goods, the motivation of self-interest is utterly insufficient. In its extreme form, self-interest is based on the anthropological assumption that the individual person is an autonomous and completely independent person who has to care about himself or herself exclusively. Commitment for others is only acceptable if it helps or at least does not hurt oneself. Any sacrifice for others has to be rejected. This view expresses the ideal of "the self-made person," vigorously defended by philosophers such as Ayn Rand (1957/2005, 1964). However, it ignores the fundamental fact that humans are relational beings, who are shaped by and, in turn, can shape, relations with other people.

The production of public goods is based on human relatedness and needs other-regarding motivations such as gratitude for the gifts received, entrepreneurial spirit and service to others. Commitment to public goods does not earn immediate rewards, may offer uncertain personal benefits in the future and can even demand personal sacrifices. But, not infrequently, it is actually made because the interests of other people count, their rights are to be respected and the needs of the community and society should be addressed. Therefore, other-regarding motivations are indispensable for creating public wealth – a topic that will be further discussed in Chapter 10.

Notes

1 The term "public bad" is used in economics as the symmetric of the term "public good" because of its characteristics of non-excludability and non-rivalry and its negative impact on people and nature. Air pollution is an obvious example of a public bad. For current definitions of public bads, see Kolstad (2010).

2 Here the term "public good" is used in a broad sense that includes immaterial goods such as trust based on expectations; see the definition of social capital in Chapter 4 and Kaul 2003 in this chapter.

3 Later on new types of goods were introduced such as "club goods," which are non-rivalrous but excludable, and "common resources" or "common pool resources," which are rivalrous but non-excludable (see Windsor 2018a).

4 The thought process of this conceptual development is well explained to non-specialist readers by David Warsh (2006) in *Knowledge and the Wealth of Nations: A Story of Economic Discovery* (particularly pp. 276–88).

5 Black et al. (2009, 409) define shadow prices as "prices of goods, services, and resources that are proportional to true opportunity costs for the economy, taking account of any externalities.... In an economy with no market failure, market prices and shadow prices would be equivalent. In

an economy with market failure ... actual and shadow prices do not coincide." However, to the extent that this no-coincidence can be estimated, a kind of shadow price can be approximated. There is a large literature on shadow prices and how they can be approximated in practice. They also require government action to set.

6 Similarly, Daron Acemoglu and James Robinson (2012) argue that if nations want to have success, they need inclusive economic institutions to succeed. Many people have discussed these issues, including old and new institutionalists, the latter including Douglass North.

7 See Marvin Brown's analysis in *Civilizing the Economy* (2010), chapter 2.

6 | Wealth Creation Is about Producing and Distributing Wealth

For too long, the purpose of business and the economy has been economic growth, usually measured in terms of GDP and regardless of its environmental impact. In Chapters 4 and 5, this narrow and misleading focus on economic growth has been rectified by defining wealth in a comprehensive sense. Accordingly, it comprehends the total amount of economically relevant private and public assets including natural, economic, human and social capital ("stocks") with their changes over time ("flows").[1] However, it still remains to be seen *how* the generation of wealth should be understood. Is it first and foremost a production process whose output is subsequently distributed to consumers and investors – in line with the saying that one has to bake the cake first before it can be shared? In other words, production first and distribution second? Or does distribution come first and production second? This question has divided the ideological Right from the ideological Left for many years, the first claiming the priority of production (for example, in supply-side economics [Roy 2018a]) while the second prioritizes distribution and fairness (for example, certain theories of justice such as John Rawls's *A Theory of Justice* [1971]).

A closer look at the generation of wealth reveals that it includes not only a productive, but also a distributive dimension. The distributive dimension permeates all stages of wealth creation, from the preconditions to the generation process, the outcome and the use for and allocation within consumption and investment. In fact, the productive and the distributive dimensions of wealth creation are intrinsically interrelated and cannot be separated into different subsequent phases. Before the creation begins, the original endowment of resources is necessarily shaped by a certain pattern of distribution (that is, who owns natural, economic, human and social capital; and whether it is private or public). During the process, multiple allocation and price decisions are made, which have far-reaching distributive implications and consequences. The outcome of the process clearly shows distributive structures with winners and losers. And the use of wealth – be it for consumption or investment purposes – involves many distributive implications, even before the government redistributes wealth through taxes and subsidies. Therefore, wealth creation as understood in this book is about both producing and distributing wealth.

Given the intrinsic relations between the productive and the distributive dimensions of wealth creation, it is easy to understand that a comprehensive conception of economic history – as proposed by Douglass North – includes "(1) the overall growth of the economy over time and the determinants of that growth (or stagnation or decline) and (2) the distribution of income within that economy in the course of its growth or decline" (North 1972, 468). Obviously, this also holds true for the comprehensive conception of wealth creation.

The importance of growth and equitable distribution for sustainability was emphasized also by Robert Solow, Nobel Laureate in Economics:

In many ways, the more equitable the growth, the more sustainable it's likely to be, because there will be less controversy, less disagreement, less resistance, and also there's an enormous amount of talent in populations that needs to be tapped. Excluding some parts of the population, whether by gender, age, or ethnicity, from the benefits of growth loses the talents that they have. So in my view, it is not only desirable that they go together, it's useful that they go together. (Quoted in World Bank 2008, 62)

Moreover, both the Stiglitz-Sen-Fitoussi Report (Report 2009) and the OECD Report *How's Life? 2013* (OECD 2013a) highlight the importance of the distributive dimension of wealth creation. The first report recommends "to give more prominence to the distribution of income, consumption and wealth" (Recommendation 4) and "quality-of-life indicators in all dimensions covered should assess inequalities in a comprehensive way" (Recommendation 7). The second report writes that "[t]he distribution of outcomes is emphasised as a key aspect of current well-being throughout *How's Life?*, but it may also be an important characteristic to investigate in capital stocks" (OECD 2013a, 178; see 193–94 and Figure 4.2 in Chapter 4).

It comes as no surprise that the distributive dimension of wealth creation has gained much attention in recent years. For practical reasons, it highly matters to people how they are affected by wealth creation. And for theoretical reasons, most influential market models – particularly general equilibrium models (see Eatwell et al. 1989) – ignore or downplay the distributive implications of market transactions. They presuppose the distribution of original endowments of resources and silently accept the outcomes based on the Pareto-efficiency criterion, which does not allow for exchanges with decreasing benefits for trading partners.

As a result of these practical and theoretical reasons, a vast literature has emerged to present and analyze increasing inequalities of income and wealth with far-reaching consequences for people's well-being. Between 2008 and 2015, the Organisation for Economic Cooperation and Development (OECD) published numerous reports on the trends and causes of rising income inequality among its member countries (for instance, OECD 2013a, 2013b, 2015a, 2015b). The World Economic Forum (2015) publishes annual global risks reports consistently identifying inequality as a major risk factor. In his 2015 encyclical, Pope Francis urged the world to care for our common home by relating "climate change and inequality" (Pope Francis 2015). The United Nations addresses inequality explicitly in two of its seventeen Sustainable Development Goals (SDGs 2015; see Chapter 2). Social scientists, especially economists, have focused on the topic, including Robert Frank (2007), Paul Krugman (2009), Antony Atkinson (2015) and François Bourguignon (2015), as have the authors of three books presented here: Thomas Piketty's (2014) *Capital in the Twenty-First Century,* Joseph Stiglitz's (2012) *The Price of Inequality* and Richard Wilkinson and Kate Pickett's (2009) *The Spirit Level: Why Equality Is Better for Everyone* (discussed in Tsui et al. 2018, 2019).

In exemplary ways, these three books point out the challenges of extreme income inequality, briefly outlined in the following, and discuss negative impacts of income inequality on people and society, the need for a just social order and the conviction that changes are possible. The authors call for the courage to pursue positive solutions, but each has a unique perspective. Piketty, a French economist, presents a large database showing the dynamics of income and wealth distribution over 120 years across twenty-nine countries. Stiglitz, US Nobel Laureate in Economics, investigates the interplay of market forces, political machinations and consequences on income inequality for the US economy and society. British epidemiologists Wilkinson and Pickett focus on the twenty-three wealthiest OECD nations. They provide robust evidence that gross inequality tears at the human psyche and creates anxiety, distrust and an array of mental and physical ailments.

These three studies examine economic inequality including income (flows) and wealth (stocks) – as this book proposes – the first two analyzing in depth its causes and negative effects and the third focusing on its impact on people and society. Moreover, the relationship between inequality and public wealth requires a great deal of scrutiny (patently clear in the Covid-19 pandemic). Obviously, these questions are highly complex and would need extensive discussion, which goes beyond the scope of this book. Suffice to insist that the distributive dimension of wealth creation is essential and needs thorough analysis and effective policies.

Thomas Piketty: Capital in the Twenty-First Century

Piketty puts the debate on the distributional question at the heart of economic analysis. Rather than denouncing inequality or capitalism, he suggests ways to best organize society and identifies institutions and policies most appropriate for achieving a just social order. Critical of mainstream US economics, abstract theory and mathematical excess, he tries to answer fundamental questions using publicly accessible data and a minimal theoretical framework. Highly aware of the complex history of income and wealth, he cautiously draws lessons from the past to predict the future.

Written in a clear, compelling and readily accessible style, the 685-page book includes an introduction, sixteen chapters, conclusions and a large appendix. The data clearly indicate that countries vary substantially in the rise and fall of income and wealth inequality because of various economic and noneconomic factors with multifaceted impacts.

Chapter 8, titled "Two Worlds," explains quite different patterns in France and the United States regarding the evolution of inequality from 1910 to 2010. In France, the evolution was simple: from 1980 to 2010, the top decile (10 percent) in total income (capital gains and wages) maintained its same share, whereas the top centile (1 percent) increased its wage share by 30 percent during the 2000s in the last decade. The top 0.1 percent and 0.01 percent had even greater increases. In the United States, inequality transformation was more complex. From 1980 to 2010, the top decile (10 percent) increased its share of total income (including wages and capital gains) from 35 percent to 48 percent, the top 10 percent to 5 percent (annual incomes $108,000 to $150,000 in 2010) remained at about 12 percent and the top 5 percent to 1 percent (annual incomes $150,000 to $352,000 in 2010) slightly increased from 13 percent to 16 percent. However, the top 1 percent (annual incomes above $352,000 in 2010) jumped from 10 percent to 20 percent, an increase of 100 percent (compared with a 30 percent increase in France). Most notable is that among the top 5 percent, almost 90 percent of the total income came from employment; less than 10 percent came from capital income. For the majority 95 per-cent, capital earnings were miniscule.

The data clearly show that since the 1970s, the United States, among all developed economies, has experienced the largest increase in income inequality and, based on projections, will continue to hold this position. How did it happen? Piketty concludes that it "reflects the advent of 'supermanagers,' that is, top executives of large firms who have managed to obtain extremely high, historically unprecedented compensation packages for their labor" (2014, 302). Consequently, corporate pay policies and practices are fueling US income inequality.

Joseph Stiglitz: The Price of Inequality

Economists largely support and non-economists can easily understand this clearly written 414-page book. In ten chapters Stiglitz criticizes the excessive gap of "the 1 percent and the 99 percent" in the United States. In chapter 1 he writes that there are

certain stark and uncomfortable facts about the US economy: (a) Recent US income growth primarily occurs at the top 1 percent of the income distribu-tion. (b) As a result, there is growing inequality. (c) Those at the bottom and in the middle are actually worse-off today than they were at the beginning of the century ... and (i) America has more inequality than any other advanced industrialized country; it does less to correct these inequalities, and inequality is growing more than in many other countries. (Stiglitz 2012, 25)

Against these inconvenient truths, Stiglitz refutes, with relevant empirical data, four retorts by the American Right: that lifetime inequality is not bad, poverty in America is not real, statistics are misleading and inequality can be economically and morally justified and, thus, should not be reduced, which would "kill the golden goose" and make even the poor suffer.

In chapters 2 and 3 Stiglitz discusses the interconnected political and economic causes of inequality. Although market forces shape the degree of inequality, government policies shape market forces, which becomes especially clear when Stiglitz compares the United States with other advanced industrialized countries. Current US political processes help the wealthy at the expense of the majority population – for example, through government-provided hidden and open transfers and subsidies, laws that make the marketplace less competitive, lax enforcement of competition laws, monopoly rents and government munificence. Real market forces also contribute to inequality, shaped by politics and societal changes and explainable by the difference between rent seeking and productive activity. Stiglitz presents a long list of examples in finance, manufacturing, discrimination, labor relations, corporate governance and globalization of trade and capital markets.

In the early 1980s, just as markets started delivering more unequal outcomes, tax policies began favoring the top (for example, by lowering tax rates on capital gains). Rather than bringing more work and better savings, the policies increased inequality. Stiglitz's sobering look at the functioning of markets, politics, societal norms and social institutions reveals multiple causes of widening inequality. Further explaining how inequality depresses national output, economic stability, economic efficiency and growth, Stiglitz writes:

> The big puzzle we presented in the last chapter was how, in a democracy supposedly based on one person one vote, the 1 percent could have been so victorious in shaping policies toward its own interests. We described a process of disempowerment, disillusionment, and disenfranchisement that produces low voter turnout, a system in which electoral success requires heavy investments, and in which those with money have made political investments that have reaped large rewards – often larger than the returns they have reaped on their other investments. (2012, 146)

In other words, economic power brings political power, which further contributes to economic power and further deepens inequality between the 1 percent and the 99 percent with far-reaching consequences for the economy, polity and society.

Richard Wilkinson and Kate Pickett: The Spirit Level

This relatively small (274-page) book, divided into sixteen chapters, is filled with surprising data and insightful discussions about the human cost of income inequality among the twenty-three wealthiest nations.

Income inequality, in this book, is defined as the difference in income between a nation's top 20 percent and bottom 20 percent, using the average of OECD data from 2003 to 2006. The authors replicate the results using data from the fifty US states, with income inequality defined with the Gini coefficient using data from 1999. The appendix explains how the authors selected the countries and provides information on the data sources.

The book focuses on income inequality at the society level, but in the final chapter the authors point to the role of the corporation: "Turning corporations loose and letting the profit motive run amok is not a prescription for a more livable world" (Wilkinson & Pickett 2009, 235). They write:

The institutions in which we are employed are, after all, the main source of income inequality. It is there that value is created and divided between the various gradations of employees. It is there that the inequities, which necessitate redistribution, are set up. And it is there that we are most explicitly placed in a rank-ordered hierarchy, superiors and inferiors, bosses and subordinates. (2009, 249–50)

Wilkinson and Pickett present research showing that rank-ordered hierarchies have devastating consequences extending far beyond subjective happiness. Inequalities influence objective well-being in diverse areas, such as homicide, obesity, infant mortality, mental illness, teenage births, social mobility, life expectancy, imprisonment rates, levels of trust in society, drug and alcohol addiction and children's educational performance. Even more sobering is that income inequality hurts all income categories – hence the subtitle, "Why Equality Is Better for Everyone."

The authors dispel the misconception that average income brings well-being. They show that economic development boosts well-being, measured by life expectancy, only in the early stages. Income and life expectancy are unrelated in countries that have average national income of more than $20,000 per person. In general, in national and census data from fifty US states, any index of health and social problems is strongly correlated with income inequality.

What might explain these findings? The authors suggest that income inequality brings social distance and stratification, causing individuals to experience anxiety, shame, humiliation, loneliness, embarrassment, depression and stress, and it triggers "fight or flight" physiological responses. Prolonged stress suppresses immunity and causes numerous health, education, psychological and behavioral problems. The United States leads the twenty-three most developed countries in terms of the highest income inequality and the poorest performance on all health and social indicators, while Scandinavian countries (Norway, Sweden, Finland and Denmark) have the lowest income inequality and the highest well-being levels. Furthermore, the relatively more equal countries maintain creativity and quality of life: they are more innovative and have a wider sense of social responsibility, as indicated by a greater recycling rate. Finally, the authors call for a social movement to increase awareness of the ills of inequality and to influence governments and corporations to take measures to increase income equality.

As the summaries of these three books show, inequalities of income and wealth are highly complex issues and have far-reaching consequences for the well-being of people and societies. In order to deeply understand and effectively address these challenges, it does not suffice to describe and analyze the distributive patterns; rather, they have to be seen as interconnected with the productive structures and processes. Only then can the creation of wealth be fully understood and successfully advanced.

The "East Asian Miracle" may serve as an example to illustrate the interconnectedness of the productive and the distributive dimensions of economic growth (see Chapter 3). It demonstrates that, under certain conditions, high growth rates are correlated with substantial reduction of inequality and poverty (discussed in Enderle 1995).

In its Policy Research Report *The East Asian Miracle* the World Bank (1993) identifies eight High-Performing Asian Economies (HPAEs) which share some economic characteristics that set them apart from most other developing countries. These HPAEs are: Japan (124 million people), the four "Tigers": Hong Kong (6 million), the Republic of Korea (44 million), Singapore (3 million), Taiwan (21 million) and the three newly industrialized economies of Southeast Asia: Indonesia (184 million), Malaysia (19 million) and Thailand (58 million), making a total population of approximately 459 million.

Although the HPAEs are highly diverse in natural resources, population, culture and economic policy, they have in common rapid, sustained growth between 1960 and 1990, in itself unusual among developing countries, combined with highly equal income distribution. The World Bank Report says:

When the East Asian economies are divided by speed of growth, the distribution of income is substantially more equal in the fast growers ... For the eight HPAEs, rapid growth and declining inequality have been shared virtues ... The developing HPAEs clearly outperform other middle-income economies in that they have both lower levels of inequality and higher levels of growth. Moreover, ... improvements in income distribution generally coincided with periods of rapid growth. (World Bank 1993, 30)

This combination of rapid growth and decreasing inequality is an extraordinary fact and deserves to be called a "miracle." It runs counter to the widely held economic theory that economic growth must necessarily be linked with increasing inequality.[2] Rather, the East Asian economies prove the contrary is possible. Moreover, these astonishing examples show that lower income groups do not have to wait for the "trickle-down" effect of economic growth from the top of the income distribution. In fact, a substantial reduction of poverty has taken place in HPAEs.[3]

In conclusion, wealth creation is not simply a production process, but involves both a productive and a distribution dimension, which are closely interconnected. Therefore, issues of unequal distribution are not just an afterthought of economic growth, and economic inequality cannot be understood and addressed without analysis of the productive side. Obviously, the question of ethical evaluation of the process of wealth creation is inescapable.

Notes

1 See also the limited role of GDP in the OECD well-being conceptual framework in Figure 4.1.
2 Sometimes one refers to the "Kuznets curve" that expresses this inverse U-shaped relationship. In fact, Kuznets investigated the relations between growth and income distribution in numerous studies but did not claim that such a link is necessary (see Kuznets 1955, 1959, 1966). For a recent discussion about growth, inequality and poverty reduction, see Bourguignon 2019).
3 Some explaining factors of the "miracle" are discussed in Enderle (1995). It goes without saying that this "miracle" provoked controversial reactions and would need further examination (see Dutt 1990).

7 | Creating Wealth Involves Material and Spiritual Aspects

Talking about wealth and its creation, one might think, first, of merely material things, goods and services, money, cash and securities, manufacturing, buildings, shipping and other things. However, a closer look reveals that wealth creation – if understood in a comprehensive sense like here – cannot be just a material matter, but necessarily involves a spiritual dimension as well. What material and spiritual aspects mean and how they belong together and relate to each other will be explored and discussed in this chapter.

Because wealth comprehends all four types of capital – natural, economic, human and social – it cannot be merely material. Human capital means healthy and educated people, and social capital consists of trust relations between people and economic actors. The capability approach, explained in the next chapter, enriches our understanding that being healthy and educated and enjoying trust relations are not just exterior attributes, but characterize "real freedoms that people enjoy" (Sen 1999, 3). Moreover, capabilities closely relate to nature (natural capital) and material things (economic capital) and therefore necessarily interpret the material world in one way or another.

Illustrations of Wealth Creation with Spiritual Aspects

Three examples of wealth creation at the micro-, meso- and macro-levels of analysis may illustrate how the material and the spiritual aspects are essential and interdependent. First, we look at the experience of a poor woman in Bangladesh, who received a micro-loan from the Grameen Bank to create wealth at a very basic level:

It took a few weeks for Aleya and her friend to form their group. "When I went to the bank, they told me to get five people," she explained. "They said, 'Your spirit must be in agreement; you have to share opinions about things; and you can't be in a group with someone who eats from the same cooking pot as you."

Aleya borrowed 2,000 takas [about 50 USD; added by G.E.] the first time. She received 1,900 takas in hand (5 percent was deposited into the Group Fund). She bought a cow and sold milk, earning between 10 and 20 takas each day. Each week she paid her installment of 40 takas and deposited a few takas in her savings. "At first it was difficult, but I had no complications."

Over the next fifty weeks, Aleya set aside 163 takas for her interest payment. (The bank was then charging 16 percent interest calculated on a declining balance.) An additional 41 takas had to be paid into the Emergency Fund (25 percent of the interest). At the end of the year, the cow belonged to her.

"How did you feel then?" I asked.
"Inside, my heart and mind stayed the same," she said. "But I also felt happy."
"Then?"
"Then I said, 'The cow is ours.'" (Bornstein 1996, 80)

Although very poor, this woman did not spend the borrowed money for consumption, but "opened her business" and invested it in a cow that produced milk, which she could sell for money. She created economic capital (a stock) that generated revenue over many years (flows). She turned the cycle of poverty of loans for consumption resulting in more debts into the cycle of wealth creation. At the same time, this material process involved a spiritual process, beginning with Aleya's determination to pay back the loan, supported by the group, through to enjoying the freedom she gained and the pride that the family owned the cow. With this freedom she was able to feed her children and allow them to go to school. Obviously, the spiritual side of this process cannot be overlooked.

A second example – at the meso-level – is the Japanese enterprise Matsushita Electric whose philosophy is summarized in *Not for Bread Alone*[1](Matsushita 1984). Its founder Konosuke Matsushita started the business in 1917 with a square, battery-powered flashlight and expanded it in the 1920s to include wiring fixtures, bicycle lamps, electric heating devices, radios, dry-cell batteries and many other products. On May 5, 1932 he explained his business ethos and management ethic to all his employees:

The mission of a manufacturer is to *overcome poverty*, to relieve society as a whole from the misery of poverty and *bring it wealth*. Business and production are not meant simply to enrich the shops or the factories of the enterprise concerned, but all of society. And society needs the dynamism and vitality of business and industry to generate wealth. Only under such conditions will businesses and factories truly prosper ... The real mission of Matsushita Electric is to produce an inexhaustible supply of goods, thus *creating peace and prosperity* throughout the land. (Matsushita 1984, 22; emphasis added)

In 1933 Matsushita set forth the seven principles of leadership, which have shaped the company's policy, culture and conduct over decades, supported by the "Peace and Happiness through Prosperity" Institute (established in 1946; www.php.co.jp/en). The principles highlight the importance of "the spirit," namely the spirit of service through industry, of fairness, of harmony and cooperation, of courtesy and humility, of accord with natural laws and of gratitude. Although Matsushita did not use the terms "spiritual" and "spirituality" (which probably would not have been understandable at that time), there is no doubt that he wanted business to bring deep meaning to people and society, greatly transcending "business as usual."

To illustrate the spiritual aspect of wealth creation at the macro-level, we may recall the buildup of close economic, social and political relations between France and West Germany after 1945, embedded in the European Economic Community (EEC) (1957–93) and the European Union (EU) (since 1993). Having waged three increasingly atrocious wars, both countries resolutely turned around and became friends, based on increasingly connected ties, in order to make war impossible in the future. They have arguably created comprehensive wealth involving spiritual as well as material aspects. As testimony of this successful development, the Treaties of Rome (1957), Maastricht (1992) and Lisbon (2009) highlight the key goals of the EEC and EU with the firm foundation on human rights and fundamental freedoms. The Treaty of Rome states in Article 2:

The European Economic Community shall have as its task, by establishing a common market and progressively approximating the economic policies of Member States, to promote throughout the Community a harmonious development of economic activities, a continuous and balanced expansion, an increase in stability, an accelerated raising of the standard of living and closer relations between the States belonging to it.

A common market was thus established where people, goods, services and capital can move freely, and the conditions were created for prosperity and stability for European citizens, ushering in the longest period of peace in written history in Europe (https://europa.eu/euro pean-union/eu60_en).

The Treaty of Maastricht expressed in its preamble the resolution to mark a new stage in the process of European integration undertaken with the establishment of the European Communities. It recalled – after the fall of the Berlin wall in 1989 – the historic importance of the ending of the division of the European continent and the need to create firm bases for the construction of the future Europe.

The consolidated Treaties of Maastricht and Lisbon (2010) confirm the Union's attachment to the principles of liberty, democracy and respect for human rights and fundamental freedoms and of the rule of law. Article 2 highlights the fundamental values:

The Union is founded on the values of respect for human dignity, freedom, democracy, equality, the rule of law and respect for human rights, including the rights of persons belonging to minorities. These values are common to the Member States in a society in which pluralism, non-discrimination, tolerance, justice, solidarity and equality between women and men prevail.

Article 3 states the Union's aim to promote peace, its values and the well-being of its people. In particular, it addresses the free movement of persons within the Union's borders and appropriate measures of external border controls (Article 3.2), the establishment of an internal market (Article 3.3) and the Union's relation with the wider world (Article 3.5).[2] In Article 6 the Union recognizes the rights, freedoms and principles set out in the Charter of Fundamental Rights of the European Union (2000) (Article 6.1) and commits itself to accede to the European Convention for the Protection of Human Rights and Fundamental Freedoms (Article 6.2).

As these excerpts of the three treaties show, the EEC and the EU constitute more than simply the formation of an economic, political and legal union of member states including the former enemies and now friends of France and Germany. With its strong emphasis on values, the Union clearly has an ethical and spiritual dimension, and the wealth creation between France and Germany has been a substantial and indispensable contribution to peace in Europe.[3]

Conceptual Clarifications

In order to clarify the meaning of the material and spiritual aspects of wealth creation, it will be helpful to reflect on the anthropological foundation of the human person. If the person constitutes an intimate unity of body and soul, the material and spiritual aspects cannot be separated from each other; although distinct, they are interconnected and influence each other in multiple ways. If, however, this intimate unity is dissolved and body and soul form separate entities, the material and the spiritual aspects take on their own dynamics. When the material aspects dominate, one ends up with a materialistic anthropology; and when the spiritual aspects prevail, a spiritualistic anthropology results. Both views distort the comprehensive conception of wealth creation.

In history, wealth creation has often been ignored, disregarded or even treated with contempt. These attitudes depend on the valuation of the material world and the "bodiliness" of the human person as well as on the notion of creation. If the material world is considered inferior or even evil and if hostility towards the human body prevails, wealth cannot avoid sharing these qualities and is likely to be denigrated. Operating under those assumptions, it becomes nonsensical to produce such wealth, were it not for another, really valuable purpose. Moreover, without proper understanding, the creation of wealth cannot be fully appreciated for its capacity to serve as a purpose of economic activity that matters more than the possession and acquisition of wealth. It is fair to say that the determined affirmation of wealth creation as both good and necessary constitutes an essential prerequisite for thriving economies and businesses in the long run.

In contrast to the spiritualistic view of wealth creation, the materialistic view values material matters the most, if not as the only important things. It takes shape in countless fashions: as tireless greed, acquisitive spirit, nonsensical hoarding of money, endless accumulation of capital, profit maximization at any cost, exuberant consumerism, unbridled materialism, growth and competition. By ignoring the spiritual side of wealth creation, humans are abused and mistreated as merely bodily objects, and nature is exploited and destroyed, losing its life-sustaining role for the planet earth.

Having critiqued the materialistic and spiritualistic views, how best can we define the meaning of spiritual and spirituality? The adjective *spiritual* goes back to the early Christian Latin *spiritalis* (or *spiritualis*), translating Pauline *pneumatikós* (first letter of Paul to the Corinthians 2:13–3:1), along with its antonym *carnalis* (unspiritual or natural) and rapidly became common (Köpf 2012). It means the things Paul speaks of in words, which are not taught by human wisdom, but by the Spirit. The noun *spiritualitas* did not appear until the fifth century and then only sporadically. However, the growing popularity of the term *spirituality* and its equivalents in other western languages in religious and theological literature is a twentieth-century phenomenon. Today the term is applied indiscriminately to non-Christian religions, a usage pioneered by Vivekananda in 1893 at the first World's Parliament of Religions in Chicago. In the late twentieth century "faith and spirituality in the workplace" – used as inclusively as possible of all religious traditions as well as of those who see themselves as "spiritual but not religious," agnostic, or atheistic – became an emerging field in research and practice (Pauchant 2002; Giacalone & Jurkiewicz 2003/2010; Zsolnai 2004; Boukaert & Zsolnai 2011; Neal 2013; Gröschl & Bendl 2015; Chatterji & Zsolnai 2016; Syed et al. 2018).

Spirituality has become almost a buzzword, appearing in a wide variety of meanings and causing quite a lot of confusion. In their introductory chapter, Robert Giacalone and Carole Jurkiewicz provide much clarification of the definitions, the dimensionality and the manifestations (attributes versus activities) of spirituality. A representative sampling of fourteen definitions of "spirituality" in the literature include, among others, the following notions (Giacalone & Jurkiewicz 2010, 7):

- The personal expression of ultimate concern.
- The presence of a relationship with a higher power that affects the way in which one operates in the world.
- A way of being and experiencing that comes about through awareness of a transcendent dimension and that is characterized by certain identifiable values in regard to self, life, and whatever one considers to be the ultimate.
- That vast realm of human potential dealing with ultimate purposes, with higher entities, with God, with life, with compassion, with purpose.
- The animating force that inspires one toward purposes that are beyond one's self and that give one's life meaning and direction.

As these definitions show, spirituality relates to an ultimate reality and can be summarized, in Judy Neal's words, as "the experience of a transformative connection" (Neal 2013, 735). It is highly relevant for a comprehensive understanding of wealth creation at all three levels of analysis: straightforward for employees and leaders (at the micro-level), easily understandable for business organizations (at the meso-level) and more difficult to comprehend with regard to entire systems (at the macro-level).

In the last thirty years a kind of spiritual awakening among business practitioners and scholars (particularly in the United States) has occurred in struggling with spirituality and faith in the workplace (Neal 2013, 3–5) – thus focusing on the micro- and meso-levels. Giacalone and Jurkiewicz (2003/2010) define workplace spirituality as "aspects of the workplace, either in the individual, the group, or the organization, that promote individual feelings of satisfaction through transcendence" (p. 13). Their 524-page *Handbook of Workplace Spirituality and Organizational Performance* presents thirty-two contributions on theoretical developments, conceptualizations and practical applications of workplace spirituality.

Interestingly, this handbook hardly mentions or addresses the relationship between spirituality and religion and faith. It therefore does not come as a surprise that – although ten years later – the 769-page *Handbook of Faith and Spirituality in the Workplace: Emerging Research and Practice* (Neal 2013) appeared. In seven parts it discusses basic issues in faith and spirituality in the workplace, religious perspectives of faith at work, mapping the territory for theory and research, cross-disciplinary perspectives, faith and spirituality at work assessments and integrating scholarship and practice, and concludes with reflective essays from the pioneers.

In order to elucidate the research field of spirituality and religion at work, Kelly Phipps and Margaret Benefiel (2013) discuss three types of "juxtapositions" of spirituality and religion in the literature: the mutually exclusive, the overlapping and the synonymous types. Accounting for different cultural contexts and research needs, the authors offer six propositions: (1) It must be allowed to speak of spirituality without speaking about religion, if necessary. (2) Various expressions of spirituality and religion should be allowed and protected, based on individual rights. (3) A variety of cultural contexts should be explored and dialogue should be fostered between those who see the relationship of work and faith in different ways. (4) Avenues in research should be opened in ways that mirror the work world as it currently exists (be it secular or shaped by certain religions). (5) Religion and spirituality should be treated as distinct but overlapping constructs. (6) Future researchers should specify whether they are studying spirituality, religion or both.

To explore and examine spirituality and religion in entire systems (at the macro-level) is much more demanding and delicate, given the immense complexity, diversity and pluralism of these systems. Nevertheless, a globalizing world exposes spiritualities and religions to face each other and can help to discover commonalities. Two initiatives in the 1990s were valuable attempts to unite world religions on a common ethical ground for living and working together on the planet Earth. At the World's Parliament of Religions 1993 in Chicago, the *Declaration Toward a Global Ethic* initiated the *Manifesto for a Global Economic Ethic* published in 2009 (Enderle 2018a), and in 1994 a group of distinguished Jewish, Christian and Muslim leaders from business, academia and religious institutions promulgated the *Interfaith Declaration of International Business Ethics* (Enderle 2018b; also Enderle 2003b). To merely mention these initiatives may suffice for now since the role that spirituality and religions may play for creating wealth in business will be further explored in Chapter 10 and exemplified in Chapters 17 and 18.

While these initiatives assign an active role to religions for a global ethic, they do not use the term "spirituality" (which, though, may be included). But, as the remarks about faith and spirituality at work underline, spirituality has its own characteristics that apply not only to religious, but also to agnostic and atheistic people and organizations. It is therefore imperative to develop a global spirituality, which can be embraced by religious and nonreligious constituencies as well, including individuals, organizations and institutions. Because human rights today are widely recognized – though not undisputed – universal ethical standards, we urgently need "a spirituality of human rights." It does not exist today, but it can and should be developed in the years to come.

Notes

1 The title refers to the answer of the fasting Jesus to the devil who tempted him "to command this stone to become a loaf of bread." Referring to the Hebrew Bible (Deuteronomy 8:3), Jesus replied that "one does not live by bread alone" (Luke 4:4).

2 The precise wording of Articles 3.2, 3.3 and 3.5 is the following:

(3.2) The Union shall offer its citizens an area of freedom, security and justice without internal frontiers, in which the free movement of persons is ensured in conjunction with appropriate measures with respect to external border controls, asylum, immigration and the prevention and combating of crime.

(3.3) The Union shall establish an internal market. It shall work for the sustainable development of Europe based on balanced economic growth and price stability, a highly competitive social market economy, aiming at full employment and social progress, and a high level of protection and improvement of the quality of the environment. It shall promote scientific and technological advance.

(3.5) In its relations with the wider world, the Union shall uphold and promote its values and interests and contribute to the protection of its citizens. It shall contribute to peace, security, the sustainable development of the Earth, solidarity and mutual respect among peoples, free and fair trade, eradication of poverty and the protection of human rights, in particular the rights of the child, as well as to the strict observance and the development of international law, including respect for the principles of the United Nations Charter.

3 The role of commerce, prosperity and economic growth for advancing peace has been insufficiently discussed in the literature, despite outstanding examples such as Fort (2011), Friedman (2005), Steinmann (2006), Williams (2008) and the publications of the above-mentioned institute "Peace and Happiness through Prosperity."

4. A concrete example of spirituality – well familiar to the author – is the Ignatian spirituality in the Christian tradition. James Martin compares spirituality to a bridge, which can take many different forms and offers a distinctive "passage" to God. The Ignatian "bridge" is supported by four "arches:" (1) Finding God in all things. (2) Becoming a contemplative in action. (3) Looking at the world in an incarnational way. (4) Seeking freedom and detachment. (Martin 2012, particularly 1–28).

8 | Creating Sustainable Wealth in Terms of Human Capabilities

Wealth creation must be "sustainable," fulfilling the demand "to meet the needs of the present without compromising the ability of future generations to meet their own needs," as defined by the World Commission on Environment and Development (WCED; see Chapter 2). While this definition clearly presupposes a wide, intergenerational time horizon, it does not specify "the needs" of the present generation and "the ability" of future generations to meet their own needs. I therefore suggest adopting Amartya Sen's "capability approach" in order to substantiate the concepts of needs and capabilities in this definition of sustainability. Sustainable wealth creation is hence assessed in terms of human capabilities.

A concise summary of the capability approach can be found in the Stiglitz-Sen-Fitoussi Report:

This approach [to measuring quality of life] conceives a person's life as a combination of various "doings and beings" (functionings) and of his or her freedom to choose among these functionings (capabilities). Some of these capabilities may be quite elementary, such as being adequately nourished and escaping premature mortality, while others may be more complex, such as having the literacy required to participate actively in political life. The foundations of the capability approach, which has strong roots in philosophical notions of social justice, reflect a focus on human ends and on respecting the individual's ability to pursue and realise the goals that he or she values; a rejection of the economic model of individuals acting to maximise their self-interest heedless of relationships and emotions; an emphasis on the complementarities between various capabilities; and a recognition of human diversity, which draws attention to the role played by ethical principles in the design of the "good" society. (Report 2009, 42)

Before discussing the features, strengths and limitations of this approach in detail, a short historic overview of its development advanced by Sen and Nussbaum will be helpful. Sen began to focus on capability in his Tanner Lecture at Stanford University in 1979 in the specific context of evaluating equality ("Equality of What?" in Sen 1982, 353–69). In *Poverty and Famines* (Sen 1981), the term of capability is not yet mentioned (while the concepts of entitlements and the ability to command enough food play a key role). Shortly after, the notion of capability gained much attention and elaboration in the context of development, well-being and poverty, liberty and freedom, living standards and development, gender bias and sexual divisions, and justice and social ethics. Among the numerous publications, one might mention *Commodities and Capabilities* (1985), *Inequality Reexamined* (1992) and "Capability and Well-Being" (Nussbaum & Sen 1993b). In *Development as Freedom* (1999) the capability approach takes center stage and is, again, masterly presented in *The Idea of Justice* (2009; see also 2017a).

Nussbaum connected the capability approach with Aristotelian ideas in the 1980s and jointly edited the book *The Quality of Life* with Sen (Nussbaum & Sen 1993a). She made pioneering contributions to the development of this approach and published numerous books and articles, documented in her book *Creating Capabilities* (Nussbaum 2011), which is a lucid masterpiece on capabilities and human development.

The capability approach starts from the experience that "all over the world people are struggling for lives that are worthy of their human dignity" (Nussbaum 2011, 1). As there is an enormous diversity of lives, many plagued by poverty, disease, disability and violence, the search for a better world and more just societies appears inescapable. The question then arises how these lives can be compared – or what "informational basis" is adequate – in order to evaluate and reduce injustices and advance good societies.

Critique of Utility-Based and Resource-Based Approaches

This question is of paramount importance for empirical and theoretical studies as well as for ethical evaluations and public policies. It is inescapable on the assumption discussed in Chapter 6 that wealth creation includes not only a productive, but also a distributive dimension. If one chooses an informational basis that does not allow for interpersonal comparisons, one cannot, strictly speaking, make social judgments. This outcome was famously demonstrated by Kenneth Arrow's "Impossibility Theorem" (Arrow 1963).

Also, "the new welfare economics," spearheaded by Lionel Robbins in the 1930s, rejects interpersonal comparisons of utility and uses only one criterion of social improvement, namely the "Pareto criterion" (Hammes 2018). This accounts only for the utilities of each person *separately*. Accordingly, the situation x of a group (or a country) is better than the situation y of this group (or country), if at least one person has more utility in x than in y and everyone has at least as much utility in x as in y. A situation is then described as "Pareto optimal" or "Pareto efficient" if and only if there is no other feasible situation that is superior to it in terms of the Pareto criterion. This means that Pareto optimality ignores the issue of the distribution of utilities and does not account for anything other than utilities (such as freedoms, rights or opportunities). It goes without saying that, in comparing situations of men and women, ethnic groups and entire nations, this criterion would generate bizarre results.

Because interpersonal comparisons are necessary for investigating and assessing social states of affairs, one may ask for the appropriate informational basis of comparisons. Broadly speaking, two influential sets of approaches can be distinguished. The first set is based on subjective feelings of persons and has been advocated, historically and most prominently, by utilitarianism with its different versions: the hedonistic view of utility as pleasure, utility as desire fulfillment and utility as preference satisfaction. More recently, studies of subjective well-being (that is, about whether people are "happy" and "satisfied" with their lives) have been undertaken, and these studies show that it can be made amenable to systematic quantification (see Report 2009, 145–51).

The second set of approaches is based on "objective" resources such as income and wealth, which are discussed as "primary goods" in John Rawls's *A Theory of Justice* (1971). Moreover, in the economics field, the welfare economics tradition and the theory of fair allocation have developed ways to include non-market aspects of quality of life into a broader measure of well-being (Report 2009, 153–55).

While Sen acknowledges the legitimacy and usefulness of subjective and objective approaches to quality of life, presented in the Report, for certain purposes, he strongly criticizes the utility-based and the resource-based approaches. The utility-based approaches suffer from two fundamental flaws. First, they aggregate the utilities simply by summing them together (an arithmetic addition), which is called "sum-ranking." Therefore, the distribution of utilities among individuals becomes irrelevant. Second, utilities are subjective, mental entities, which are shaped by the environments to which individuals have been exposed for a long time.

The utilitarian calculus based on, say, happiness can be deeply unfair to those who are persistently deprived, such as the traditional underdogs in stratified societies, oppressed minorities in intolerant communities, precarious sharecroppers living in a world of uncertainty, sweated workers in exploitative industrial arrangements, subdued housewives in deeply sexist cultures. The hopelessly deprived people may lack the courage to desire any radical change and often tend to adjust their desires and expectations to what little they see as feasible. They train themselves to take pleasure in small mercies. The practical merit of such adjustments for people in chronically adverse positions is easy to understand: this is one way of making deprived lives bearable. But the adjustments also have the incidental effect of distorting the scale of utilities. (Sen 2008, 18–19)

Sen's critique of the resource-based approaches (particularly Rawls's notion of primary goods) is based on a differentiated understanding of the relation between goods and persons and the fundamental value of a person's real freedoms. Sen distinguishes different categories that are involved in the relation between a good (say, a bike) and a person (Sen 1982, 30):

goods >>> characteristics >>> *conversion into:* >>> functioning >>> capability
(e.g., a bike) (e.g., transport)   (e.g., moving)   (e.g., able
                                                                                    of moving)

"Characteristics" are qualities of goods, whereas "functioning" relates to a person's *use* of those characteristics, for example, *a bike* provides transport while *a person* moves and can move with it. The crucial point in this relation is that the goods with their characteristics are means to achieve the ends of the person. They are not identical with, but *converted* into the functionings and capabilities of the person. This conversion of goods in general and primary goods in particular depends on the characteristics of the person.

For example, a person who is disabled may have a larger basket of primary goods and yet have less chance to lead a normal life (or to pursue her objectives) than an able-bodied person with a smaller basket of primary goods. Similarly, an older person or a person more prone to illness can be more disadvantaged in a generally accepted sense even with a larger bundle of primary goods. (Sen 1999, 74)

Against Rawls's use of primary goods, Sen insists that the conversion problem that affects significantly disabled people should be addressed by choosing the informational basis with the focus on functionings and capabilities. After all, "the magnitude of the global problem of disability in the world is truly gigantic. More than 600 million people – about one in ten of all human beings – live with some form of significant disability" (Sen 1999, 258).

Sen's emphasis on finding an adequate informational basis for comparing human lives can be explained by his life-long concern for the poor and his search to engage ethics and economics into productive interdisciplinary communication. On the one hand, the informational basis must reach the lives and freedoms of people; on the other hand, it has to be objective enough to allow for interpersonal comparisons. Moreover, it must include all people and hence be globally applicable. Thereby, both commonalities and diversities of human lives have to be taken into account, avoiding ethical imperialism as well as ethical relativism. Finally, the informational basis should allow sufficient room for multiple ethical theories.

Essential Elements of the Capability Approach

Having discussed the importance of an adequate informational basis for interpersonal comparisons and criticized different prominent approaches, we ask what the capability approach can offer (for a scholarly discussion of Sen's capability approach, see Cortina 2013). What are its essential elements? As Nussbaum writes, the key question for an adequate informational basis is, "What is each person able to do and to be?"

The approach takes *each person as an end*, asking not just about the total or average well-being but about the opportunities available to each person. It is *focused on choice or freedom*, holding that the crucial good societies should be promoting for their people is a set of opportunities, or substantial freedoms, which people then may or may not exercise in action: the choice is theirs. It thus commits itself to respect for people's power of self-definition. (Nussbaum 2011, 18)

The importance of each person as an end, with his and her choice or freedom, and the claim to be respected, has universal validity and holds for all people in all cultures and religions. It is noteworthy that the concentration on capabilities of persons does not imply "methodological individualism," which assumes that individuals with their thought, choice and action are detached from the society in which they exist. "The capability approach not only does not assume such detachment, its concern with people's ability to live the kind of lives they have reason to value brings in social influences both in terms of what they value (for example, 'taking part in the life of the community') and what influences operate on their values (for example, the relevance of public reasoning in individual assessment)" (Sen 2009, 244). In other words, it would be "a significant mistake" (Sen) to interpret the capability approach in an individualistic sense. Sen emphasizes that:

the freedom of agency that we individually have is inescapably qualified and constrained by the social, political and economic opportunities that are available to us … It is important to give simultaneous recognition to the centrality of individual freedom *and* to the force of social influence on the extent and reach of individual freedom. To counter the problems that we face, we have to see individual freedom as a social commitment. (Sen 1999, xi–xii)

A further feature of the capability approach is a pluralist understanding of value:

The approach is resolutely *pluralist about value*: it holds that the capability achievements that are central for people are different in quality, not just in quantity: that they cannot without distortion be reduced to a single numerical scale; and that a fundamental part of understanding and producing them is understanding the specific nature of each. (Nussbaum 2011, 18–19)

To illustrate, it does not make sense to curtail to one single indicator among the following capabilities: being adequately nourished, escaping premature mortality, reading, calculating and writing, doing "decent work" (that includes many substantive elements) and having leisure time. It is noteworthy that the Stiglitz-Sen-Fitoussi Report, too, emphasizes a range of features in people's lives:

that are important either intrinsically, as objective expressions of a good life, or instrumentally, to achieve valuable subjective states or other objective goals. Some of these features may be conceived as referring to particular functionings (that is, descriptions of people's doings – for example, working, commuting – and beings – for example, being healthy or educated) while others may be conceived as freedoms in particular domains (for example, political voice and participation). (Report 2009, 156)

Finally, Nussbaum emphasizes the value perspective of the capability approach:

The approach is *concerned with entrenched social injustice and inequality*, especially capability failures that are the result of discrimination or marginalization. It ascribes an urgent *task to government and public policy* – namely, to improve the quality of life for all people, as defined by their capabilities. (Nussbaum 2011, 19)

While the capability approach offers an adequate informational basis for interpersonal comparisons in general, it is particularly apt to shed light on poverty and inequalities and to guide public policies to address these issues. This does not require an all-encompassing theory and policy. But a focus on a limited set of issues – or what Sen calls a "partial ordering" – suffices (see Sen's extensive discussion of his view of how to approach justice in Sen 2009).

These essential elements of the capability approach (see Box 8.1), are shared by Sen and Nussbaum (and many other scholars). However, there are also differences between the two authors, which may be indicated briefly, but not pursued further in this book. Nussbaum calls her approach the "Capabilities Approach," pointing to the plurality and qualitative distinctness of the most important elements of people's quality of life (see Nussbaum 2011, chapters 2 and 4; also Sen 2005, 157, 160). She explicitly grounds her theory of fundamental political entitlements in human dignity and employs a specific list of ten "central capabilities." They constitute a minimal threshold level that a political order must at least secure to all citizens: life; bodily health; bodily integrity; senses, imagination, and thought; emotions; practical reason; affiliation; relating to other species; play; and control over one's environment, politically and materially. In line with Rawls's political liberalism, her capability-based theory of justice refrains from offering a comprehensive assessment of the quality of life in a society. But it also comprehends the capabilities of nonhuman animals.

In contrast, Sen abstains from establishing a specific list of (basic) capabilities, leaving its specification to public reasoning (although he thinks some capabilities, for example, health and education, are particularly important). A main concern of his has been to identify capability as the most pertinent space of comparison for purposes of

---

Box 8.1 Human capabilities

To measure the quality of life, the human capability approach conceives a person's life as a combination of various "doings and beings"
(functionings) and of his or her freedom to choose among these functionings (capabilities). Some of these capabilities may be quite elementary, such as being adequately nourished and escaping premature
mortality, while others may be more complex, such as having the
literacy required to participate actively in political life.
  Essential elements:

- Focus on the person's real choice or freedom: Each person is taken as
  an end.
- Resolutely pluralist approach about value: Capability achievements
  that are central for people are different in quality, not just in quantity. Therefore, they cannot without distortion be reduced to a single
  numerical scale (for example, being adequately nourished and escaping premature mortality). A fundamental part of understanding and
  producing them is understanding the specific nature of each.
- Concern about entrenched social injustice and inequality, especially
  capability failures that are the result of discrimination or
  marginalization.

---

quality-of-life assessment, which can be the basis for a comprehensive
quality-of-life assessment in and between nations and other groups (see
Report 2009). Such a project, in turn, goes beyond the deliberately
limited aims of Nussbaum's political liberalism. Sen, however,
develops a theory of justice in a very broad sense. "Its aim is to clarify
how we can proceed to address questions of enhancing justice and
removing injustice, rather than to offer resolutions of questions about
the nature of perfect justice" (Sen 2009, ix). Moreover, Sen does not
extend his theory to nonhuman animals' capabilities.

Limitations of the Capability Approach

As Sen readily admits, the capability approach also has its limitations.
For instance, it cannot pay adequate attention to fairness and equity
involved in procedures (that is, the process aspect of freedom) that
have relevance to the idea of justice (Sen 2009, 295–98; this point,

though, is criticized by Nussbaum 2011, 67). Moreover, capabilities, unlike human rights, are not moral claims that involve duties (Sen 2005, 2009, 370–76; see Chapter 12).

Another limitation – and a critique to some extent – has to do with the notion of wealth. Sen agrees with Aristotle that "wealth is evidently not the good we are seeking; for it is merely useful and for the sake of something else" (Sen 1999, 14; also Sen 2009, 253). Wealth is not something we value for its own sake. It is only an "admirable general-purpose means for having more freedom to lead the kind of lives we have reason to value" (Sen 1999, 14).

This is a narrow, material understanding of wealth, reflecting a certain underestimation of the material world and the "bodiliness" of the human person (see Chapter 7). If the material world is considered inferior and merely instrumental, wealth cannot but share these qualities and is likely to be undervalued. If it has no intrinsic value, it is not a place where deeper meaning can be searched for and found. It therefore matters to acknowledge that wealth creation involves a spiritual side as well.

Concluding Remark

To understand wealth creation in terms of human capabilities puts people center stage. It is about "a process of expanding the real freedoms that people enjoy" (Sen 1999, 3). The importance of each person as an end, with his and her choice or freedom, and the claim to be respected has universal validity and holds for all people in all cultures and religions. The capability approach provides a solid informational basis for interpersonal comparisons. It is resolutely pluralistic about value, requires public scrutiny and reasoning, and is concerned with entrenched social injustice and inequality.

9 | *Creating Means Making Something New and Better*

In his captivating historical account *The Wealth and Poverty of Nations: Why Some Are So Rich and Some So Poor* (1999), David Landes discusses the question of why the Industrial Revolution happened in Europe, a relatively poor world region at that time, and not in the Middle East, with its high Islamic culture, nor in China, the richest country in the middle of the second millennium. His short answer points to the Europeans' cultivation of invention (called "the invention of invention" by some authors) as well as the European *joie de trouver* or the pleasure in what is new and better. These developments arose due to much less interference by religion (as in the case of Islam) or the state (as in the case of China):

> The Europeans ... entered during these centuries [of the Middle Ages] into an exciting world of innovation and emulation that challenged vested interests and rattled the forces of conservatism. Changes were cumulative; novelty spread fast. A new sense of progress replaced an older, effective reverence for authority. This intoxicating sense of freedom touched (infected) all domains. These were years of heresies in the Church, of popular initiatives that, we can see now, anticipated the rupture of the Reformation; of new forms of expression and collective action that challenged the older art forms, questioned social structures, and posed a threat to other polities; of new ways of doing and making things that made newness a virtue and a source of delight; of utopias that fantasized better futures rather than recalled paradises lost. (Landes 1999, 57–58)

Landes first describes organizational innovations and adaptions in polities and commerce (chapter 3). He then explains technological innovations with the help of several examples: the water wheel, eyeglasses, the mechanical clock, printing and gunpowder (chapter 4). Critical in this process were not only the inventions – numerous happened in other parts of the world as well – but also the fact that they were made feasible in economic and financial terms. For these applications, he asserts, the market plays a crucial role[1]:

Enterprise was free in Europe. Innovation worked and paid, and rulers and vested interests were limited in their ability to prevent or discourage innovation. Success bred imitation and emulation; also a sense of power that would in the long run raise men almost to the level of gods. (Landes 1999, 59)

This look at the history highlights the importance of "making" – not only imagining – something new. It can lead one to believe that the new will necessarily be better. In fact, very often innovation is unquestionably assumed to make things not only new but also better. However, we also know from history that innovative technology was used to kill thousands of people. Therefore, in defining the "creation" of wealth, both elements need to be stressed: the making of something new that is also better.

It seems obvious, but nevertheless deserves emphasis, that wealth creation is more than both possessing and acquiring wealth, since it constitutes a special form of increasing wealth. According to Jacob Viner, "Aristotle ... insisted that wealth was essential for nobility, but it must be inherited wealth. Wealth was also an essential need of the state, but it should be obtained by piracy or brigandage, and by war for the conquest of slaves, and should be maintained by slave works" (quotation in Novak 1993, 105). In the course of history, the colonial powers acquired a great deal of wealth, usually with no regard for legal and ethical concerns, which, by and large, amounted to a redistribution rather than a creation of wealth. In the capitalistic system, the "acquisitive spirit," the "accumulation of capital," and the "acquisition of companies" do not necessarily entail the creation of wealth, properly speaking. It is, therefore, crucial to investigate precisely what this concept of "creation" means.

To create is to make something new and better. It is an innovative activity that is constantly searching for improvement, in part by being pushed by competition, also and foremost for the sake of a better service to people and the environment. Examples can be found in rich and poor countries and in many economic activities, ranging from the Grameen Bank in Bangladesh (www.grameen-info.org) to environmental pioneers such as Rohner Textil in Switzerland (see Gorman et al. 2003, 109–45) and the medical device corporation Medtronic in the United States (www.medtronic.com).

On a national scale, the meaning of wealth creation can be easily understood against the backdrop of the debacle of a war. In the aftermath of the Second World War, Germany and Japan had to create, to a large extent, new economies; and China, after the traumatic civil war of the Cultural Revolution (1966–76), engaged in a transformation process from a centrally planned to a market-oriented economy. In those situations, creating wealth is a national objective that mobilizes a great many forces for a new and better future.

Wealth creation as understood in this book involves many aspects of ethical innovation that are explored and developed in *Ethical Innovation in Business and the Economy* (Enderle & Murphy 2015). Therefore, in the following, several aspects are briefly explained, namely conceptual, theoretical and methodological clarifications and systemic changes for ethical innovations, while individual initiatives for ethical innovations and examples of innovative and ethical organizations are presented later in Part III of this book (particularly Medtronic, Grameen Bank, Unilever Sustainable Living Plan and Rohner Textil AG).

Conceptual, Theoretical and Methodological Clarifications

Innovation has become a catchword to attract a great deal of attention in business and economic policy and far beyond. It is praised as a key driver of increasing productivity and thus economic growth. Companies and countries that are in the forefront of innovation are said to win the race for global advantage. So what do we mean by innovation?

There are multiple definitions of innovation, which might be appropriate in accordance with specific contexts. For example, the OECD Reports (2012, 2013b) use the OECD/Eurostat (2005) definition of innovation as "new and/or significant improvements to existing goods and services." It goes beyond a "technology-based perspective" and includes "frugal innovations" (modifying existing technologies or products so as to supply lower-income markets) and "grassroots innovations" (adopting novel approaches to using existing technologies in a given local context). Given the wide range of definitions, I propose a few conceptual clarifications (see Enderle 2015c).

In their excellent book, *Innovation: A Very Short Introduction*, Mark Dodgson and David Gann define innovation as "*ideas, successfully applied in organizational outcomes and processes*" (2010, 14).[2] The authors focus on innovations other than those described as "continuous improvement" that tend to be routine and highly incremental in nature. Their concern lies rather with ideas that stretch and challenge organizations as they attempt to survive and thrive. "By concentrating on innovations beyond the ordinary that occur in both the outcome of organizational efforts and the processes that produce them, we capture a great degree of what is generally understood to be innovation" (p. 14). The wide range of phenomena that fit this definition is extensively discussed in their book and others. It also includes the "quality changes," which, according to the Stiglitz-Sen-Fitoussi Report, should be accounted for in measuring produced capital (see Chapter 4).

This definition points to two components, which characterize, in varying forms, many other definitions as well: innovation is the novel outcome of human intellect and the realization thereof in concrete matters. On the one hand, innovation originates from human thought and imagination, the search for and finding of ideas; on the other hand, it is about making the ideas work and applying them successfully to the material world. Imagination is crucial, but only as the first step. Successful application is the necessary second step. Therefore, innovation should not be equated with imagination and invention, since innovation includes both thinking and doing. As mentioned, this crucial distinction has been emphasized by Landes with regard to the Industrial Revolution that happened in Europe.

The first component of "*ideas*" (beyond the ordinary) points to human ingenuity driving individuals and teams and allowing for a wide range of gradual to radical innovation. The second component (that is, "*realization in concrete matters*") relates to doing, making and behaving and the context or framework in which innovation appears. But it also stresses the importance of successful application, meaning innovation made feasible in economic and financial terms. The electric car can serve as an example to illustrate the difference: as long as electric cars remain so costly and inaccessible that only the wealthy can buy and use them, innovation has not yet "created the market."

Obviously, *success* can be defined in different ways. A helpful economic distinction is proposed by Bryan Mezue, Clayton Christensen and Derek van Bever (2015) who identify three varieties: (1) "*Sustaining innovation*" – that helps to replace old products with new and better ones (which is, by nature, a substitutive process). (2) "*Efficiency innovation*" – that helps companies to produce more for less. (3) "*Market-creating innovation*" – that transforms products and services so costly and inaccessible that only the wealthy can buy and use them, into offerings cheap enough and accessible enough that they will reach an entirely new population of customers. This variety of innovation creates new growth and new jobs. Referring to the example of the electric car, it might have become a "sustaining innovation" previously in the 1970s; however, only now does it have the opportunity to become an "efficiency innovation" and a "market-creating innovation" (that is, successful in the triple sense).

Innovation defined as the successful application of ideas or the accomplishment of a worthwhile objective (Dees et al. 2001, 162) *implies an evaluation of what success or an accomplished worthwhile objective is*. It involves certain norms and values, which might be ethical or unethical. In other words, such ethical implication is unavoidable; it is not only about "doing" but also about doing "the right thing." Admittedly, Dodgson and Gann do not elaborate the ethical dimension in their "very short introduction" to innovation. But in the last chapter on building a smarter planet, they explicitly speak of greater ethical and responsible decision-making, sustainability, intuition and judgment, tolerance and responsibility, diversity of interests and cross-cultural sensitivities. It is no exaggeration to say that building a *smarter* planet implies building a *more ethical* one.

Furthermore, as Dodgson and Gann emphasize, innovation (as process) is risky in multiple respects and can lead to *failure* and fear. Numerous applications of ideas do not succeed, and change just for the sake of change is not the way to go. Nonetheless, the attitudes of *curiosity, risk-taking and "the joy of finding"* (see Landes 1999), supported by an environment that provides free space, are essential for innovation. It goes without saying that, along with risk and uncertainty, the ethical assessment and guidance of innovation becomes even more challenging.

In line with the three-level conception of business ethics (see Chapter 2), Dodgson and Gann (2010, 22 and 26) distinguish the level of *individual* innovators, entrepreneurs and managers (for example, Thomas Edison); the level of business strategy for *organizational* innovation (for example, IBM); and the level of economics for *national* innovation performance (which should be supplemented by *global* innovation systems; see Atkinson & Ezell 2010). It is noteworthy that each level has its particular challenges of complexity, predictability and governance; further, the more aggregate the level is, the more complex, the less predictable and the more difficult it becomes to govern the challenges (see the Level I, II and III Technology in Allenby & Sarewitz 2011).

In *practical* terms, one can distinguish *seven forms of innovation* situated mainly at the micro- and meso-levels (see Kickul & Lyons, 2012, 45–46):

(1) Creating new products, services, programs or projects.

(2) Producing a new process or delivering an existing product, service, program or project (for example, Habitat for Humanity).

(3) Delivering an existing product, service, program or project to a new or previously under-served market (for example, Grameen Bank).

(4) Utilizing a new source of labor or other production input (for example, Greystone Bakery of Yonkers).

(5) Implementing a new organizational or industrial structure (for example, community development banks).

(6) Implementing new ways of engaging "customers" or target beneficiaries.

(7) Utilizing new funding models.

To sum up, innovation consists of the following features: It means the successful application of ideas beyond the ordinary that can lead to gradual change or great disruption. It is about making something new, which has ethical implications. It requires curiosity and a risk-taking attitude. It can occur at the individual, organizational and/or systemic levels and take multiple forms of products, services, processes, business models, systemic disruptions and other changes (see Box 9.1).

George Brenkert's (2015) contribution to *Ethical Innovation in Business and the Economy* seeks to start a discussion about moral innovation itself, its role in business and how such innovations might be evaluated. His conceptual and theoretical clarifications provide a solid foundation for the theme of *Ethical Innovation . . .* in general and for several chapters in particular (chapters 4, 6, 7, 10, 12, 13 and 14). Despite the significance of innovation, he notices that the area of morality has been quarantined against any innovations. Yet moral innovation involves something distinctively new in that it alters how people believe and behave regarding some aspects of their lives. Brenkert explores fascinating perspectives of this woefully under-discussed topic in ethics as well as in business ethics.

> ### Box 9.1 Creating means making something new and better: ethical innovation
>
> Innovation differs from imagination and invention by transforming new human thinking into new practical doing, making and behaving. Innovation in business and the economy means making things new and feasible in economic and financial terms, implying an ethical dimension. I propose to define creativity not merely as a cognitive activity like imagination and invention (as Kickul & Lyons 2012 do). Rather, creating means making something new and better, thus combining thinking and doing together, although in a less specific way than innovation.

When facing complex ethical problems, assigning responsibility is a difficult undertaking with far-reaching consequences. If it were merely a matter of either taking individual responsibility or relying on institutions alone, shortcut solutions would be quickly at hand. Thomas Beschorner and Martin Kolmar (2015) address this foundational issue by arguing for a multi-level approach that rejects this either/or thinking. They propose using an extended transaction cost approach (inspired by economics) in order to determine a fair sharing of moral responsibilities among individual and organizational actors and social institutions. As moral agency and institutions are interdependent – which is quite obvious from a dynamic perspective – they not only shape but also are shaped by each other. This multi-level approach implies that governance is important at each level and requires coordination to address complex ethical problems. It informs a useful space for bottom-up movements to be discussed in chapters 6, 7, 10, 12 and 14 (see also Chapter 18 in this book).

While Brenkert and Beschorner and Kolmar deal with basic conceptual and theoretical problems, the chapter by Christoph Luetge and Matthias Uhl (2015) focuses on an innovative methodology, that is, on an experimental approach to ethics. The contributions of experimental disciplines are particularly important if business ethics is to be understood as an interdisciplinary field that includes not only a normative-ethical but also a descriptive-explicative dimension. After a brief summary of experimental philosophy and experimental ethics with its philosophical precursors, the chapter explores future opportunities and key research questions of experimental ethics. Drawing on recent ethical experiments, it discusses practical implications and possible types of criticisms.

Systemic Changes for Ethical Innovations

Patricia Werhane and David Bevan (2015) take up a critical view of present day "market capitalism." They rectify the widely held misinterpretation of Adam Smith's understanding of free enterprise and demonstrate with numerous examples the flourishing drive of alternative businesses in different parts of the world. This constructive trend from the bottom up is articulated and exemplified also in other chapters of *Ethical Innovation* ... particularly in chapters 3, 7, 10, 12 and 14.

While concrete examples of social innovation always contain descriptive and normative aspects, the following chapter by Gene Laczniak and Nicholas Santos (2015) proposes a normative-ethical model for marketing. It outlines what is owed to vulnerable, impoverished consumers when they enter into marketplace transactions with more powerful sellers. Needless to say, such a model is relevant for developing and developed countries alike. The authors identify, discuss and justify five prescriptive components of the so-called Integrative Justice Model: (a) authentic engagement without exploitative intent, (b) co-creation of value with customers, (c) investment in future consumption; (d) genuine interest representation and (e) focus on long-term profit management.

Finally, the chapter by Peter John Opio (2015) opens up a widely ignored but hugely important new perspective on business and the economy as we normally understand them. His contribution is based on groundbreaking experiences in African countries and shows that innovation can – and not seldom does – happen in informal firms and economies, arising, again, from the bottom up. This innovation is vital for the survival of the poor. As with other innovations, however, it merits ethical scrutiny and examination. At the same time, it can inspire businesses in the formal economies to become more creative, which has been demonstrated by the outstanding examples of the Nigerian Nollywood film industry and the cellphone-based M-Pesa banking from Kenya.

As these groundbreaking contributions show, ethical innovation is an enormous challenge that needs to be addressed from a big variety of angles, thoroughly and in a sustained fashion. Therefore, in a modest way, this book on *Corporate Responsibility for Wealth Creation and Human Rights* also aims to be an innovative project in multiple respects, in business, economic and ethical terms, of theoretical and practical relevance, providing new and better ways to cope with globalization, sustainability and financialization. In Part I, the comprehensive conception of wealth creation with its seven features opens radically new perspectives on what wealth is and how it works. In Part II, the United Nations Framework and Guiding Principles on Business and Human Rights provide specific global ethical standards for business enterprises around the world – an achievement that has never happened in the history of humankind before. Finally, in Part III, the unique application of wealth creation and human rights offers clear and substantive guidance for the ethics of business organizations.

Notes

1 In addition to the market, Landes also acknowledges other important reasons for the "invention of invention": the Judeo-Christian values of respect for manual labor, subordination of nature to man and the sense of linear time (Landes 1999, 58–59).

2 Like Landes, the authors, in 2008, define the term as follows: "Innovation is much more than invention – the creation of a new idea and its reduction to practice – and it includes all the activities required in the *commercialization* of new technologies (Freeman & Soete 1997). Essentially, innovation is the successful commercial exploitation of new ideas. It includes the scientific, technological, organizational, financial, and business activities leading to the commercial introduction of a new (or improved) product or service" (Dodgson et al. 2008, 2; emphasis in the original).

10 | *Wealth Creation Needs Self-Regarding and Other-Regarding Motivations*

Key Role of Motivation in Any Economic Activity

The seventh feature of wealth creation highlights the key role motivations play in any economic activity. However, this feature is often taken for granted, simply described and hardly scrutinized. As explained in Chapter 1, the engineering approach to economics basically disregards motivations and primarily focuses on logistical issues: What means should one choose in order to achieve as efficiently as possible, under very simple behavioral assumptions, goals that are given from elsewhere? In contrast, the ethics-related approach, advocated in this book, explicitly accounts for human motivation and the judgment of social achievements that cannot be disconnected from the ethical questions of the good: How should I/we live and how should I/we foster a good society? (See Chapter 1).

Motivations are also an essential component of any economic system properly defined. Jürgen Kromphardt (1991) criticizes the characterizations of economic systems, which only use one dominant system criterion, be it capital for capitalism or the market for the market economy (see Enderle 2018c). A pertinent analysis of economic systems, according to Kromphardt, identifies three essential components with the following criteria: (1) Criteria of ownership and rights of disposal: Who participates in the economic processes of planning, decision-making and controlling with regard to production, distribution and consumption? (2) Criteria of information and coordination: With the help of what information systems are individual decisions coordinated? And (3) criteria of motivation: What objectives do various decision-makers pursue and how do they behave in carrying out their decisions? (see Enderle 2018c). Given this three-pronged conception of the economic system, the question of motivation deserves full attention.

In addition, the question of motivation is highly relevant when considering the role of religions to support a common ethical ground, as in the *Manifesto for a Global Economic Ethic* and the *Interfaith Declaration of International Business Ethics*, briefly presented in Chapter 7. Inspired by Rawls's "idea of an overlapping consensus" (Rawls 1993, 133–72),[1] a pluralistic society with different and opposing religious and philosophical "conceptions of the good" (such as Christianity, Hinduism and utilitarianism) needs a common ethical ground, which is valid for *all* human beings, in order to survive and flourish. How then can the complex relationship between those comprehensive conceptions and the limited common ethical ground be understood? It is helpful to distinguish four different levels of this relationship: heuristic, motivational, normative-ethical and implementational levels (see Enderle 1997). While at the normative-ethical level, the content must be identical (for example, the Golden Rule and the four Directives of the *Manifesto for a Global Economic Ethic*[2]), there can be a great variety at the other three levels.

To illustrate this multi-level relationship, Christian ethics may serve as an example. Its distinctiveness has been intensely discussed (see Curran & McCormick 1980; Auer 1984/2016; Bobbert & Mieth 2015) and a wide consensus has emerged that at the normative-ethical level, Christians and non-Christians share much common ground. But at the heuristic, motivational and implementational levels, Christian ethics significantly differs from other ethics and worldviews; it is very specific and, at the same time, important to support the common ethical ground. The Hebrew bible and the New Testament as well as the Christian traditions offer plenty of models of ethical conduct, which can be used as heuristic lenses to help human beings better understand present ethical challenges and to look for ethical solutions in a wider and longer lasting horizon of sense ("Sinnhorizont"). In addition, Christian ethics provides a wide range of strong motivations to act ethically, namely, to listen to the Word of God, to discern and do God's will, to follow the example of Jesus, to forgive and try again, to live ethically in spite of the sinful conditions of human beings, to be aware of the importance of ethical decision-making in view of the Last Judgement and other motivations. Furthermore, numerous forms of liturgy and services, rites, symbols and institutional frameworks may help strengthen the resolve of Christians to live up to their ethical norms.

As these brief remarks indicate, motivations constitute an essential part of economics understood in the ethics-related sense, of economic systems and of religious and non-religious worldviews. Hence they are also essential for the conception of wealth creation. So, what motivates people, companies and countries to engage in wealth creation? Common answers in the economic, sociological and psychological literatures are self-interest, greed, the will to survive, the desire for power aggrandizement, the enjoyment of riches and the glory, honor and well-being of nations. However, these motivations, taken individually or in various combinations, are rarely related specifically to the creation of wealth, but instead drive economic activities in general and, most often, merely incite the acquisition and possession of wealth. When economic activities clearly focus on wealth creation, other motivations such as the entrepreneurial spirit, the desire to serve others and the *joie de trouver* become more important. In Landes's judgment (1999, 58), it was this "joy of finding" that was the distinctive motivation in medieval Europe – as compared to Islamic countries and China – which prepared the Industrial Revolution (see Chapter 9).

Obviously, the question of motivation pertains to all features of wealth creation as explained in the previous chapters; but it is particularly pertinent to the notion of wealth as a combination of private and public wealth. If the distinctive characteristics of private and public wealth explained in Chapter 5 are taken seriously, two fundamentally different types of motivations are indispensable in order to create wealth in the comprehensive sense: self-regarding and other-regarding motivations (Randels 2018a, 2018b).

As indicated in Chapter 5, the motivation of self-interest (an important type of self-regarding motivation) undoubtedly plays an important (though not exclusive) role to produce private goods and create private wealth. This could be observed, for example, in China's "entrepreneurial decade" in the 1980s, mainly in rural areas, guided by "directional liberalism" (Huang 2008; Enderle 2010a, 2013c). The reform strategy aimed at allowing some economic freedom and creating private wealth "outside the system" in order to drive the growth of the economy, which preceded the reform "inside the system," primarily in urban areas. In other words, private wealth creation was given a leading role that got its credibility (understood as a public good) from Deng Xiaoping. Important slogans encouraged people to "jump into the sea" (that is, to start one's own private business and to "make money") and propagated the belief that "first some should get rich for the benefit of the whole country." Private wealth creation was also enhanced by "soft infrastructure" and improved education; (at least) it did not worsen health care provisions and contributed, in turn, to creating these public goods.

Self-Interest Fails to Create Public Wealth

However, when it comes to creating public wealth, the motivation of self-interest is utterly insufficient, for economic and non-economic reasons alike. Because public wealth is defined by non-rivalry and non-excludability, the "free-rider problem" exists; that is, people take advantage of being able to use public wealth without paying for it. Self-interest does not motivate the creation of public wealth. Whoever is engaged in creating public wealth cannot expect a reward equivalent to the time and effort put into such engagement. Rather, one has to accept or at least put up sacrifices in one form or another – against one's own self-interest.

Self-interest maximization as the intelligent pursuit of self-interest – attributed to the so-called *homo oeconomicus* or "economic man" (Hargreaves-Heap & Hollis 1987; Mansbridge 1990; Kirchgässner 2008) – is quite a narrow view of rationality and has effectively dominated contemporary economics. It has strongly influenced the theory of rational choice and economic behavior, and many of the central theorems of modern economics significantly depend on it (for example, the Arrow-Debreu theorems on the existence and efficiency of general equilibrium in a competitive economy without externality and without increasing returns). It also has had an enormous practical impact on business and economic life. Moreover, it is widely used – beyond economics – in "rational choice" models in politics and the investigations on "law and economics" and shapes a great number of institutional designs. This self-interest view is often related to and justified by the writing of Adam Smith, "the father of modern economics," who supposedly understood each human being as tirelessly promoting his own particular interest (and nothing else). However, this interpretation of Smith is hardly accurate and does not stand the test of historical scrutiny (Sen 1987, 22–28).

In the ideal-type case of neoclassical economics, self-interest maximization means that the agent has complete, fully ordered preferences over the full range of consequences of his feasible actions. He has perfect information and can calculate exactly all possible outcomes of his preferences. Having done his calculation, he chooses the action, which satisfies (that is, maximizes) his preferences better (or at least no worse) than any other action. A more sophisticated model looks at the risks of several possible consequences of each action and the (subjective) probability distribution for the consequences. The agent assesses the expected utility by discounting each consequence and chooses the action with the highest expected utility. Similarly, rational choice theory defines rational maximizing behavior according to Gary Becker as follows: "All human behavior can be viewed as involving participants who (1) maximize their utility (2) from a stable set of preferences and (3) accumulate an optimal amount of information and other inputs in a variety of markets" (Becker 1976, 14; quoted in Sen 2002, 27).

In his critique of self-interest maximization Sen points to theoretical, conceptual and empirical problems. Self-interest maximization is more than internal consistency and belongs to the ethics-related approach insofar as it includes an external reference, that is, the value of self-interest, to which all decisions have to be oriented. Decisions are rational only insofar as they serve directly or indirectly the self-interest of the person. The person may value anything including the actions and states of other persons, but he includes them in his rational choice – out of "sympathy" or "antipathy" (Sen) – only to the extent that they affect his own well-being and advantage. However, this narrow view of rationality is highly questionable because it refuses to recognize any value other than self-interest that might guide human behavior. Modelling economic and rational behavior in this way is a radical simplification that qualifies all human behavior – if not motivated by self-interest – as irrational, hence dissociating individual behavior from values and ethics (other than the value of self-interest).

Sen rightly also criticizes the concept of utility-maximizing behavior because in a large part of modern economics (inspired by the theory of "revealed preferences"), the distinction is not made between utility as maximand and utility as the person's self-interest or well-being (that is, for what the maximand is to be maximized). Therefore, as Sen critically notes, "[A] pair of distinct delineations is used, typically implicitly (by calling both ideas 'utility'), to get an empirical rabbit out of a definitional hat" (Sen 2002, 27).

In addition to these theoretical and conceptual problems, the narrow rational view of self-interest maximization leads to serious descriptive and predictive problems in economics because human behavior is often shaped by other values as well. Behavioral economics has shown that motivations such as fairness and commitment (beyond self-interest) do exist and can be strong drivers for human behavior. If they are not taken into account, the predictions of human behavior can be seriously flawed (Mullainathan & Thaler 2000; Thaler 2009).

The economic literature presents three reasons for the failure of self-interest to produce public goods and to create public wealth.

The *first* reason concerns the relationship between motivations and consequences of actions. It rejects the view that the strict separation between individual motivations and public consequences has been crucial for the success of modern economies. This currently widely held view draws on the famous fable of the bees by B. Mandeville (1714) as well as the working of the "invisible hand" according to A. Smith. In fact, both authors are of the opinion that the actual consequences of actions can considerably differ from the intended ones. "Private vices" generate "public benefit," and the "invisible hand" (invoked by Smith in his two works only twice) effectuates a relatively equal distribution of life necessities among all citizens despite the accumulation of wealth by the rich (Smith 1759, 184–85); further, in foreign trade, it yields better results than if well-intended people want to achieve the public welfare directly (Smith 1776, 456).

It is certainly correct that in a modern economy with a highly complex division of labor, the interconnections between individual motivations and public results are not unequivocally direct. The loosening of these relations provides more freedom to the individuals and seems to be necessary in a pluralistic society. However, by demanding such a strict separation, the baby is poured out with the bathwater. The separation cannot actually be carried out. Individual motivations cannot but influence decisions about public goods and thus should be taken into consideration when analyzing the decision-making process. To ignore these interconnections seems to indicate a rather naive view that shies away from perceiving different power relations involved in those processes and, by doing so, actually accepts them.

A *second* reason for the failure in producing public goods lies in the fact that individual preferences and costs can be concealed from the public decision-makers and thus can be captured only with great difficulty. A number of attempts to provide this information have proven to be insufficient: voluntary agreement on the distribution of marginal gains from public goods, incentive compatible mechanisms of taxation, voting on public goods, cost-benefit analysis, ability of tax payers to move to those communities that supply the required set of public goods and so on. Usually these attempts are based on the motivational assumption that individuals disclose their preferences and costs to government only as far as they can maximize their own advantages. However, empirical investigations cast doubt on this assumption and suggest more complex motivational structures.

Yet, even if the simple assumption of maximization held true from a realistic point of view, facing the great importance of public goods, one would also have to ask whether or not this assumption is acceptable from an ethical point of view. A further difficulty (a *third* reason for market failure) arises even if the preferences are revealed. According to the impossibility theorem of K. J. Arrow (1963), it is not possible, for a pluralistic society, on the basis of a few plausible assumptions to deduce a collective welfare function out of individual preferences (which do not need to be egotistical). Applicable to public goods, this theorem has devastating implications. Either in a pluralistic society one accepts a strictly individualistic philosophy and must do without public goods that require collective preferences, or one wants public goods and must therefore reject a strictly individualistic philosophy. In other words, one cannot have both, a strictly individualistic philosophy and public goods.

In sum, these critical reflections suggest that self-interest as a prevailing self-regarding motivation in economics and other social sciences fails in creating public wealth. However, if the wealth of a country, a region or the entire world is conceived as a combination of private and public wealth – the view explained in Chapter 5 – other-regarding motivations are not negligible at all. Rather, they are indispensable to create wealth in a comprehensive sense at all levels of the economy.

Other-Regarding Motivations Are Indispensable for Creating Public Wealth

Of particular importance and urgency are other-regarding motivations for the creation of *public wealth in the global economy,* involving both theoretical and practical aspects (see Kaul et al. 1999a; Kaul 2003). From a theoretical point of view, the simplistic behavioral assumptions, particularly of self-interest and profit maximization, should be replaced by more differentiated assumptions that better reflect the reality of human action. From a practical point of view, those "ethical resources" needed for the worldwide production of public goods should be better used and cultivated. Both theoretical and practical points of view, which influence each other, are of paramount importance for the building up of a united world community that is capable and willing to come to grips with and solve global problems.

Regarding the basic assumptions in mainstream economic analysis, Amartya Sen (1997) observes "an interesting asymmetry" between the treatment of "business principles" and "moral sentiments" (or ethical resources). While business principles (essentially, directly or indirectly, restricted to profit maximization) are very rudimentary and extend to virtually all economic transactions, the ethical resources are considered highly complex (because they originate from many different kinds of ethics); their validity, however, is allegedly restricted to a very narrow realm, and these resources virtually have no impact on economic behavior. Sen criticizes this asymmetry, especially that the principle of profit maximization in today's international economy shows "little empirical evidence and not much analytical plausibility" (Sen 1997). He advocates the replacement of this rudimentary assumption by more complex assumptions. Only if different *sociocultural factors* are integrated into the economics models, economic successes and failures, including successful and failed provisions of public goods, in the different parts of the world can be understood and explained.

Beyond their relevance for explanation, more differentiated sociocultural assumptions in economic models are *also of normative-factual importance*, for often rudimentary assumptions of self-interest and profit maximization are not only taken as explanatory variables, but also as normative demands indicating how economic actors *should* behave. Since rudimentary assumptions already capture the reality of the global economy poorly, it is not difficult to anticipate that all the more their normative usage can entail devastating consequences.

Therefore, the required extension of the paradigm must capture more accurately the sociocultural richness in which transnational business operates today and also must include "moral commitments" that, going beyond self-interest, are indispensable for producing public goods. In fact, such public goods already exist to some extent. By applying this more sophisticated approach, the "East Asian miracle," for instance, can be better explained from the ethical perspective of "a morality of inclusion" (see Enderle 1995). Similarly, as for other, including western, cultures, if the assumptions of economic models contained a higher degree of nearness to reality, the already existent and used "ethical resources" (such as a sense for the common good, solidarity and justice) would be taken more seriously for public goods. Then the pessimistic outlook about the provision of public goods could be mitigated (see, for instance, Braybrooke & Mohanan 1992; Kerber 1993; Brieskorn 1997).

Nevertheless, despite the extended and differentiated paradigm, many grave problems *of a normative-ethical and practical nature* (which go beyond the cognitive perspective) remain. Global public goods can only be produced and sustained if supported by a global ethical consensus. In other words, a global ethos is required that, on the one hand, is supported by various ethical traditions of religious and non-religious origins and, on the other hand, provides a "common ground" (or an "overlapping consensus" in John Rawls's terminology) that transcends individual traditions. It seems to me that the strength of Hans Küng's approach (developed in Küng 1998, 1999) above all lies in the "support" of the global ethos by religious traditions.

In addition to the theoretical perspectives, the problems of public goods in a global economy, first and foremost, give rise to enormous practical challenges. Only if sufficient "ethical resources" are actually mobilized will humankind be capable of solving immense common problems. As discussed above, an ethos of mere (even enlightened) self-interest of groups, nations and corporations is not up to these challenges. Also a secular ethos, ignoring religious traditions (to which, after all, a large majority of humankind adheres), cannot match them. The religious traditions offer indispensable "ethical resources" for the provision of global public goods because, in one form or another, they have always promoted common goods that transcend single human beings. However, for religious traditions too, these global challenges are new. Each tradition must find the right relationship with those who differ, in the global context, from their own adherents in terms of race, gender, culture, politics and faith.[3]

To conclude this chapter on the need for self-regarding and other-regarding motivations, we may recall Jane Mansbridge's manifesto *Beyond Self-Interest*, in which she writes:

I would argue that most human institutions, including family, elections, tax collection, and war, to name some obvious examples, are predicated on equally mixed motives. As empirical social science stops ignoring this reality and starts exploring duty and love with the same intensity it has recently given self-interest, the resulting analyses are likely to become more useful to those engaged in collective action. (Mansbridge 1990, xiii)

Notes

1 "Inspired" by Rawls means that the "overlapping consensus" consists of common norms and values (that is, a "common ethical ground"), which are free-standing (as Rawls claims) and can be justified by different philosophical and religious traditions (which goes beyond what Rawls claims).
2 The Manifesto is based on "the fundamental principle of humanity" that recognizes – notwithstanding differences between cultural traditions – the inalienable dignity of each human being that is the basis for the esteem, defense and fulfillment of their human rights. It is contained in the Golden Rule "What you do not wish done to yourself, do not do to others" and further developed with four basic values, which can be found in all great religious and ethical traditions of humankind: (1) Non-violence and respect for life (or the demand "You shall not kill!"). (2) Justice and solidarity (or the demand "You shall not steal!"). (3) Honesty and tolerance (or the demand "You shall not lie!"). (4) Mutual esteem and partnership (or the demand "You shall not commit sexual immorality!").
3 This was one of the fundamental questions addressed to the faith traditions by Gerald Barney during the Parliament of World's Religions 1993 in Chicago (Barney et al. 1993).

PART II

Human Rights as Public Goods in Wealth Creation

Introduction

Promulgated over seventy years ago – in 1948 – the Universal Declaration of Human Rights (UN 1948) was a milestone in the history of humankind and formulated, for the first time, a common worldwide moral foundation for the living together of human beings on the planet Earth. The Declaration was and still is an enormous challenge, which is very far from being fully addressed. Its validity is called into doubt and threatened by people, organizations and states in all regions of the world, in recent times particularly by authoritarianism and populist, nationalistic and fundamentalist movements.

Nevertheless, with the UN Global Compact (2000), the UN Framework (2008) and UN Guiding Principles on Business and Human Rights (2011), the human rights agenda has expanded to the business sector and, in turn, has been strengthened by the "National Action Plans for Human Rights (2016–2020)" launched by numerous governments (including Argentina, Australia, Germany, Italy, Sweden, the United States and many more; see BHRRC). Moreover, the responsibility for human rights has been extended beyond business and government to non-state actors such as universities, civil society organizations and religious communities (see Kirchschläger 2017).

For a clear understanding of human rights we may draw on the works of the philosophers Alan Gewirth (1984) and Henry Shue (1996) and the "architect" of the UN Framework and Guiding Principles on Business and Human Rights John Ruggie (UN 2008a, 2011; Ruggie 2013). Gewirth distinguishes five components (or "elements") of a claim-right (that is, a right that claims to be respected): (1) the subject of the right, (2) the nature of the right, (3) the object of the right, (4) the respondent of the right and (5) the justifying basis or ground of the right (see P.II.1).

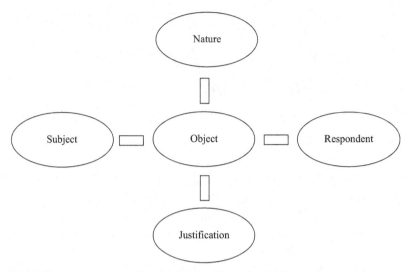

P.II.1 Five components of a claim-right (Gewirth 1984)

By applying this distinction to human rights, we can distinguish difficult from less difficult questions. It is fair to say that a relatively big, worldwide consensus exists with regard to the subjects of human rights (component 1): all human beings without exception are subjects of these rights, including present and future generations. This focus on the subjects is important because all human beings possess these rights in virtue of their humanity, regardless of whether the rights are fulfilled or not. As for the objects of human rights (component 3), they consist of what is necessary for a life with dignity, which comprehends civil, political, economic, social and cultural demands. They have to be defined more precisely according to the socio-economic and socio-cultural as well as historic contexts. Thus it is more difficult to agree upon this component. For example, a decent standard of living varies greatly across countries, but it can be determined within a certain range of imprecision.

Much more difficult is it to find a consensus with regard to the other three components. In many situations there are several or even multiple respondents (component 4) so that a fair allocation of responsibility to all respondents (say, to individuals, organizations and states) can be extremely difficult. The nature of human rights (component 2) means that, as minimal requirements, these rights trump any other claims and do not allow for trade-offs. At the same time, these requirements can take different forms of obligations – an important distinction which is often overlooked. Following Shue (1996), Ruggie (2013, UN 2008a) distinguishes: the (direct and indirect) "respect" for human rights (as the "responsibility" of business enterprises); the "protection" against human rights violations by third parties (as the "duty" of states); the provision of access to "remedy" human rights violations (as the obligation of both business and states); and the "promotion" of human rights (as the obligation of other actors). Finally, the justification of human rights (component 5) is the most difficult task in contemporary pluralistic societies. However, this does not mean that one should abandon it; rather, justifications from different philosophical and religious perspectives are urgently needed.

Given this differentiated understanding of human rights, two flawed and widespread notions of human rights can be avoided. The distinction between positive and negative rights is based on the view that a negative right to freedom means non-interfering with the right holder's decisions and actions, while a positive right, say, to certain economic and social goods, entails that others (for example, the government) have a positive obligation to fulfill the rights of the right holder (see discussion in Arnold 2018a). Shue (1996) rejects this distinction as artificial and inconsistent with social reality. He argues that this distinction refers to the duty (that correlates to the right) – not to the right itself – and "negative rights" entail both negative and positive duties. For example, the right of physical security (not to be killed, tortured, abused or violently threated) requires not only negative steps to refrain, but also positive steps such as law enforcement agencies and a criminal justice system.

Another common, though flawed view of human rights interprets the assertion of human rights in an individualistic sense as if it meant an egoistic claim that places the right holder's interests above all others' interests and the common good of the community and ignores the correlating duties and responsibilities. Rather, the differentiated understanding of human rights connects unambiguously the subjects with the respondents of human rights. It affirms that each human being has the same human rights and no one can be excluded. It is a strong advocate of and calls attention to those who suffer from human rights violations. And it provides the conditions for the survival and flourishing of communities.

Having outlined the understanding of human rights in general terms, we now relate it as the normative-ethical perspective to the creation of wealth explained in Part I of this book. As noted in Chapter 1, wealth creation is conceived in an "ethics-related" sense, which includes human motivation and the judgment of social achievements and is thus broader than a "value-free" logistic (or "engineering") approach to economics (Sen 1987).

This part consists of four chapters. Chapter 11 deals with the scope of human rights, which includes all human rights incorporated in the International Bill of Human Rights and eight ILO core conventions. They are indivisible and interrelated and can be impacted by any actor in society, be it government, business, any other non-state actor or individuals. This list is larger than a set of basic rights (Shue 1996) and shorter than the amount of rights that might be granted in a democratic country. What they mean concretely is illustrated by thirty-five vivid stories celebrating the Universal Declaration of Human Rights (Amnesty International 2009). In Chapter 12 the binding nature of human rights is discussed in moral terms: the moral reality of human rights, their moral minimum without trade-offs and their distinctiveness from other moral obligations, expectations and ideals. Chapter 13 presents cost-benefit considerations about human rights. Human rights are conceived not only as constraints of wealth creation, but primarily as goals and means that support the process of wealth creation. Finally, Chapter 14 qualifies human rights as ethically demanded global public goods and explores some implications for appropriate institutions and motivations.

11 | *All Internationally Recognized Human Rights Are at Stake*

After the launch of the United Nations Global Compact in 2000 by Kofi Annan, Secretary-General of the United Nations, the Sub-Commission on the Promotion and Protection of Human Rights was charged with specifying the principles of human rights and labor rights stated in the Global Compact and developing "Norms on the Responsibilities of Transnational Corporations and Other Business Enterprises with Regard to Human Rights." In 2003, the Sub-Commission published the so-called Draft Norms, which limited business responsibilities to economic, social and cultural rights, but wanted to make them legally binding (UN 2003). However, these Draft Norms ran into fierce opposition by business and were finally dropped. A new attempt to specify business responsibilities in terms of human rights was undertaken by John Ruggie as the Special Representative of the Secretary-General and succeeded with the UN Framework (UN 2008a) and UN Guiding Principles on Business and Human Rights (UN 2011), followed by "An Interpretive Guide" (UN 2012a). These documents, unanimously enforced by the United Nations Council on Human Rights, declare all internationally recognized human rights relevant for business, namely civil, political, economic, social and cultural rights, including the right to development. These rights are based on "social expectations" and businesses are required to consider them in "due diligence processes"; however, they are not legally binding.

The reasons for including all internationally recognized human rights resulted from multiple consultations Ruggie and his team conducted with business enterprises, civil society organizations, governmental agencies and other stakeholders. It turned out that companies can impact any human rights situation. Hence, the UN Framework should not be limited to economic, social and cultural rights, but also include civil and political rights and the right to development as well.

Ruggie's Report to the Human Rights Council in 2008 explains "why any attempt to limit internationally recognized rights is inherently problematic" (UN 2008a, §52). He draws from a study of 320 cases (from all regions and sectors) of alleged corporate-related human rights abuses, published on the Business and Human Rights Resource Centre website from February 2005 to December 2007, and concludes:

There are few if any internationally recognized rights business cannot impact – or be perceived to impact – in some manner. Therefore, companies should consider all such rights. It may be useful for operational guidance purposes to map which rights companies have tended to affect most often in particular sectors or situations. It is also helpful for companies to understand how human rights relate to their management functions – for example, human resources, security of assets and personnel, supply chains, and community engagement. Both means of developing guidance should be pursued, but neither limits the rights companies should take into account. (UN 2008a, §52)

To summarize, business impact on human rights includes the following rights (UN 2008a, § 52):

Labor rights: Freedom of association; right to organize and participate in collective bargaining; right to non-discrimination; abolition of slavery and forced labor; abolition of child labor; right to work; right to equal pay for equal work; right to equality at work; right to just and favorable remuneration; right to a safe work environment; right to rest and leisure; right to family life.

Non-labor rights: Right to life, liberty and security of the person; freedom from torture or cruel, inhuman or degrading treatment; equal recognition and protection under the law; right to a fair trial; right to self-determination; freedom of movement; right of peaceful assembly; right to marry and form a family; freedom of thought, conscience and religion; right to hold opinions, freedom of information and expression; right to political life; right to privacy; right to an adequate standard of living (including food, clothing and housing); right to physical and mental health; access to medical services; right to education; right to participate in cultural life, the benefits of scientific progress and protection of authorial interests; right to social security.

Four years later, all internationally recognized human rights relevant for businesses are listed in *The Corporate Responsibility to Respect Human Rights: An Interpretive Guide*, published by The United Nations Human Rights Office of the High Commissioner. They are based on the International Bill of Human Rights and eight core

Table 11.1 *International Covenant on Civil and Political Rights (ICCPR)*

Article 1: Right of self-determination

Articles 2 to 5: Overarching principles

Article 6: Right to life

Article 7: Right not to be subjected to torture, cruel, inhuman and/or degrading treatment or punishment

Article 8: Right not to be subjected to slavery, servitude or forced labor

Article 9: Right to liberty and security of the person

Article 10: Right of detained persons to humane treatment

Article 11: Right not to be subjected to imprisonment for inability to fulfil a contract

Article 12: Right to freedom of movement

Article 13: Right of aliens to due process when facing expulsion

Article 14: Right to a fair trial

Article 15: Right to be free from retroactive criminal law

Article 16: Right to recognition as a person before the law

Article 17: Right to privacy

Article 18: Right to freedom of thought, conscience and religion

Article 19: Right to freedom of opinion and expression

Article 20: Right to freedom from war propaganda, and freedom from incitement to racial, religious or national hatred

Article 21: Right to freedom of assembly

Article 22: Right to freedom of association

Article 23: Right of the protection of the family and the right to marry

Article 24: Rights of protection for the child

Article 25: Right to participate in public life

Article 26: Right to equality before the law, equal protection of the law and rights of non-discrimination

Article 27: Rights of minorities

---

conventions of the International Labour Organisation (ILO) (UN 2012a, 87–89):

The International Bill of Human Rights consists of the Universal Declaration of Human Rights and the main instruments through which it has been codified: the International Covenant on Civil and Political Rights and the International Covenant on Economic, Social and Cultural Rights. Similar provisions in the two Covenants stipulate non-discrimination and gender equality as overarching principles to be applied in conjunction with specific rights. Both Covenants recognize and define in more detail the rights in the Universal Declaration. (see Tables 11.1 and 11.2)

Table 11.2 *International Covenant on Economic, Social and Cultural Rights (ICESCR)*

Article 1: Right of self-determination
Articles 2–5: Overarching principles
Article 6: Right to work
Article 7: Right to enjoy just and favorable conditions of work
Article 8: Right to form and join trade unions, and the right to strike
Article 9: Right to social security, including social insurance
Article 10: Right to a family life
Article 11: Right to an adequate standard of living. (This includes the right to adequate food, the right to adequate housing and the prohibition of forced evictions. This right has also been interpreted to comprise the right to safe drinking water and sanitation.)
Article 12: Right to health
Article 13 and 14: Right to education
Article 15: Right to take part in cultural life, to benefit from scientific progress, and of the material and moral rights of authors and inventors

Table 11.3 *ILO core conventions*

- Freedom of association and collective bargaining
- Elimination of forced and compulsory labor
- Elimination of discrimination in employment and occupation
- Abolition of child labor

The Declaration on Fundamental Principles and Rights at Work, adopted by ILO in 1998, committed members to respect four fundamental principles and rights at work, each of these supported by two ILO conventions (see Table 11.3).

It is noteworthy that the G4 Sustainability Reporting Guidelines of the Global Reporting Initiative (updated in July 2018) include the two sub-categories Labor Practices and Decent Work and Human Rights (www.globalreporting.org). In line with the UN Guiding Principles on Business and Human Rights, they comprise the standards of the International Bill of Human Rights and the ILO Declaration on Fundamental Principles and Rights at Work (along with regional conventions and conventions protecting the rights of individuals).

Moreover, there are many "aspects" that provide insights into human rights performance and impacts in other sub-categories of the G4 Guidelines. While these Guidelines are voluntary to the full discretion of the organization and not a "responsibility" of business enterprises (as is the case with the UN Guiding Principles), they are nonetheless a valuable tool for companies to "take responsibility" and improve their social performance.

These internationally recognized rights amount to a total of thirty human rights (UN 2008a, ICCPR Art. 6-26 and ICESCR Art. 6-15; see UDHR 1948). All thirty human rights are necessary for a human life with dignity – neither a small set of "basic rights" nor a proliferation beyond thirty rights. They define the contents (or "objects" in Gewirth's [1984] terminology) of rights and concretize to some extent what human dignity means in these respects. But they are not specific enough and need to be determined further in the specific socio-economic, socio-cultural and historic contexts of the right holders. For example, the right to privacy in the digital age has a different specific content compared to this right before the digital age. Or the right to an adequate standard of living is specified differently in a low- and in a high-income country (see, for instance, the study of poverty in Switzerland in Enderle 1987).

Moreover, caution is in place when the language of human rights is used in a non-western context. Without being declared as such, labor rights can play important roles to move toward a more Confucian, family-like community in the workplace (Kim 2014). Or the right of protection for the child can be understood – without human rights language – in a civil-war-torn country with child soldiers such as Sierra Leone.

In discussing the contents of human rights, three further characteristics should be briefly addressed: their indivisibility, interdependence and interrelatedness. Daniel Whelan (2010) presents an interesting account of the usage of these terms from the antecedents of the Universal Declaration of Human Rights to the Optional Protocol to the International Covenant on Economic, Social and Cultural Rights in 2009 and focuses on the relationship between the two grand categories of human rights – civil and political rights on the one hand and economic, social and cultural rights on the other hand. He defines the words "interdependent" and "interrelated" as "bringing together ... two or more things into a mutual harmony" while "they still acknowledge separateness," whereas the word "indivisible" means "incapable of being divided, in reality or thought" (p. 6). Whelan assumes rightly that the Universal Declaration – without using the word "indivisible" – forms an organic unity of both grand categories of human rights. They are not conceived as separate entities, which then could be brought together through interdependent and mutually related ties. Rather, they are "indivisible." This view, however, was questioned during the periods of the "Postcolonial Revisionism: 1952–1968" and the "Economic Justice: 1968–1986" and was reaffirmed in the period of the "Restoration: 1986–2009."

Granted the unity of all thirty human rights, two questions remain, namely (1) whether, and if so, how, particular human rights (beyond the two grand categories) can be conceived as indivisible, interdependent and interrelated and (2) whether there is another and a better way to ground the indivisibility of human rights than by relying on modern political and economic institutions as suggested by Whelan.

The first question can be addressed by defining indivisibility, interdependence and interrelatedness in a sense (slightly) different from Whelan's definition. The unity or indivisibility of human rights can be maintained if they are conceived as distinct – rather than as separate – anchored in the human person and not allowing for trade-offs. While they are incapable of being divided, they relate to each other and depend on each other in specific ways. For example, the right to education is essential to the right to participate in public life; the right not to be subjected to slavery, servitude or forced labor is necessary for the right to work; the right to an adequate standard of living implies the rights to liberty and security of the person; and the freedom of association entails the right to form and join trade unions and the right to strike.

As for the question of grounding the indivisibility of human rights, Whelan's proposal of grounding it in modern institutions seems to argue only from a legal perspective, that is, how human rights incorporated in laws can be enforced by institutions. What is missing is a moral (or ethical) perspective that is prior to the legal incorporation and takes "the moral reality of human rights" (Tasioulas 2007) seriously. Johannes Morsink provides a thorough moral foundation in *Inherent Human Rights* (2009). Moreover, as Shue (1996) forcefully argues, the perspective of human rights holders (the "subjects" who suffer from human rights violations) should not be confused with the perspective of the "respondents" (Gewirth 1984) of human rights that might be expressed by institutions and/or interactions of individuals. The next chapter takes up the moral reality of human rights and elucidates their moral dimension to some extent.

12 | *Human Rights Constitute Minimal Ethical Requirements*

The previous chapter identified and discussed to some extent the contents of the thirty human rights as they are recognized internationally at present. By doing so, we get a concrete understanding of what is at stake with human rights. It helps to critically assess the prolific rhetoric of official documents and particular campaigns (such as those for and against abortion) as well as the growing oblivion to human rights of workers and immigrants. Having focused on the contents of human rights, we now can turn to addressing their moral quality and legitimacy. Therefore, this chapter discusses the nature of human rights – that is Gewirth's second component of human rights – and presents his approach to justification – that is the fifth component (see Introduction to Part II). Subsequently, human rights are related to Sen's capability approach and defined as minimal ethical requirements without addressing the wide range of ethical obligations and ideals above this fundamental minimum (see De George 2010).

In his illuminating introduction to *Human Rights: Moral or Political?* Adam Etinson (2018, 1–38) starts with the observation that human rights have various "natures" or mode of existence: human rights (plausibly) exist as moral rights, on the one hand, but also as socially, politically and legally practiced rights, on the other. These two approaches often clash in the so-called "Orthodox-Political debate" between "Orthodox" and "Political" theorists. Etinson carefully presents and comments on these approaches and concludes that they do not necessarily conflict with each other and can be complementary. In this book I endorse his view and briefly present the two approaches.

The Moral Reality of Human Rights

The "Orthodox" approach conceives of human rights as natural rights or moral rights that humans have simply by virtue of being human. Before this term was introduced by John Tasioulas (2010), Gewirth had already provided in the 1980s a precise definition of the nature of human rights: They are *"personally oriented, normatively necessary moral requirements"* that every human has the necessary goods of action (Gewirth 1984, 2; emphasis in the original). "Personally oriented" means that the requirements are owed to distinct subjects or individuals for the good of those individuals; hence they are not just consequential upon or instrumental to the fulfillment of aggregative or collective goals. "Normatively necessary" indicates the moral status, meaning that compliance with them is morally mandatory. Finally, "moral requirements" include three aspects: (1) they are necessary needs that qualify the relationship between the subjects and objects of human rights; (2) they are justified entitlements regarding the relationship between objects and their justifying basis; and (3) they are claims or demands addressed to and imposed on other persons, communities and institutions.

Given this definition, what does it mean that human rights "exist"? Commenting on Thomas Jefferson's famous statement that all humans "are endowed by their Creator with certain inalienable rights," Gewirth writes:

It is not the case that humans are born having rights in the sense in which they are born having legs. At least, their having legs is empirically verifiable, but this is not the case with their having moral rights. The having or existence of human rights consists in the first instance not in the having of certain physical or mental attributes, but rather in certain justified moral requirements, in the three senses of "requirement" mentioned above. (Gewirth 1984, 3)

Gewirth defends this Orthodox approach against the Political approach, which holds that human rights exist, or persons have human rights only when and insofar as there is social recognition and legal enforcement of all persons' equal entitlement to the objects of human rights. He argues that "if the existence of human rights depended on such recognition or enforcement, it would follow that there were no human rights prior to or independent of these positive enactments" (1984, 3).

Similarly, Thomas Nagel makes the uncompromising statement:

The existence of moral rights does not depend on their political recognition or enforcement but rather on the moral question whether there is a decisive justification for including these forms of inviolability in the status of every

member of a moral community. The reality of moral rights is purely normative rather than institutional – though of course institutions may be designed
to enforce them. (Nagel 2002, 33)

Referring to the context of globalization, Tom Campell and Seumas
Miller (2004) emphasize the high moral importance of human rights
beyond the conformity to human rights laws and explore their practi-
calities for organizations operating in both private and public spheres
(relevant in Part III of this book).

Furthermore, John Tasioulas (2007) defends "the moral reality of
human rights" against the Political approach by arguing that "the
international regime of human rights is not morally self-evaluating;
instead, its legitimacy depends on its conformity with independent
moral standards, including genuine human rights" (p. 75). He supports
the Orthodox approach that "which human rights exist is a *moral*
question to be distinguished from the predominantly *institutional*
question of the extent to which they are recognized, respected, or
enforced" (p. 75). In line with Gewirth, he stresses the perspective of
the subjects (that is the individuals) while allowing much variety in
identifying the respondents, be they persons or institutions:

Human rights are moral entitlements possessed by all *simply in virtue of their
humanity*. It seems to follow from this definition that no account needs to be
taken of individuals' special relationships to persons, groups, and institutions
in determining which human rights exist. And this is so even if the human
capacity for entering into such relationship is a relevant consideration in
identifying human rights. (p. 76; emphasis in the original)

With regard to the objects of human rights, he claims – similarly,
though less precisely than Gewirth – that "the rights must have a
tolerably determinate content independently of any subsequent institutional specification they might receive. If they did not, there would be
no warrant for treating them as human rights in the first place" (p. 76).

It is noteworthy that the International Bill of Human Rights and the
eight ILO core conventions do not use explicit moral language, nor do
the UN Framework and Guiding Principles on Business and Human
Rights. Nevertheless, these rights arguably can be interpreted as moral
rights while leaving open their moral justification (see Enderle 2014b).

Human Rights Also Exist Today as Explicitly Recognized Norms of Popular Morality, Political Practice and Legal Institutions throughout the World

In addition to the moral reality of human rights, Etinson draws attention to the fact that human rights are also standards that many people around the world happen to *believe* in (as popular moralities) and, moreover, are norms deeply embedded in contemporary politics and law – domestically, regionally and internationally (Etinson 2018, 2). Ruggie's consultations on business and human rights around the world are a vivid testimony of this reality, let alone the International Bill of Human Rights and the big number of National Action Plans for Human Rights (see Chapter 11).

As Etinson affirms, this mode of existence is of enormous practical and theoretical significance (pp. 2–3). Without real-world belief in the importance of human rights, as well as recognition in politics and enforcement through law, the promise of human rights would hardly ever be fulfilled. And without this reality, philosophy would not be so challenged as it is today to help us make sense of our ideals and practices as they *are* and help us reimagine them as they *ought* to be.[1]

Given the importance of both modes of existence of human rights, it would be shortsighted and unwise to assert one mode and reject the other. For the implementation of human rights their moral reality matters as much as their institutionalization. Both modes relate to each other, although in different and complex ways. The Orthodox approach affirms the grounding priority of human rights as moral rights and criticizes the Political approach to the extent that it denies their moral existence. Therefore, as an Orthodox proponent, Tasioulas (2007) objects to Raymond Geuss's "enforceability" argument (that moral beliefs only exist if they are enforceable) and Onora O'Neill's claimability thesis (that only universal liberty rights, not welfare rights, can impose "negative" duties to refrain from harming others in various ways). On the other hand, Political proponents make the valuable point that human rights have a functional role and – in many, but not all cases – need to be enforced by law in order to facilitate stable and predictable social relations.

Three Types of Obligations to Secure Human Rights

In elucidating the nature[2] of human rights, a further aspect should be addressed. It has been advanced by the UN Framework for Business and Human Rights (UN 2008a), following the distinction proposed by Shue (1996) who identifies three principles or types of obligations: to "protect" human rights, to "respect" human rights and to provide access to "remedy" for human rights violations. All three types define ethical requirements in the relationship between subjects (individuals) and respondents: protect refers to states; respect relates to business enterprises; and remedy concerns both (for more, see Chapter 15).

The obligation to *protect* means protection against human rights abuses by *third* parties. Human rights need protection against any violation wherever it comes from. The binding nature is uncompromising.[3] The obligation to *remedy* requires to addressing *actual* human rights violations, which exist, but should not be tolerated. And the obligation to *respect* involves three demands of having no *adverse human rights impacts through the own activities* of business enterprises and states, namely the demand:

(a) to avoid *causing* such impacts and address them when they occur;
(b) to avoid *contributing* to such impacts and address them when they occur; and
(c) to seek to *prevent* or *mitigate* such impacts that are *directly linked* to their operations, products or services by their business relationships, even if they have not contributed to those impacts. (UN 2011, Principle #13)

It is noteworthy that adverse human rights impacts are at the center of the UN Framework for Business and Human Rights. They emphasize the significance that human rights are normatively necessary moral requirements, which have to be fulfilled. This can be done by different actors and in different ways. One crucial criterion applicable to states and business enterprises is the actor's adverse impact of its own activity defined by the three ethical demands. It also applies to other actors such as universities, civil society organizations, and religious communities (see Kirchgässner 2017). If the normatively necessary moral requirements are not fulfilled, the failing respondents need to be brought to account.

Gewirth's Approach to Justifying Human Rights

Having discussed some features of the nature of human rights (that is, their moral existence and the protect-respect-remedy obligations), we now turn to the question of how human rights can be justified. An example of a rational, defensible, well-thought-out theory is Gewirth's approach. In his keynote address to the XXI World Congress of Philosophy in 2003 (adapted in Gewirth 2007), Gewirth presents a concise account of the approach he has developed in his scholarly work over the years (Gewirth 1978, 1982, 1996). It attempts to overcome the weaknesses of other approaches. The appeal to self-evidence in Jefferson's statement mentioned above lacks universal firmness: "what is self-evident to one person may not be self-evident to others, some may, in fact, regard it as moronic or worse" (Gewirth 2007, 221). Religious justifications such as the Judeo-Christian belief that all humans as children of God have moral rights would not convince a non-believer. And "secular thinkers, including Kant and John Rawls, have tried in various ways to ground human rights in certain procedural considerations," but – in Gewirth's view – not successfully.

To begin with, Gewirth proposes to examine the objective *context* in which the concept of rights has its chief and necessary justifying basis. The question is:

When we say that someone has a right to something, what is the more general conceptual area or independent variable to which we are appealing in justification of this claim?

And Gewirth suggests that this conceptual area is *human action*:

It is the concept of action that underlies and justifies the invocation of rights. To see this, we must note that the concept of a right is a moral concept before it is a legal one; and the general context of all morality is *action*. For all moralities, amid their various conflicting contents, require that persons act in certain ways. The specific kinds of action that are upheld are, of course, very different, especially as concerns the root principles to which they appeal: thus the religious moralist differs from the atheist moralist, the communist moralist differs from the libertarian, the aesthete differs from the Benthamite utilitarian, and so forth. Nevertheless, all these different moralities agree in setting forth requirements for action. It is from the necessary conditions of action that moralities come to prescribe rights. (Gewirth 2007, 221–22)[4]

Thus the concept of action is the independent variable for all rights and has certain necessary conditions which justify the move from the proposition "A is human" to the proposition "A has certain moral rights." While actions have varying contents, they all have two generic features in common: *voluntariness* or *freedom* and *purposiveness* or *intentionality* that Gewirth calls at its fullest successful extent *well-being*. The feature of freedom assumes that the right bearers have autonomy: they can control their behavior by their unforced choice while having knowledge of relevant circumstances. And the feature of well-being assumes that agents act with some end in view, some purpose they want to achieve. Thus they have the abilities and conditions that are at least minimally needed for all successful action. As *basic* well-being, the abilities and conditions include having life, physical integrity, and mental equilibrium. As *non-subtractive* well-being, they are needed in order to maintain undiminished one's level of purpose-fulfillment such as not being lied to, not having promises to oneself broken, and so forth. And *additive* well-being consists of abilities and conditions that are needed for increasing one's level of purpose-fulfillment, for example, education, self-esteem and other conditions making progress in one's ability of agency.

In short, the two generic features of freedom and well-being constitute the necessary conditions of human action that serve as the independent variables of all rights. They are akin to Sen's fundamental distinction between "freedom of processes" and "substantive opportunities," which will be discussed later on. They can be also related to the Kantian approach that focuses on the autonomy of the person and to the Aristotelian approach that emphasizes the goods necessary for human flourishing.

In the next step of the justification, referring to his books (1978, 1982, 1996), Gewirth argues that "every agent must regard his freedom and well-being as necessary goods for him, since without freedom and well-being he would not be able to act at all or with general chances of success in achieving his purposes" (Gewirth 2007, 222). Therefore, the agent must hold that he (or she) has rights to freedom and well-being.

However, if the agent then is denied his rights and other persons are permitted to interfere with his having freedom and well-being, the agent would contradict himself: freedom and well-being are not necessary goods for him and he does not have these rights. Moreover, since he is a prospective purposive agent who claims these rights for himself, he must accept – in order not to contradict himself – that all prospective purposive agents have these rights, which are now qualified as moral rights. In conclusion, the existence of human rights is established on the basis that all humans are actual, prospective, potential agents and must be similarly treated as the formal conception of justice requires (that is to treat equals equally and unequal unequally).

Three clarifications are in place that explicate the substantive concept of justice. First, the argument does not claim that any necessary good for the agent can provide the basis for a right. Hence, one cannot say, "I must have a ten-speed bicycle; it is a necessary good for me, so I have a right to it." The necessary good has to be an intrinsic ability of agency based on reason and a universal good of purposive action that stands the test of non-contradiction. Second, the agent's claim of rights to the features of action does not mean that the rights pertain to what the agent necessarily has *already*. It sometimes happens that purposive actions are not successful and agents do not have the non-subtractive and additive abilities to attain these necessary goods of well-being. Although well-being in its full scope cannot be achieved, it is at least intended. Third, even with regard to the right to freedom and basic well-being, it is claimed by the person not only as a present or actual agent, but also as a prospective agent, although he does not necessarily have freedom and well-being. Moreover, there is always the possibility of interference with his agency and hence of his lacking the freedom and well-being that agency requires. Thus the right to have freedom and well-being is claimed within this broader, prospective context. (As for human beings who are so deficient mentally or physically that they cannot engage in full-fledged purposive agency, Gewirth addresses this question with the principle of proportionality explained elsewhere.)

To summarize Gewirth's justification, there are two grounds on which human rights are normatively mandatory:

First, on the substantive ground that their objects, what they are rights to, are the necessary goods of action; and, second, on the formal ground that any attempt to violate them involves the agent in self-contraction, for he is then in the position of denying that his victim, as a prospective purposive agent, has the same generic rights he must claim for himself.

We may also call this principle of human rights the principle of generic consistency (PGC) because it combines the formal consideration of consistency with the substantive consideration of the generic features and rights of action. It is this principle that underlies the moral requirement both of human rights and global justice. (Gewirth 2007, 224)

In appreciation of Gewirth's work on human rights that dates back to the 1980s, but arguably has not found its deserved recognition among scholars, the following features of his contribution to the philosophical justification of human rights may be highlighted (see Enderle 1987, 169–73, 180–81). His profound and well-thought-through argumentation starts from the generic features of human action. By doing so, he sets his approach, from the beginning, on the basis of universality and makes it independent of any kind of morality. The necessary features of human action are identified as freedom and well-being. Freedom is not conceived as metaphysical or political freedom, but as freedom of action. By equally valuing freedom and well-being, Gewirth rejects both the priority of freedom and the primacy of welfare rights (Golding 1984) and provides a solid foundation for overcoming the fruitless dispute in human rights discussions between civil and political rights on the one hand and economic, social and cultural rights on the other. Moreover, with his precise way of reasoning he succeeds to demonstrate the relevance of logic for ethics in the sense that, while logic cannot directly answer fundamental ethical questions, it can exclude inconsistent answers and thereby offer indirect solutions.

My critique concerns in particular two points (see also Regis 1984). Although rational argumentation – undervalued by many contemporaries – should play an important role in the human rights debate, one might still ask whether Gewirth overextends the limits of rational ethics. Isn't it reasonable and often experienced in real life that not only reason and rationality but also affectedness ("Betroffenheit") and compassion ("Mitleid") can have a functional role in justifying human rights (see Ebeling 1984; Morsink 2009)? If so, any rational ethics should be embedded in a broader context in which affectedness and compassion are indispensable aspects.

With such a broader conception of ethics, I may raise a second critical remark about Gewirth's approach. He speaks of "generic features," "prospective, purposive agents" and "moral rights"; but he does not specify these agents, the subjects of human action, more precisely. In other words, Gewirth's concept of the person becomes visible only in a rather vague sense, either by alluding to it (for instance, human rights as attributes of persons) or by not treating this question explicitly (in contrast to authors such as Melden 1977 and Parfit 1984). Ethics cannot but relate to anthropology.

Human Rights Related to Sen's Capability Approach

As explained in Chapter 8, the capability approach puts people on center stage beyond utility- and resource-based approaches and provides a solid informational basis for interpersonal comparisons and economic and social policies, focusing on the key question: "What is each person able to do and to be?" So how are human rights related to capabilities? As Sen points out, "[T]he two concepts – human rights and capabilities – go well with each other, so long as we do not try to subsume either concept entirely within the territory of the other" (Sen 2005, 151). Accordingly, four commonalities and differences are briefly discussed in the following.

First, capabilities express real freedoms people possess, and can help identify the contents of rights. For example, to be able to read and write indicates what (basic) education means; or to be able to be protected against gender discrimination implies being treated equally. Thus human rights are *entitlements* to *capabilities* and specify substantive *opportunities*. In checking the International Bill of Human Rights, one can find many rights, which are backed up by capabilities.

Second, other rights such as the right to a fair trial or the right of aliens to due process when facing expulsion cannot be adequately supported by capabilities, which are characteristics of individual advantages. These rights qualify the *process* aspect of freedom – not its opportunity aspect. Sen explains this difference with the "harsh" example of giving health care to women and men. If they are given the same care, women tend to live longer than men. Concerned only with capabilities (and nothing else) and, particularly, with equal capability to live long, one would have to conclude that men should be given more medical attention than women in order to counteract the natural masculine handicap. However, process equity would be violated if women get less medical attention for the same health problems than men. Therefore, a theory of human rights – like a theory of justice – should address both aspects of freedom, the capability as well as the process aspect.

Third, a controversial question concerns *the list of capabilities and human rights*: what capabilities and what rights should be included?

As mentioned in Chapter 8, Sen abstains from establishing a specific list of capabilities, leaving its specification to public reasoning, while Nussbaum proposes a specific list of ten "central capabilities" based on her theory of fundamental political entitlements. In Chapter 11 the UN Framework and the UN Guiding Principles on Business and Human Rights refer to the International Bill of Human Rights and ILO Core Conventions and include thirty rights, which are potentially relevant for business enterprises. These varying numbers reflect different approaches, which are not necessarily contradictory. All three approaches focus on the contents of the persons' capabilities and rights, respectively, and do not directly identify the respondents, that is, who is responsible to realize these capabilities and human rights. Nussbaum's central capabilities constitute a minimal threshold level that any political order must at least secure to all citizens. According to the socio-political context, they can be concretized and expanded and incorporated as entitlements in national legislation and international agreements. The thirty internationally recognized human rights express the demands of all human beings as established in international accords and can be partially supported by capabilities. Sen's open list of capabilities is supposed to be specified by the goals of social initiatives and movements, which stand the test of public reasoning.

Fourth, in his book *The Idea of Justice* (2009) Sen does not propose an ideal theory of justice (or a "transcendental institutionalism" approach). His approach is more action-oriented that gets its agenda from urgent justice and human rights challenges (called a "realization-focused comparison" approach; pp. 1–27). For him, the justification of human rights lies in public reasoning. To assess the ethical claims of human rights and the challenges they may face, he requires some test of open and informed scrutiny:

The status of these ethical claims must be dependent ultimately on their survivability in unobstructed discussion. In this sense, the viability of human rights is linked with what John Rawls has called "public reasoning" and its role in "ethical objectivity". (Sen 2004, 349; referring to Rawls 1971, 1993, 110–13)

"Unobstructed" open public discussion implies the acceptance of equality of human beings, that is, no one is excluded. Although such discussion is hardly possible, if not impossible, in politically and socially repressive regimes, it is essential not only for the defense but also for the dismissal of human rights claims. Criticizing Rawls's limitation of the domain of public reasoning to a given society alone, Sen demands that the discussion include – even for domestic justice (if only to avoid parochial prejudices and also to examine a broader range of arguments) – views from "a certain distance" as required already by Adam Smith. While the universality of human rights has been rejected by many authors over centuries (for example, Edmund Burke, Rosa Luxemburg, Samuel Huntington and Gertrude Himmelfarb), Sen extensively explains his own view in his chapter "Culture and Human Rights" (Sen 1999, 227–49), which can be summarized as follows: "The championing of open public discussion, tolerating and encouraging different points of views, has a long history in many countries in the world" (Sen 2004, 352). In agreement with Sen, one can make a strong case that justification of universal human rights needs public reasoning that is not limited to national or ethnic borders. However, this still leaves wide room for different and more elaborated ways of justifying human rights, be it with the approach proposed by Gewirth or others (see Etinson 2018; Morsink 2009).

Human Rights as Minimal Ethical Requirements in the Context of Morality and Ethics

In concluding this chapter, it is important to emphasize that morality and ethics[5] cover a much broader range of ethical obligations and ideals, including, for example, the rule of reciprocity, the values of generosity and gratitude and the character traits or virtues of courage and integrity. Human rights are only minimal ethical requirements, which, of course, does not mean that they are less important. They are fundamental and do not allow any trade-off. They provide the common ethical ground that is particularly challenged in pluralistic societies. It is ethically not possible to achieve ethical ideals while violating minimal ethical requirements. One cannot maximize a certain variable (for instance, utility) by disrespecting minimal ethical demands in such a way that the better becomes the enemy of good. Moreover, human rights do not constitute simply exterior conditions for human flourishing; rather, they are an integral part of it.

To talk about "ethics" in very general terms, to demand "ethical" conduct from individuals or companies or to blame them for unethical behavior can be confusing unless a distinction is made between different levels of the binding nature of ethical claims. In his book *Competing with Integrity in International Business*, De George distinguishes three levels and applies them to firms in international business: minimal ethical requirements, positive obligations beyond the minimum and aspirations for ethical ideals (De George 1993, especially 184–93). Enderle & Tavis (1998) applied this distinction to "the balanced concept of the firm."

The *first* level includes basic ethical norms of not doing harm instantiated in seven guidelines for multinational corporations.[6] The contents of these guidelines have to be specified at a more concrete level, which is where most difficulties arise. However, as for these minimal requirements, it is fair to assume that consensus can be attained even in a pluralistic society. If it is not achieved in a society, business cannot survive.

Positive obligations beyond the minimum, the *second* level of ethical claims, are to create and maintain trust relationships with the stakeholders, to help employees in need, to compensate the community for the damage unintentionally done by the firm, to engage for fair market conditions, etc. Here it is certainly more difficult to find consensus than in the first case. Still, a certain set of positive obligations of the firms is necessary for the effective and thriving functioning of the economy.

Thirdly, moral actors – individuals as well as companies – are characterized by aspiring to ethical ideals, if they are to overcome purely reactive behavior and take a pro-active stance. These aspirations are able to mobilize a great deal of motivation and energy in the economic, social and environmental realms. To a large extent, these aspirations create the very specific identities and missions of companies. To reach a consensus for these positive aspirations in a pluralistic society at the societal level is neither possible nor desirable, whereas, at the corporate level, a certain consensus seems to be required for corporate effectiveness.

This application to corporate conduct can illustrate the general importance of the triple distinction of minimal ethical requirements, social obligations and aspirations for ethical ideals. It greatly matters for understanding the binding nature of human rights and will be further discussed in Part III, Chapters 17 and 18.

Notes

1 A powerful statement for human rights is the *Human Development Report 2000*. See Fukuda-Parr 2004.

2 According to Gewirth (1984; see Introduction to Part II), the binding nature of human rights is the second component of a claim-right. Here it is further qualified with Shue's (1996) three types of obligations to protect, respect and remedy.

3 This obligation might be too demanding in the case of failing states. Still, the rights to physical security (according to Shue 1996) continue to exist and have to be protected by the state or an alliance of public and private actors.

4 This holds true for virtue ethics as well since virtues consist of dispositions to *act* in certain ways.

5 De George (2010) offers a thought-out and useful definition of morality and ethics: "Morality is a term used to cover those practices and activities that are considered importantly right and wrong; the rules that govern those activities; and the values that are embedded, fostered, or pursued by those activities and practices" (12). And: "In its most general sense, ethics is a systematic attempt to make sense of our individual and social moral experience, in such a way as to determine the rules that ought to govern human conduct, the values worth pursuing, and the character traits deserving development in life" (13). In contrast, the adjectives moral and ethical are used here synonymously.

6 The seven guidelines are as follows: American multinationals should: (1) do no intentional direct harm; (2) produce more good than harm for the host country; (3) contribute by their activity to the host country's development; (4) respect the human rights of their employees; (5) respect the local culture and work with and not against it – to the extent that local culture does not violate ethical norms; (6) pay their fair share of taxes; (7) cooperate with the local government in developing and enforcing just background institutions (De George 1993, 42–58).

13 | Cost-Benefit Considerations about Human Rights as Goals, Means and Constraints

To apply cost-benefit analysis to human rights seems to be unusual, if not inappropriate, if human rights have to be respected for their own sake, regardless of the consequences. Intrinsic values like human rights should not be instrumentalized for other values. How can one put a price on the right to life? What are the costs and benefits of a fair trial? How does one assess the consequences of the workers' right to freedom of association? Clearly, there are many good reasons for being cautious about cost-benefit analysis. However, this does not mean that it should be rejected entirely, as strictly deontological ethics claims. Rather, it is advisable to differentiate the understanding of cost-benefit analysis.

Multiple Approaches of Cost-Benefit Analysis

Cost-benefit analysis (CBA) can be defined in a variety of ways.[1] As Sen (2000) suggests, one can distinguish between the foundations of the general approach to CBA and additional requirements that make CBA more specific. While there is wide consensus on the foundational principles among those who accept CBA in one way or another, the specification of additional requirements takes many different forms, in particular the mainstream approach to CBA that "uses a formidable set of very exacting requirements" (p. 932).

The basic rationale of CBA lies in the idea that things are worth doing if the benefits resulting from doing them outweigh the costs (p. 934). Decisions and actions do have consequences, be they "positive" or "negative," and their evaluation with "pro" and "contra" arguments often points to some benefits and costs. Sen refers to the big irrigation project of the Narmada Dam in India, which was justified with a CBA carried out by the government. At the same time, opponents to this project pointed to the "human costs" that were ignored or not adequately considered. In sum, the framework of costs and benefits has a very extensive reach and can be used to assess alternative choices and their advantages in a wide variety of problems, from economic development or the quality of life to the extent of inequality, poverty or gender disparity (p. 934).

The foundational principles, supported by a wide consensus, include explicit valuation, broadly consequential evaluation and additive accounting. First, explicit valuation – as opposed to rhetoric of advocacy – demands full explication of the reasons for making a decision, rather than relying on unreasoned conviction or on an implicitly derived conclusion. This demand of accountability is particularly important for public decisions. Second, broadly consequential evaluation expands the narrow notion of consequences in terms of happiness and the fulfillment of desire (in the utilitarian sense) and includes also whether certain actions have been performed or particular rights and freedoms have been violated. Against the strictly deontological view of just doing one's duty, irrespective of consequences, in CBA the "wellness" of the outcome must take note inter alia of the badness of violation of rights and duties. Third, additive accounting points to the fact that CBA looks for the value of net benefits after deducting costs from benefits (p. 938). Different kinds of benefits are put together through a selection of weights, while costs are understood as foregone benefits. Thus, benefits and costs are defined, ultimately, in the same "space" and can be expressed with concave functions that respond positively to benefits and negatively to costs. Additive accounting can take multiple forms, but it implies the cost of some limitation such as relatively marginal changes (which cannot be discussed here further). To conclude, these three foundational principles define the general approach to CBA. On the one hand, it sharply differs from the strictly deontological view of consequence-independent obligations; on the other hand, it allows for a great variety of additional requirements.

According to Sen (2000), additional requirements of CBA concern structural demands, evaluative indifferences and market-centered valuation. As for *structural demands,* maximization is required (which means not to choose an alternative that is worse than another that can be chosen instead), but completeness of evaluation (that each consequence be identified and known with the definitive and unique weights at the appropriate points) or optimization (that the best alternative must be chosen) are not required. Complete knowledge and expected value reasoning are undoubtedly helpful; however, substantially important decisional concerns risk being neglected. Moreover, because factual presumptions of valuation may change over time, there is need for iterative exercises of valuation (see "contingent valuation" applied to environmental interventions).

With regard to *evaluative indifferences*, it is important to note that mainstream CBA neglects considerations of actions, motives and human rights. It is indifferent to the intrinsic value of freedom. And it does not assess value modification caused by movements of people from one cultural setting to another (for example, from rural to urban areas) and ignores the question in terms of with which values – the prior or posterior beliefs – the assessment should occur. Undoubtedly, it is not easy to account for these evaluative aspects; however, at least their neglect should be flagged and the results of CBA should be interpreted carefully.

A third group of additional requirements concerns *market-centered valuation*. Mainstream CBA primarily relies on market valuation by using willingness to pay as the key indicator. While the market allocation system and the market analogy have the merits of being sensitive to individual preferences and being able to deal with relative weights, they also have basic limitations. CBA as an application of welfare economics is based on the rationale of a potential Pareto improvement (Mishan 1988, xxiii) and thus neglects distributional issues. It attaches the same weight to everyone's dollars, irrespective of the poverty or the opulence of the persons involved, and does not account for any distributional changes resulting from the projects supported by CBA, since in the market system persons are only valued on willingness to pay. When it comes to public goods, market analogy valuation involves additional problems. People will not easily reveal their willingness to pay, when they are not also asked for their actual demand for that payment. And when they are asked, they may distort their revealed willingness to pay for strategic reasons, causing the free rider problem. Furthermore, willingness to pay is hard to estimate in contingent valuation procedures, which use CBA based on existence values of prized components of the environment (for example, to prevent an oil spill).

As this overview of multiple approaches of CBA shows, the general approach allows for a big variety of CBAs. When additional requirements are imposed – including structural demands and evaluative indifferences – gains can be achieved mainly in convenience and usability while losses occur mainly in the reach of the evaluative exercise. The mainstream approach of CBA is a strong and very special version of CBA. It is grounded in the foundational principles, requires structural demands and evaluative indifferences and, furthermore, values the costs and benefits with the logic, or in analogy with the logic, of the market allocation. Sen concludes his assessment as follows:

The market analogy has merits in the case of many public projects, particularly in providing sensitivity to individual preferences, relevant for efficiency considerations (in one form or another). Its equity claims are, however, mostly bogus, even though they can be made more real if explicit distributional weights are introduced (as they standardly are not in the mainstream approach). The use of compensation tests suffers from the general problem that they are either redundant or entirely unconvincing. Even the efficiency claims of the mainstream approach are severely compromised in the case of many public goods, and much would depend on the nature of the valuations in question ... *The spectacular merit of the informational economy of the market system for private goods ends up being a big drag when more information is needed than the market analogy can offer.* (Sen 2000, 951; emphasis added)

As Sen's extensive and differentiated discussion reveals, the "discipline" of cost-benefit analysis includes a wide range of concepts. Thereby the mainstream approach plays a dominant role, which, though, does not mean that other approaches are irrelevant. The foundational principles matter for any approach and additional requirements can take many forms.

An illuminating example of a powerful critique of mainstream cost-benefit analysis is Giulia Wegner and Unai Pascual's article "Cost-benefit analysis in the context of ecosystem services for human well-being: A multidisciplinary critique" (2011). Ecosystem services consist of life-supporting services (for example, the recycling of nutrients, the assimilation of waste and the regulation of climate, watershed and pests/diseases) and provisioning services (for example, water flow, domestic crops and livestock and wild plants and animals). Combined with human-related assets (for example, man-built infrastructure, knowledge, networks), they provide tangible and intangible benefits to humans such as food, hydroelectric power, a stable climate and psycho-physical equilibrium. *When applied to public ecosystem services, mainstream CBA fails* in many respects and thus should be *replaced by a pluralistic framework* composed of a heterogeneous set of value-articulating instruments that are appropriate to the specific context within which decision-making takes place. The authors argue that within this pluralistic framework CBA may remain an appropriate tool to examine the contingent trade-offs of local policies with limited impacts on ecosystems and their services.

Given the great variety of CBA approaches, several important aspects should be distinguished: (1) What are the objects to be analyzed? Public policies of governmental agencies covering fiscal policy, transport, education, health and the environment or business strategies of firms examining the creation and elimination of jobs, relocation of headquarters and investment in foreign countries? (2) In whose interests are the costs and benefits analyzed? For the decision maker – be it the government, the firm or its CEO – or for a broader constituency – all citizens, powerful lobbies, marginalized groups, shareholders alone or all stakeholders (including shareholders)? (3) What time perspective is adopted? A short-term or a long-term perspective – the term of office, the quarterly report or the well-being of the present and future generations, the lasting health of the firm? While these distinctions are important for any CBA, they matter in particular for CBA of human rights.

A General CBA Approach to Human Rights with Limited Additional Requirements

In applying CBA to human rights, we may use Sen's framework and the three aspects mentioned above.[2] The foundational principles require explicit valuation, broadly consequential evaluation and additive accounting. The reasons for making decisions involving human rights as both goals and means have to be fully explicated and accounted for.[3] This means that not only the outcomes but also the processes (for example, whether human rights are respected or violated as goals and as means) should be included in the evaluation. Moreover, a kind of additive accounting should take place that calculates the value of net benefits after deducting costs from benefits. This can be done – at least partially – by using the capability approach applied to the policy in question (see Chapter 8).

An additional requirement of CBA involving human rights is maximization (that is, not choosing an alternative that is worse than another that can be chosen instead). But it is not required that each consequence be identified and known with the definitive and unique weights at the appropriate points (that is, completeness of evaluation) nor that the best alternative must be chosen (that is, optimization). Furthermore, evaluative indifference of human rights is not acceptable since actions and motives can be accounted for. In contrast to the mainstream approach to CBA, market-centered valuation is not suitable for CBA of human rights because it is based on willingness to pay, does not generally address distributional issues and cannot account for many public goods. Hence, similar to the pluralistic framework of Wegner and Pascual (2011), it is necessary to discuss other methods of valuation below (see also research opportunities in Chapter 20).

The distinctions of objects, interests and time perspectives – relevant for CBA in general – apply also to CBA of human rights. The *objects* of CBA can include any of the thirty human rights incorporated in the International Bill of Human Rights and the ILO Core Conventions (see Chapter 11). However, depending on the focus of public and corporate policies, some rights are directly at stake – be it as goals, means or constraints – while other rights are not relevant in these contexts. For example, the public policy to ensure the right to security of the person (protection against terrorism) may demand high economic and other costs, while its fulfillment can also yield significant and even more economic and other benefits. Or the implementation of the right to health for all citizens may require high fiscal expenses in the government's budget; however, it also may bring even more economic and other benefits to citizens, the economy and society at large. With regard to corporate policy, the abolition of child labor in global supply chains may entail increasing financial costs for factories (by paying higher wages for adult workers) as well as for affected families (by losing additional income from their children); however, freed from labor, children can benefit from basic education, enjoy their childhood and become, as adults, bread-winners for their families, while factories are incentivized to improve their productivity (by paying higher wages) and to strengthen the engagement of their workers. Another example is freedom of association and worker participation (discussed extensively in Chapter 20). To establish well-functioning freedom of association and worker participation in the workplace (even if legally required) can involve substantial financial and other costs for the company (by supporting the worker organization, foregoing work time and slowing down decision making processes); on the other hand, the company can benefit in multiple ways (by avoiding reputational risk, improving corporate decision-making and strengthening a culture of mutual respect and collaboration). In sum, the CBA of human rights should include both costs and benefits in financial and economic terms as well as in social, psychological and other terms. What Richard Musgrave said of a theory of public finance also holds true for CBA of human rights: "A theory of public finance remains unsatisfactory unless it comprises both the revenue and expenditure sides of the fiscal process" (Musgrave 1969, 797).

The second aspect of CBA distinguishes *in whose interests* the costs and benefits are analyzed. Ideally speaking, one would assume that the decision maker takes into account the interests of all those who are affected positively or negatively by the proposed policy, that is, not only his or her own interests or the interests of a particular group. Governments would care for all people affected by their policies, and companies would take all stakeholders seriously. However, realistically speaking, decision makers often put their own interests first beyond the interests of others. Political leaders may do so out of personal ambition or in favor of their own party. In business, a case in point is the widespread practice and theoretical claim "to make the business case" for a good cause, be it in a narrow or a broader sense.

Dorothée Baumann-Pauly and Michael Posner (2016) assess this view with regard to human rights. Making the business case for human rights means demonstrating theoretically or practically that human rights programs and policies lie in the self-interest of the company. Unfortunately, there is scant literature on the relationship between corporate performance and fulfilling human rights. This lack of empirical studies, though, does not come as a surprise, given the complexity of conceptualizing and measuring either variable that is even greater for human rights than for environmental sustainability (see the CBA for public ecosystem services mentioned above). One would have to determine the precise criteria of the economic, social, environmental and human costs and benefits, to aggregate them in an appropriate fashion and to define and account for the suitable time perspective.

Despite these difficulties, within large corporations the business case for human rights is internally debated; the costs of human rights commitments are considered and weighed against the benefits, which will accrue to the company and its relevant stakeholders. For example, the World Business Council for Sustainable Development issued the Action 2020 plan to demonstrate that human rights are good for business (WBCSD 2016). Five reasons are given for the business case: (1) It's a risk management strategy. (2) It's cheaper to prevent than to cure. (3) It levels the playing field. (4) It reinforces corporate values. (5) It's a competitive advantage.

Baumann-Pauly and Posner (2016) distinguish the negative and the positive business cases for human rights. The negative version focuses on the risks to a company's reputation if action is not taken. The risks can be substantial (for instance, in the mining industry) and are treated as legal or public relations problems while disregarding the underlying rights problems. According to the authors:

[W]hen companies apply a purely economic rationale to their operations and focus only on the pressure to achieve maximum short-term financial returns, they often decide that the potential negative impact on human rights problems simply does not outweigh the time, money and attention it would take to deal effectively with the complex issues that underlie many business and human rights challenges. In effect, they decide to accept such costs as unavoidable but manageable costs of doing business. (pp. 15–16)

In contrast, the affirmative business case for human rights is proactive and innovative, takes the opportunities as well as the challenges of human rights seriously, incorporates human rights into the core business strategies as part of the future business model and adopts a long-term perspective that is good for the overall health of the company as distinct from profit maximization (see Bower & Paine 2017). The benefits for the corporation arise, for example, from the hiring and retention of outstanding employees convinced by its business model, the respectful corporate culture providing greater freedom to innovate and improve product quality, the attraction of investors committed to "responsible investing" (PRI 2018) and the support by critical stakeholders who acknowledge corporate legitimacy. Corporations like Hewlett Packard, Nike and Unilever seem to understand that the business case can involve win-win strategies for both business and society. While acknowledging such good examples, the authors persuasively argue that shared responsibility among business and multiple stakeholders is needed to foster the positive business case for human rights.[4]

The third aspect of CBA in general and for human rights in particular concerns the appropriate choice of the *time horizon*. For both public and corporate policies human rights are supposed to be secured forever; they are not meant to lose their binding force when jeopardized or violated. For example, the right not to be subjected to torture, cruel, inhuman and/or degrading treatment or punishment holds under all circumstances, even in wartime. And the right to an adequate standard of living is imperative, regardless of the age of the person. Given the unshakeable standing of human rights, their fulfillment cannot depend on short-termism, that is, the exclusive focus on the short term while completely disregarding the longer term. The longer-term commitment requires the investment of resources and time, which are costs that can be substantial. However, a CBA of human rights should not only count the costs, but should also reckon the benefits that can be even more substantial than the costs. Moreover, it is crucial to consider the distribution of both costs and benefits, which is normally disregarded by the mainstream approach of CBA. Accounting for human rights in public and corporate policies needs long-term thinking as a kind of responsible investing (see Bekink 2016).

While CBA was originally developed in economics (Musgrave 1969; Mishan 1988) and has then unfolded in multiple forms in various disciplines (Sen 2000), other assessment tools have been created because of critical limitations of many CBA techniques and applied to a variety of fields (see overview in Götzmann 2017). The environmental impact assessment (EIA) identifies, predicts, evaluates and mitigates the biophysical, social and other relevant effects of development proposals before major decisions are taken and commitments made. The social impact assessment (SIA) includes the processes of analysis, monitoring and managing the intended and unintended social consequences, both positive and negative, of planned interventions (policies, programs, plans, projects) and any social change processes invoked by those interventions, aiming at a more sustainable and equitable biophysical and human environment. Similarly, the environmental, social and health impact assessment (ESHIA) integrates EIA and SIA with human health concerns. The human-rights based approach (HRBA) was introduced for the field of international development cooperation. More recently, different strands of human rights impact assessment (HRIA) have emerged for evaluating the areas of development, the right to health, children's rights, business activities, international trade and investment – as guidance for public authorities. According to the World Bank and the Nordic Trust Fund (2013), HRIA can be defined as "an instrument for examining policies, legislation, programs and projects and identifying and measuring their effects on human rights" (p. 1). HRIA can be a stand-alone approach focusing exclusively on human rights impacts, or the assessment of human rights impacts may be incorporated within other appropriate processes (for example, ESHIA), granted human rights are accounted for comprehensively.

HRIA has become an important instrument not only for public policies, legislation, programs and projects but also increasingly for assessing business activities. The UN Guiding Principles on Business and Human Rights (UN 2011) demand that business enterprises "respect human rights" and have "human rights due diligence processes" in place to "identify, prevent, mitigate and account for how they address their impacts on human rights" (UN 2011, Principle 15, also 17 and 18). What this means will be discussed extensively in Part III of this book, which focuses on the ethical responsibilities of business enterprises to create wealth and respect human rights.

Notes

1 There is a vast literature on cost-benefit analysis, to name a few: Musgrave 1969; Kelman 1981; Mishan 1988; Brent 1998, 2018; Adler 2012; Windsor 2018b.
2 This general CBA approach equally applies to human rights conceived as "public goods," as it is argued in Chapter 14.
3 This can be done within the framework of business ethics as a goal-rights-system (Enderle 1998).
4 The report "The business case for protecting civic rights" (The B Team 2018) examines the economic impact of respect for civic rights and civic space. It shows that limits on important civic freedoms are linked to negative economic outcomes. In countries of the Middle East and North Africa, sub-Saharan Africa and East Asia economic growth rates are especially linked to the state of civic rights.

14 | *Human Rights as Public Goods*

Why Public Goods and Global Public Goods?

Conceiving of human rights as public goods may sound strange, for two reasons in particular. How can and should human rights be considered "goods" in the first place? Does this conception not give way to "commodification" that turns things such as intrinsic values into commodities, which are just economic goods that can be bought and sold? This danger already appeared in Chapter 13, where cost-benefit considerations were applied to human rights. It seems even more serious when human rights are taken as goods. And why can and should human rights be characterized as "public" goods? What public goods means exactly is hardly understood in common language and mostly ignored in the praise of the market economy.

To respond to the accusation of commodification, one can rightly argue that human rights involve an economic dimension. But this does not mean that they are purely economic goods. Rather, they can include other dimensions as well – for example, social, cultural and legal dimensions – which are particularly visible in public goods. As for the widespread ignorance of the notion of public goods, instead of avoiding this term, it would better serve the common understanding to clearly articulate and explain this key concept of basic economics.

As explained in Chapter 5, the public good is defined by two formal criteria of non-excludability and non-rivalry in consumption. Because of its formal distinction, it can mean a positively or a negatively valued content – that is, a public "good" or a public "bad" – which therefore needs ethical evaluation. Due to the free-rider problem and the prisoner's dilemma, a public good cannot be properly traded on the market nor imputed with a price. In contrast, the private good is excludable and rivalrous; it is traded on the market and imputed with a price. Between these extreme poles of pure public and pure private goods, there is a wide variety of mixed goods with varying degrees of excludability and rivalry. Impure public goods are goods that only partly meet either or both of the defining criteria. However, for practical reasons, they can be included in pure public goods because "many of the implications of publicness remain salient even when a good is only partly nonrival or partly nonexcludable" (Kaul et al. 1999b, 4). Moreover, public goods can be "final" goods or "intermediate" goods, the latter being instrumental for producing private or other public goods.[1]

The reach of public goods depends, in principle, on the extent of their impact (their "publicness"), be it positive or negative. A safe neighborhood might be limited to the local level ("a local public good"). A fair and effective health care system might affect people at the national level ("a national public good"). A war might strike a whole region ("a regional public bad"). In addition, due to globalization and other factors, public goods and bads are going global.

In *Global Public Goods: International Cooperation in the 21st Century* Inge Kaul, Isabelle Grunberg and Marc Stern (1999a), along with two dozen contributors, provide a groundbreaking overview and analysis of global public goods. Key concepts are carefully defined. Multiple case studies address topics such as equity and justice, market efficiency, environment and cultural heritage, health, knowledge and information, and peace and security. Policy implications are presented, followed by extensive and far-reaching conclusions. The authors point to public bads, which are international – and particularly global – and severely affect national and individual well-being: banking crises, internet-based crime and fraud and increased risks of ill-health due to escalated trade and travel and the world-wide spread of drug abuse and smoking. Among public goods, they particularly mention the rapidly growing number of international regimes that provide common frameworks for international transport and communication, trade, harmonized taxation, monetary policy, governance and much more. They define:

global public goods as outcomes (or intermediate products) that tend towards universality in the sense that they benefit all countries, population groups and generations. At a minimum, a global public good would meet the following criteria: its benefits extend to more than one group of countries and do not discriminate against any population group or any set of generations, present or future. (Kaul et al. 1999b, 16)

Their typology of global public goods distinguishes three main classes, according to the policy challenges they pose: (1) *Natural global commons* such as the ozone layer or climate stability whose collective action problem is one of overuse. (2) *Human-made global commons* encompassing scientific and practical knowledge, principles and norms, the world's common cultural heritage and transnational infrastructure such as the internet. Their main challenge is underuse. (3) *Global policy outcomes* including peace, health and financial stability, whose collective action problem is undersupply. All classes and types of global goods can be categorized in terms of benefits based on their non-excludability and non-rivalry, while corresponding bads can be distinguished in terms of costs also based on their non-excludability and non-rivalry. For example, the global public good of the atmosphere (climate) yields benefits from which no one can be excluded, but its consumption is rivalrous. If overused, the costs of the corresponding global public bad are difficult to be avoided by anyone and its impact on one person does not reduce its impact on others. (Kaul et al. 1999c, 452–61)

Having briefly outlined the conception and relevance of global public goods in general, this typology, which includes principles and norms, also illuminates the understanding of human rights as public goods at all levels, from the local to the global. By using this typology, important public features are highlighted in a number of human rights chosen from the list of thirty human rights in Chapter 11. More examples are discussed, to a larger or smaller extent, in various chapters of this book, particularly the right to just and favorable conditions of work (Chapter 19) and the right to freedom of association (Chapter 20).

Identifying Human Rights as Public Goods

Human rights are often understood as individual claims addressed to governments or other actors (for example, corporations, educational institutions, particular groups or persons) while ignoring their public good characteristics. As long as human rights are respected, they are normally taken for granted (like clean air) and not noticed as essential conditions for living with dignity in society. When they are violated, they become conspicuous, especially to the immediate victims of violation, and subsequently to a broader public.

After the Second World War Martin Niemöller (1892–1984), a German Protestant pastor, came to understand that he and many others had failed to stand up to the Nazi regime in the mid-1930s. His famous confession of personal guilt showcases the violation of human rights as public goods.

First they came for the Communists, and I did not speak out – because I was not a Communist. Then they came for the Trade Unionists, and I did not speak out – because I was not a Trade Unionist. Then they came for the Jews, and I did not speak out – because I was not a Jew. Then they came for me – and there was no one left to speak for me. (Quoted in Bergen 2018)

More recent examples of drastic violations of human rights are the persecution of the Rohingya minority by Myanmar state forces in 2015 with the resulting refugee crisis (BBC 2018), and the killing of the Saudi journalist Jamal Khashoggi on October 2, 2018 in the Saudi consulate in Istanbul, Turkey (Haltiwanger 2018). The Rohingya crisis dramatically demonstrates the violation of numerous human rights, particularly the rights to self-determination; life; not to be subjected to torture, cruel, inhuman and/or degrading treatment or punishment; liberty and security of the person; freedom of thought, conscience and religion; freedom of opinion and expression; and the rights of minorities. It impacts not only the nation of Myanmar but also the neighboring countries of Bangladesh and Thailand and civil organizations and international institutions in charge of refugee challenges. In the instance of Khashoggi's murder, not only were many of his rights violated – especially the rights to life; not to be subjected to torture, cruel, inhuman and/or degrading treatment or punishment; liberty and security of the person; freedom of thought, conscience and religion; and freedom of opinion and expression. Moreover, the violations of these rights as public bads also affected the profession of journalists worldwide, wide circles concerned about the freedom of speech in the media, the countries such as Turkey and the United States and, obviously, Saudi-Arabia.

According to Kaul et al. (1999c), the benefits of human rights as public goods can be distinguished based on the characteristics of non-excludability and non-rivalry. They are nonrival because the enjoyment of any right by one person does not diminish the enjoyment of any of those rights by any other person. But they are only partly nonexcludable because the access to those rights can be impeded or blocked by legal or social discrimination or the lack of economic resources (when, for example, poor people cannot benefit from the right to health care because they cannot afford the co-payments). On the other hand, the costs of human rights violations (that is, public bads) are also nonrival because the harm of the violation of any right done to one person does not reduce the harm of the violation of any of those rights inflicted on any other person; in many cases, the costs even increase enormously, as Niemöller experienced during the Nazi regime. However, like the benefits of human rights, the costs of their repression are only partly nonexcludable; it is possible for wealthy and powerful people to protect themselves and thus avoid bearing the costs, for example, against unsafe environments, poor educational institutions and epidemic diseases (see On the Media 2018).

Human Rights as Final and Intermediate Goods

Like public goods in general, human rights can be final goods (that is, goals to be achieved for themselves) or intermediate goods (that is, means to realize other goods or rights). This distinction relates to their place in the production chain and has significant policy relevance (Kaul et al. 1999a, 13–14). While the fulfillment of human rights are goals in themselves, securing certain human rights can also be instrumental to achieving the realization of other human rights as well as other public goods and private goods. For example, the rights to freedom and security of the person and to an adequate standard of living can constitute means to realize the rights to health and education, which help implement the rights to work, to a family life and to participate in public life. Beyond the fulfillment of these rights, many other positive outcomes can be achieved such as a reduction of poverty, an increase of healthy families and a more vibrant public life. Another example concerns the rights to freedom of association, to form and join trade unions and to strike. They can lead to just and favorable conditions of work, greater job satisfaction, higher productivity of the workforce and – as the Post–World-War-Two experience in western countries showed – to high economic growth and the avoidance of extreme income inequality.

On the other hand, the abuse of human rights as intermediate public goods can generate severe public bads by also violating other human rights and causing economic and social harm. Youth unemployment as nonfulfillment of the right to work can negate the right to self-determination, weaken self-esteem and push young people to leave their country. The absence of a fair and effective social security system can incapacitate the right to health of the elderly, cause anxieties among them and push them to embrace populism.

Looking from an investment perspective, in recent years human rights have become a benchmark against which ethical investing is being assessed, as documented, for instance, in the *Research Handbook on Human Rights and Investment* by Yannick Radi (2018). Ethical investing aims at changing states of affairs deemed to be unjust, degrading and inhumane, destructive to the environment and unsustainable for humankind and the Earth (Stüttgen 2019). While ethical investing has its precursors in initiatives driven by religious, political, social and ecological motivations, it has gained global awareness with the United Nations Principles for Responsible Investment (www.unpri.org) and its goals to incorporate ESG factors (that is, factors of environmental, social and governance relevance) into investment research, analysis and practice. And, under the influence of the United Nations Principles on Business and Human Rights (UN 2011), human rights are beginning to be addressed explicitly in "due diligence" processes undertaken by business (see Chapter 15). But there is still a long way to go until human rights are an indispensable part of ethical investing, as can be seen from recent literature (for example, Emunds 2014; Dembinski 2017; Radi 2018; Stüttgen 2019).

Sectorial and regional case studies can illustrate the impact of investments on human rights (Radi 2018, 345–534). In the extractive industries pressing human rights abuses tend to occur in artisanal and small-scale mining, resettlement of populations, security and labor, particularly felt at the community level. In the agricultural sector human rights concerns are associated with large-scale land acquisitions for agricultural investments. As for the fashion industry, human rights issues arise at different stages of the production process, especially worker rights. Private investments are related to the human right to water, implying substantive and procedural obligations of private companies. Three examples of Nepal, Cambodia and North India show how investors dealt with the social and political context very differently: in the first two countries very negatively and in the third country with strong positive impact.

As this brief overview shows, human rights can be pursued as final or as intermediate public goods. Another interesting example is the Chinese human rights guidance on minerals sourcing (Buhmann 2017) that seems to utilize human rights as both final and intermediate public goods. The government-related China Chamber of Commerce of Metals, Minerals and Chemicals (CCCMC) issued mining investment guidelines in 2014, followed by due diligence guidelines in 2015, which specify in detail risk-based supply-chain due diligence in order to prevent human-rights-related conflicts. Both sets of guidelines apply to approximately 6,000 companies, including most Chinese mining companies investing abroad and trading in mineral, metal and hydrocarbon products. The language of these guidelines is closely aligned with the UN Guiding Principles on Business and Human Rights and the OECD Due Diligence Guidance.[2] It provides guidance and support to companies ... "to identify, prevent, and mitigate the risks of directly or indirectly contributing to conflict, serious human rights abuse, and risks of serious misconduct" (CCCMC 2015, 3). These guidelines clearly aim at the realization of human rights as final public goods to benefit people impacted by Chinese minerals sourcing particularly in Africa. At the same time, it seems fair to interpret human rights here also as intermediate public goods, understood as means to encounter widespread criticism of China's economic engagement in Africa and build China's soft power in the global arena. Final public goods can turn into intermediate public goods and vice versa.

When dealing with final and intermediate public goods, one cannot help looking at the cost-benefit implications. As Chapter 13 has extensively discussed cost-benefit considerations about human rights, they also apply to human rights understood as public goods. In contrast to the mainstream approach to cost-benefit analysis (CBA), market-centered valuation is not suitable for CBA of human rights because it is based on willingness to pay, does not generally address distributional issues and cannot account for many public goods. Therefore, other methods of valuation are necessary, which concern the objects, interests and time perspectives of valuation. Because these methods are explained in the previous chapter, it suffices here to recall the basic points. The objects of CBA can include any of the thirty internationally recognized human rights. The CBA must account, in principle, for the interests of all those who are affected positively or negatively by the proposed policy, that is, not only the interests of the decision-makers and of particular groups. And as for the time horizon, the appropriate choice is a long-term perspective because human rights are supposed to be secured forever.

Need for Collective Actors and Other-Regarding Motivations

Having discussed the characteristics of human rights as public goods, we now turn to two far-reaching implications. First, the establishment, fulfillment and guarantee of human rights cannot be achieved by market institutions; rather, collective actions are needed at multiple levels of society. Second, self-regarding motivations alone inevitably fail to establish, fulfill and guarantee human rights; other-regarding motivations are indispensable.

As explained in Chapter 5, the market institution is very successful in providing private goods, but it fails, in principle, to produce public goods; therefore, other institutional arrangements, namely institutions for collective action, are necessary to achieve this goal. Since the Universal Declaration of Human Rights in 1948, the obligation for collective action has been placed primarily on the nation-states and their governments, although other organs of society and individuals were mentioned in the Declaration as well. In the last twenty-plus years non-state actors, too, have also been recognized as responsible for human rights, as the above discussion of global public goods and the growing influence of the UN Guiding Principles have showed.

Collective actions are necessary to ensure that no human being be excluded from the enjoyment of human rights, because individual actions alone cannot guarantee that no one be excluded. According to mainstream economic theory, without collective action, free-rider problems and prisoner's dilemmas arise and prevent non-excludability of human rights.

For proponents of an individualistic worldview, the term "collective" action may sound repressive of individual freedom. However, collective actions do not need to conflict with individual freedom. On the contrary, they can have a positive meaning, as Martin Wolf writes:

"Making choices, together, about the provision of such [public and semi-public] goods does not represent a violation of freedom, but is rather both an expression and a facilitator of that fundamental value" (Wolf 2014, xxii).

Collective action for human rights does not have to start at the global level. It can begin in personal relations, between husband and wife, parents and children, friends, colleagues and neighbors. It means recognizing the dignity and the human rights of the other person without denying other people the same dignity and human rights. While personal relations can involve many ethical obligations, human rights form an essential part of them. Specifically, they may include the rights to life, to liberty and security of the person, of the protection of the family and for the child, to a family life, and privacy. It also implies taking seriously one's own dignity endowed with human rights. Mutual respect of human rights builds strong ties between people who know each other, is based on the principle of reciprocity, embodies the Golden Rule and is a form of love. At this personal level, collective action is hardly threatened by free-rider problems and prisoner's dilemmas.

Taking human rights seriously in personal relations can provide a starting point for collective action in broader communities, in towns, cities and agglomerations, characterized by anonymous relations. Although people do not know each other personally, they still can respect each other, driven by other-regarding motivations such as empathy, caring for others and solidarity. Many civil society organizations have been established at the local, national, regional and global levels to defend particular human rights of people previously ignored by the public and governments. As examples, we may mention Amnesty International (www.amnesty.org), Human Rights Watch (www.hrw.org) and multiple Human Rights Commissions working in cities, countries and internationally. Moreover, an increasing number of business enterprises and other non-state actors have set up human rights policies to address adverse human rights impacts, joining the UN Global Compact (UNGC 2000) and following the UN Guiding Principles on Business and Human Rights (see Chapter 15).[3] At the country level, governments have issued "National Action Plans on Business and Human Rights" (Morris et al. 2018). At the regional level, human rights have become constitutive principles, for example of the European Union (see Chapter 7). And at the global level, the United Nations Human Rights Council (www.ohchr.org) is responsible for strengthening the promotion and protection of human rights around the globe and for addressing situations of human rights violations and making recommendations on them. While these collective actions at multiple levels certainly contribute, by and large, to the fulfillment of human rights, it is fair to say that they are immensely insufficient to overcome the exclusion of large populations from these public goods and secure the fulfillment of human rights to all people on the planet Earth.

Understanding human rights as public goods has a second far-reaching implication that concerns motivations. As discussed in Chapter 10, the creation and maintenance of public goods cannot be achieved with self-regarding motivations alone; they require also other-regarding motivations. Whoever is engaged in creating public goods cannot realistically expect a reward equivalent to the time and effort put into such engagement. In many cases, one has to accept or at least put up with sacrifices in one form or another. Other-regarding motivations are necessary that take the interests of other persons, groups, organizations, states, and other entities at least as seriously as one's own interest. While this holds true for public goods in general, it matters in particular for human rights.

Because human rights are considered "positive" or ethically demanded public goods (discussed in Chapter 12), the motivations to establish and fulfill human rights cannot be any type of other-regarding motivations (for example, the ultimate interest of a nation; see Chapter 10). They must be "ethical resources" – which take seriously the dignity of other people – such as a sense for the common good, care, solidarity and justice. Multiple philosophical and religious perspectives can provide this moral support. Some of them have been briefly explained in Chapters 7 and 10.

* * * * *

To conclude, in Part II we developed the normative-ethical conception of human rights as public goods in wealth creation that provides the ethical foundation of corporate responsibility to be discussed in Part III. The list of human rights includes all thirty internationally recognized rights incorporated in the International Bill of Human Rights and eight core conventions of the International Labor Organization. Human rights constitute minimal ethical requirements that stand the test of ethical reasoning. While cost-benefit analysis in the sense of rational choice theory does not apply to human rights, cost-benefit considerations can be meaningful with regard to human rights. By identifying human rights as public goods, a conceptual bridge extends to wealth creation. Human rights from the local to the global levels are non-excludable and non-rivalrous and require for their implementation collective actors and other-regarding motivations.

Notes

1 The term "instrumental" for producing private or other public goods is used here in the sense of having "instrumental" (not "intrinsic") value; it is not capital to be used up for production.

2 The complete title is "OECD Due Diligence Guidance on Responsible Supply Chains of Minerals from Conflict-Affected and High-Risk Areas."

3 Andreas Scherer and Guido Palazzo qualify this corporate engagement for human rights and public goods as "political CSR" (as a consequence of globalization). "In a nutshell, political CSR suggests an extended model of governance with business firms contributing to global regulation and providing public goods. It goes beyond the instrumental view on politics in order to develop a new understanding of global politics where private actors such as corporations and civil society organizations play an active role in the democratic regulation and control of market transactions" (Scherer & Palazzo 2011, 900–1).

PART III

Implications of Wealth Creation and Human Rights for Corporate Responsibility

15 | *The Ethics of Business Organizations Is Called Corporate Responsibility*

Focusing on the Ethics of Business Organizations

As stated at the beginning of this book, I argue for a radically new understanding of the ethics of business organizations (or business enterprises) in the global context. In Parts I and II I defined and delineated the purpose of business and the economy as the creation of wealth in a comprehensive sense, guided by thirty internationally recognized human rights. Combining the ethics-related approach to economics with the normative-ethical perspective of human rights, this vision invites practitioners and scholars "to walk on two legs" by taking seriously and integrating both economic and ethical perspectives at all levels of decision making and action in business and the economy: at the systemic (macro), organizational (meso) and individual (micro) levels. Now, in Part III, this broad vision is applied to the ethics of business organizations (at the meso-level). It is radically new by combining wealth creation and human rights in relation to business organizations in the global context. It further develops recent approaches to notions of wealth and business and human rights and builds on many achievements of business and economic ethics in the last decades, particularly with regard to corporate ethics, the notion of responsibility and the UN Guiding Principles on Business and Human Rights. It is developed within the framework of business ethics as a goal-rights-system (Enderle 1998) and explained with multiple examples in Chapters 17–20.

Corporate ethics or the ethics of business organizations as scholarly inquiry and reflection has been developed since the 1980s. In German-speaking countries corporate ethics ("Unternehmensethik") was vigorously promoted by Horst Steinmann and Albert Löhr (1990). In Europe it became a central theme in the European Business Ethics Network – EBEN (founded in 1987 in Brussels). In North America so-called "business ethics" was already emerging as an interdisciplinary field in the late 1970s (De George 1987). It included ethical questions about the free-enterprise system (at the macro-level), the study of business within this system (at the meso-level) and the morality of individuals in economic and business interactions (at the micro-level). With its strong focus on the ethics of business organizations (named also "corporate ethics" or "corporate responsibility"), North American business ethics has significantly influenced the development of business and economic ethics in Europe and other continents. Not only individuals and states but also business organizations have been increasingly held morally responsible for their conduct, often under the pressure of scandals. Moreover, farsighted entrepreneurs and managers have committed themselves on their own initiative to an ethical culture in their organizations. In such ways corporate ethics (or business ethics in a narrow sense) has given rise in the last thirty-plus years to multiple initiatives in theory and practice, often successfully; however, it is still far from becoming common practice.

At the same time, corporate ethics has taken many forms and has been called by various names: corporate responsibility, corporate social responsibility (CSR), corporate social performance, corporate citizenship, corporate accountability, triple bottom line, sustainability and other terms. There is no space to discuss these variations here since the reader can find abundant information in numerous encyclopedias (for example, Enderle et al. 1993; Werhane & Freeman 1997; Frederick 1999; Korff et al. 1999; Becker & Becker 2001; Visser et al. 2007; Crane et al. 2008; Scherer & Palazzo 2008; Brenkert & Beauchamp 2010; Kolb 2018).

In my view, an appropriate term for the ethics of business organizations (corporate ethics or business ethics in a narrow sense) is "corporate responsibility," which I explain below.[1] It involves a deep sense of moral responsibility and pertains to all dimensions of corporate performance (economic, social and environmental) comprehensively mapped with the sustainability principles of the Global Reporting Initiative (www.globalreporting.org). It stands in stark contrast to the widely used concept of corporate social responsibility or CSR (Carroll 2008), which, in my view, lacks a solid definition of "responsibility," uses the term "social" in inconsistent ways and does not articulate environmental responsibility and human rights (see an extensive critique in Enderle 2006, 2010b). The term "corporate responsibility" (without "s") is appealing to practitioners and scholars alike and frequently employed in practical language (for example, Caux Round Table 1994 and Corporate Responsibility Magazine) and academic literature (for example, Coleman 1990, chapter 6; Enderle & Tavis 1998b, UN 2008a, 2011; Carroll et al. 2012; Ruggie 2013).

Responsibility: A Key Concept in Contemporary Ethical Thinking

In observing both the usage and absence of the term "responsibility," we find an interesting phenomenon. On the one hand, the word is used in common parlance very frequently, meaning an important moral obligation. We speak of the responsibility of parents, teachers, physicians and journalists, thus often meaning role responsibilities; however, we also expect responsible behavior from organizations and institutions such as government, the private sector, the media, business schools and even perhaps wealthy nations vis-à-vis poor countries. In particular, "responsibility" has gained wide currency in qualifying leadership. Leaders must be able and willing to accept and not shirk responsibility.

On the other hand, it is striking that the term and often even the subject of responsibility was conspicuously absent, to a large extent and for many years, in the literature on leadership, in bestseller business books like *Built to Last* (Collins & Porras 1994)[2] and in many business ethics textbooks. Only in the late 2000s has the label of "responsible leadership" become a common term in the leadership literature (Maak & Pless 2006; Waldman & Galvin 2008) and then aroused a large body of publications (Frangieh & Yaacoub 2017; Miska & Mendenhall 2018).

The ethical concept of responsibility is relatively new in the history of ethics and was developed in the twentieth century by a number of scholars. The German discussion goes back to a famous lecture in 1918 by Max Weber who opposed the ethics of conviction against the ethics of responsibility, and to the phenomenological analysis in 1933 by Wilhelm Weischedel (1972) under the influence of Martin Heidegger (Enderle 1993, 42–53, 145–53). In my view, Walter Schulz offers the deepest understanding of responsibility (1972, 1989). In his masterwork *Philosophie in der veränderten Welt* [Philosophy in the World That Changed], published in 1972, he contends that the fundamental processes driving the contemporary world are culminating in the challenges of "responsibility":

Although a contemporary ethics cannot longer follow the perspective of a private and introverted morality, it absolutely must hold on the fundamental opposition between good and evil. Ethics needs to be oriented toward concrete challenges ("Sachprobleme") in view of shaping the future. (Schulz 1972, 10; translated by G.E.)

The word "responsibility" contains the idea of responding or giving valid answers to questions asked by others, similar in meaning to the word "accountability." Thus responsibility reflects the relational structure of human existence. According to Schulz, the concept of responsibility includes a polarity. On the one hand, there is the inner pole or self-commitment originating from freedom ("Selbsteinsatz aus Freiheit"). Responsibility thus rests on and requires an inner decision. A responsible person cannot hide herself behind a given role. Rather, the exercise of responsibility may demand one to act above conventional morality. Think of a whistle-blower in an oppressive corporate culture or of a conscientious objector in an army.

Ethics is founded in the 'self-commitment originating from freedom.' Although traditional ethics, in the form of the ethics of conviction, has reduced this insight, by and large, in a subjectivist manner, we still can learn from it that the self-understanding of the human being is the crucial foundation of ethics, particularly of an ethics that centers on human relationship. (Schulz 1972, 631; translated by G.E.)

On the other hand, on the opposite pole, this self-commitment originating from freedom has its point of departure and its point of destination in worldly relationships ("in welthaftem Bezug").

In as far as the human being indispensably stands in historical situations, responsibility is always *toward* [...] and responsibility *for*. This means responsibility is a category of relationship. Consequently, in an ethics of responsibility the question of interpersonal conduct must be to the fore, to be precise, as concretely as possible. (Schulz 1972, 632; translated by G.E.)

As we can see from this brief summary, Schulz vigorously rejects Max Weber's separation of an ethics of conviction and an ethics of responsibility (also Enderle 2007). He anchors responsibility in the freedom of the human person as decision maker, stretching it to an authority or addressee toward whom one is responsible and to a very concrete

---

Box 15.1 Responsibility – a key concept in contemporary ethical thinking

Responsibility: "Self-commitment originating from freedom in worldly relationships" (Walter Schulz)

Thus responsibility includes a polarity:

- The inner pole: Responsibility rests on and requires an inner decision ("self-commitment origination from freedom").
- The outer pole: Self-commitment originating from freedom has its point of departure and its point of destination "in worldly relationships."

Responsibility has three components:

1. The subject of responsibility or *who* is responsible;
2. The content of responsibility or *for what* is one responsible;
3. The authority or addressee *toward whom* one is responsible.

---

matter for which one is responsible. So responsibility includes three components: (1) the subject of responsibility or who is responsible; (2) the content of responsibility or for what one is responsible; and (3) the authority toward whom one is responsible (for example, stakeholders, tribunal, spouse or one's conscience). This distinction may help to sort out ambiguous and complex issues of responsibility and clarify the concept of corporate responsibility later on (see Box 15.1).

Because of the pervasive dominance of human institutions in our societies, ethical responsibility needs to be incorporated into these institutions as well – strongly argued by Arthur Rich, the late dean of Protestant Social Ethics, in his masterwork *Business and Economic Ethics: The Ethics of Economic Systems* (2006):

The human person is responsible not only for his behavior toward himself, for his personal interaction with those around him, and for the use or misuse of the environmental goods necessary for existence, in so far as all of this concerns him directly; he is also responsible, in so far as he is indirectly affected in all of that by the structures of the social institutions within which his life concretely takes place ... This responsibility, which is concerned about social structures and their consequences for the qualitative formation of the basic human relationships, constitutes the specifics of what is called here 'social ethics.' *Human responsibility is integrated into a whole only in social ethics understood in this sense.* (Rich 2006, 52–53; emphasis in the original)

While ethical responsibility concerns both direct and indirect human relationships, it is important to define its limitations as well. Just as it would be wrong to limit the scope of responsibility to fulfilling roles and following rules, so too it would be wrong to extend it to cover each and every object. If we were responsible for each and everything, we would end up being responsible for nothing. Richard De George's definition of responsibility offers three basic criteria, which also help determine its limitations (De George 2010, chapter 6). Acting in a morally responsible manner means to be capable of acting (causing the result of action) and to do it knowingly and willingly. Responsibility is about action and inaction (being the independent variable of all morality; see Gewirth in Chapter 12); it requires knowledge (Schulz 1972, 1989; Jonas 1984); and it is grounded in freedom (Frankl 1984; Sen 1999). Hence limitations can arise in causing directly or indirectly results of action or inaction, in lacking knowledge about the consequences, or in not being free to act or abstain from acting. It goes without saying that these limitations can take many different forms and are often difficult to determine – a subject that cannot be discussed here further (see Social Philosophy and Policy 1999, 2019; Kettner 2002).

Given the key role of responsibility in contemporary ethical thinking, it does not come as a surprise that it also plays a prominent role in the UN Framework and Guiding Principles on Business and Human Rights. We therefore present the meaning of corporate responsibility in these UN documents and, in addition, develop some ethical explications, which attempt to clarify and strengthen this framework beyond its current interpretation. Subsequently, the tripartite concept of corporate responsibility will be unfolded further in the Chapters 16, 17 and 18 and explained with two, more specific studies in Chapters 19 and 20.

Corporate Responsibility in the UN Framework and Guiding Principles on Business and Human Rights and Some Ethical Explications

Introduction

Since the turn of the millennium, the theme of "business and human rights" has been discussed with increasing urgency and in more and more circles. An important impetus was the launching of the United Nations Global Compact (www.unglobalcompact.org) in 2000 by Kofi Annan, along with the study "Human rights – is it any of your business?" by Amnesty International and The Prince of Wales Business Leaders Forum in 2000 (AI and PWBLF 2000; also MNEs and HR 1998; Avery 2000). In the intervening years, innumerable publications have appeared, among them, of particular significance, the Reports of the Special Representative of the Secretary-General of the United Nations, John Ruggie (UN 2007, 2008a, 2008b, 2009, 2010, 2011, 2012a; Ruggie 2013; Bird et al. 2014). The English title "business and human rights" sounds quite catchy since it seems to combine two things that, for many, are a contradiction in terms.

The challenge for business and human rights has arisen from the drastic expansion and impact of global markets since the 1990s, on the one hand, and the lack of capacity of societies to manage the adverse consequences of the markets, on the other. As Ruggie reports on "Business and Human Rights" in 2007, this "fundamental institutional misalignment ... creates the permissive environment within which blameworthy acts by corporations may occur without adequate sanctioning or reparation. For the sake of the victims of abuse, and to sustain globalization as a positive force, this must be fixed" (UN 2007, 3).

In order to fix this fundamental institutional misalignment, the states, transnational corporations and other business enterprises, along with other social actors, need to collaborate on the basis of an ethical framework that is built on a relatively broad, worldwide consensus. Today, such a framework is available, consisting of human rights which, since the Universal Declaration of Human Rights (UN 1948), have been further developed toward a truly global support (Burke 2010) with the acknowledgement of the "indivisibility, interdependency, and interrelatedness" of human rights (for more, see Part II).

To illustrate the importance and timeliness of "business and human rights," one might recall a few cases that have caught public attention: Shell's alleged complicity in the death of Nigerian activist Ken Saro-Wiwa (Balch 2009b); Google facing internet censorship in China (Brenkert 2009); investors asking companies in Sudan to respect human rights (Kropp 2010); sweatshops and labor relations (Hartman et al. 2003); and access to basic medicines in developing countries (Balch 2009a). An excellent on-line source of information is the *Business & Human Rights Resource Centre* with its website (www .business-humanrights.org) and *Weekly Updates.*

In order to sort out the wealth of information about business and human rights, to clarify the human rights challenges transnational corporations face and to provide guidance to meet those challenges, the United Nations Framework "Protect, Respect and Remedy" (UN 2008a), elaborated by John Ruggie, was developed and has "provided a structure for the debate and action on business and human rights to be built on" (Davis 2011, 43). There is no doubt that this structure includes many important ethical implications. However, these implications are barely articulated and most often remain hidden, perhaps in order to avoid philosophical controversies that might divert attention from taking action.

However, philosophical reflections need not necessarily distract from action; rather, they can clarify key concepts and strengthen the structure of the UN Framework. Therefore, I point out some basic assumptions of this approach and explicate several crucial ethical implications, in particular the moral status of the corporation, the notion of responsibility, the distinction of different types of obligations, and the criteria of assigning these obligations to different moral actors (based on Enderle 2014b).[3]

Basic Assumptions in the UN Framework for Business and Human Rights

A series of basic assumptions are implied in the UN Framework and can be considered plausible (see the extensive discussion about human rights in Part II):

(1) Corporate responsibility for human rights requires strategies and conduct that are ultimately oriented toward people (not things) and thus are "humanly just" (Rich 2006), aiming at the expansion of "human capabilities" (as suggested in Chapter 8).

(2) Human rights are universally valid ethical norms, which, today, have been recognized worldwide, although not undisputedly (see Chapter 11).

(3) Human rights comprehend all thirty human rights: civil, political, economic, social and cultural rights, including the right to development (see Chapter 11).

(4) Human rights are minimal ethical norms and do not encompass all ethical norms and values that are relevant for business enterprises (see Chapter 12).
(5) The justification of human rights is left open and can be approached from any philosophical or religious perspective (see Chapter 12).

Ethical Obligations of Securing Human Rights

Starting from these five assumptions, we can summarize the core problem of human rights as follows:

(1) All human rights, as minimal norms, must be secured completely.
(2) Each individual and all organs of society must contribute to meet this norm, to the extent each is capable of.

The first proposition about human rights is relatively clear and does not need here further explanation, if one can accept the assumptions mentioned above. The second proposition, however, is more difficult to understand and thus has to be scrutinized more closely. For this purpose, three aspects can be distinguished: (1) the subjects of obligations; (2) the types of obligations and (3) the criteria, on the basis of which the obligations are to be assigned to the various subjects. These three aspects can be presented with the help of a matrix, in which the rows indicate the subjects and the columns the types of obligations while the filling of the cells marks the criteria of assigning the obligations to the subjects (Figure 15.1).

Subjects of Obligations

As the Universal Declaration of Human Rights states, in principle all human beings and all organs of society are obligated to contribute to securing human rights. They include the states and their diverse organs, political and economic organizations, nongovernmental organizations, religious communities, international institutions, individuals, groups and many more. Thereby it is important to distinguish between individuals and organs of society. Apparently, ethical obligations are being assigned not only to individual humans, but also to the organs of society. Although the concept of the "moral actor" is not literally used, the Declaration of 1948 applies it substantively to the states, whereas large-scale enterprises, at that time, were not yet

	Respect		Protect	Remedy	Promote
	Direct:	Indirect (no complicity):			
States					
Transnational corporations and other business enterprises					
Other organs of society					
Individuals					

Figure 15.1 Subjects and types of obligations for securing human rights

understood as "moral actors." However, for the current discussion about corporate responsibility for human rights, the concept of the moral actor of business enterprises is of fundamental importance and thus will be discussed in Chapter 16.

Types of Obligations

Securing human rights involves not only a variety of subjects of obligations, but also different types of obligations that depend on the ways these obligations can be fulfilled. Such a typology is crucially important in order to allocate human rights in a differentiated manner.

Moreover, it helps to overcome the questionable yet widespread dichotomy between "negative" and "positive" rights by locating the difference between avoiding action (non-interference) and taking positive actions not in rights, but in correlative obligations (see Chapters 11 and 12). In line with Shue's pertinent work (1996, 35–64), three types of obligations can be distinguished: (1) the obligation to avoid violations of human rights; (2) the obligation to protect human rights by demanding recognition of the first obligation and by establishing "institutional" provisions that prevent, as much as possible, the violation of this obligation through appropriate incentive systems and (3) the obligation to provide the victims of human rights violations access to the remedy of their rights.

This triple distinction coincides, by and large, with the distinction made in the UN Framework, although the latter changed the order by placing "protect" (the second obligation) first, followed by "respect" and "remedy" (UN 2008a, esp. §§ 10–26). It assigns the obligation to protect exclusively to the state, calling it "the duty of the state." The obligation to respect relates primarily to the corporation, calling it "the responsibility of the corporation," and the obligation to remedy then relates to both the state and the corporation.

Compared to a traditional understanding of the roles of the state and the corporation, the UN Framework offers considerable progress by significantly expanding and differentiating the responsibility of transnational corporations and business enterprises. This expansion and differentiation concerns not only the responsibility of the corporation to respect, but also the duty of the state to protect and further the remedy obligations of both.

Nevertheless, the UN Framework does not go far enough for a number of authors. Because today's powerful transnational corporations should be understood as quasi-governmental institutions, their responsibility should also include the protection of human rights against third parties (Wettstein 2009, esp. 305–11). Moreover, transnational corporations should not content themselves with a defensive attitude, but adopt a proactive attitude to promote human rights (Tavis & Tavis 2009, 168).

Criteria of Assigning Obligations

As has become clear from the discussion of the subjects and types of obligations to secure human rights, the question arises about the criteria on the basis of which the different types of obligations should be assigned to the different subjects. According to a traditional understanding that prevailed after the Second World War until the end of the twentieth century, it was primarily the nation-state and, internationally, the system of all nation-states (along with their extraterritorial areas), which were held responsible to secure human rights. In contrast, a cosmopolitical view has identified a power shift, caused by globalization in the last thirty years, from nation-states to transnational corporations, and demands a redefinition and redistribution of their respective responsibilities.

In the literature, the following criteria are predominantly discussed:

1. Different roles of actors with a strict separation of private and public interests: the state is responsible for public interests, the other actors for private interests.
2. Impact of the actor on the victims of violations of human rights: intentional, unintentional.
3. Complicity: direct, indirect, beneficial, silent, and structural.
4. Sphere of influence[4] of the actor on the victims and perpetrators of human rights violations: actual and potential influence.
5. Capability of the actor to respect, protect, remedy, and promote human rights, although the actor did not cause human rights violations directly or indirectly.

For all criteria, it is assumed implicitly or explicitly that the actor has a certain space of freedom (to a varying degree) to secure human rights in one or another way (by respecting, protecting, remedying or promoting them).

Different authors employ different criteria. In the following, a short overview shows how selected authors apply the criteria to the matrix of subjects and types of obligations to secure human rights.

The Draft Norms of the United Nations (UN 2003) use the criteria "impact" (#2), "direct and indirect complicity" (#3) and "actual sphere of influence" (#4). They reject the strict separation of private and public interests (#1) and disregard the "capability of the actor." Furthermore, the Draft Norms focus only on the economic, social and cultural rights while ignoring the civil and political rights and the right to development.

The United Nations Framework (UN 2010, § 1), supported also by the Business Leaders Initiative on Human Rights (BLIHR 2009, chapter 1), comprehends, most importantly, all human rights (see Figure 15.2). It assigns the exclusive duty of protection to the state, but seems to decline a strict separation of private and public interests. The relevant criteria are "(direct) impact" (#2) and "complicity" (or "indirect impact") (#3). The criterion of the "sphere of influence" (#4) is criticized as "too broad and ambiguous" and rejected and that of the "capability of the actor" (#5) is deemed "confusing" and rejected as well (see Figure 15.2 and discussion below). The Framework only pertains to the filled-in cells and leaves the other cells empty; that is, it does not address the obligation of promoting human rights and

	Respect		Protect	Remedy	Promote
	Direct:	Indirect (no complicity):			
States					
Transnational corporations and other business enterprises					
Other organs of society					
Individuals					

Figure 15.2 UN framework for business and human rights (2008a): All rights

abstains from attributing obligations to "other organs of society" (see, for example, Kirchschläger 2017) and individuals.

Like the UN Framework, Florian Wettstein (2009) includes all human rights in the obligations of transnational corporations. But unlike the UN Framework, he extends their responsibilities far beyond the scope defined by the UN Framework, using the criteria of "impact" (#2), "direct, indirect, beneficial, silent, and structural complicity" (#3), "actual and potential sphere of influence" (#4) and "capability of the actor" (#5). The strict separation of private and public interests is rejected.

The "hybrid model" of Wesley Cragg (2010) offers a practical proposal inspired by many initiatives such as the Sullivan Principles, the Kimberly Process Certification Scheme, the Extractive Industries Transparency Initiative and the Equator Principles. It is about "specific rule systems" for selected human rights, based on the criteria of "impact" (#2) and the "specific setting" of an industry or a social conflict.

Determining Corporate Responsibility for Human Rights

After this short overview of several approaches to "business and human rights," we now attempt to determine the notion of the "responsibility" of business organizations or "corporate responsibility" for human rights. The analysis draws largely on the UN Framework and Guiding Principles on Business and Human Rights and, in addition, articulates key ethical implications.

First, the subject of corporate responsibility for human rights are business organizations, which will be extensively discussed in Chapter 16. For the time being, we only point to the key feature of being *"moral actors"* – to the extent that they are "corporate actors" – understood as collective entities capable of intending actions, carrying them out under their control and reflecting on their commitment. They can be held morally responsible for their acts, which does not hold for value-free organizations and mechanisms. Because business organizations are not ends in themselves, they are not moral persons who can claim the rights of human beings. Obviously, this concept of the moral actor indicates only the moral status of business organizations without assessing their moral quality. It is, by no means, a substitute for the responsibilities which individuals and groups carry in and for their organizations. But this concept of the moral actor is necessary in order to speak of "corporate responsibility" in a meaningful way.

Second, we apply the bipolar concept of responsibility discussed above to the business organization as a moral actor. *"Self-commitment originating from freedom"* signifies a moral commitment of the business organization that transcends its sociological role and its legal definition. This moral "anchoring" is particularly important when, in the process of globalization, the sociological and legal environment of business is changing drastically. To fix the worldwide institutional misalignment mentioned above, not only laws and regulations but also the ethical commitment of business is necessary. At the same time, self-commitment *"in worldly relationships"* means "to respect human rights" and to contribute to "remedying human rights violations." It is important to emphasize the independence of the responsibility of business enterprises from the duty of states. The Commentary of the Guiding Principle 11 makes clear that "[T]he responsibility to respect human rights ... exists independently of States' ability and/or willingness to fulfill their own human rights obligations, and does not diminish those obligations. And it exists over and above compliance with national laws and regulations protecting human rights" (UN 2011, 13).

Third, in line with the UN Framework, our approach comprehends *all* businesses. "The responsibility of business enterprises to respect human rights applies to all enterprises regardless of their size, sector, operational context, ownership and structure. Nevertheless, the scale and complexity of the means through which enterprises meet that responsibility may vary according to these factors and with the severity of the enterprise's adverse human rights impacts" (Principle 14: UN 2011, 15 and UN 2012a, 18–22).

Fourth, of far-reaching importance is the *human rights due diligence* to be exercised by business enterprises (Principles 17–21: UN 2011, 17–24 and UN 2012a, 31–63). It concerns corporate management in its entirety, taking seriously all actual and potential impacts on human rights. Therefore, due diligence demands: (1) to understand the human rights context of the countries, in which the corporation does or intends to do business, (2) to assess the corporation's own activities and (3) to analyze the corporation's relationships with business and other entities. The manner of exercising due diligence becomes an important benchmark for assessing the corporation's commitment and credibility.

Fifth, with regard to the content of corporate responsibility, we may ask whether it should be limited to a sub-set of internationally recognized human rights – as the UN Draft Norms (UN 2003) and Cragg (2010) do – or extended, in principle, to all human rights (see Chapter 11). The UN Guiding Principles include all – not only economic and social – human rights expressed in the International Bill of Human Rights and the principles concerning fundamental rights set out in the International Labor Organization's Declaration on Fundamental Principles and Rights at Work (Principle 12: UN 2011, 13–14 and UN 2012a, 9–15). Accordingly, we propose to include *all human rights* and, if appropriate, subject them to the due diligence exercise. If only a subset of internationally recognized human rights (say, economic, social and cultural rights) were relevant for corporate responsibility, business organizations would not be accountable for their adverse impact on the other internationally recognized human rights (say, civil and political rights).

While all human rights are considered relevant in principle, the types of obligations vary and can demand to protect, respect, remedy or promote human rights. Based on which criteria do business enterprises have the responsibility to "respect" human rights (see Figure 15.2)?

The Guiding Principle 13 requires three criteria: Causation, contribution, and direct linkages without contribution, namely *the criteria of direct and indirect impact* and *of complicity* (see Chapter 12). While the first two criteria are relatively undisputed, the third criterion can take on multiple forms, which are sometimes very difficult to assess. Nevertheless, these criteria apply to all business enterprises. "Such attributes as companies' size, influence, and profit margins may be relevant factors in determining the scope of their promotional CSR-activities, but they do not define the scope of the corporate responsibility to respect human rights" (UN 2010, § 58). Also, companies' capacity, whether absolute or relative to that of states, should not, as a general rule, determine corporate responsibilities for human rights (UN 2010, § 64).

As for *the criterion of sphere of influence*, it is very ambiguous and thus cannot be applied in a satisfactory manner (see Note 3). It encompasses two very different meanings of "influence": the impact of the actor on the victim and the leverage of the actor on the perpetrator of human rights violations. Moreover, it includes several notions that should be distinguished: proximity (to the victim), causation, control, benefice and political influence. Even if a powerful corporation is able to exercise the protection of human rights similarly to a governmental organ, its sphere of influence does not necessarily legitimize the exercise of its power. Due to these difficulties, the 2010 Report by John Ruggie correctly pleads for a systematic strengthening of the state duty to protect (UN 2010, §§ 16–53).

Much more difficult is it to assess the relevance of *the criterion of the actor's capability* that goes beyond avoiding the causation of human rights violation. On the one hand, the capability is a necessary condition to protect against violations by third parties. On the other hand, it is not a sufficient condition because other capable actors (for instance, fairly well-functioning states) that are legitimized to exercise this protection, can act as well. Admittedly, the situation is more complicated when the state actor possesses this capability only to a diminished degree or not at all.

Notwithstanding these difficulties, the UN Framework makes a groundbreaking and very helpful contribution to the clarification of corporate responsibility with regard to human rights and will serve as a reasonably solid foundation of "respecting human rights" in this book. It includes the following components: (1) Transnational corporations and other business enterprises have to "respect" all internationally recognized human rights worldwide. This means, they must not cause directly or be involved as accomplices directly or indirectly in human rights violations. (2) In order to perceive and fulfill these responsibilities, companies have to exercise "due diligence" (that is, to be committed) to examine, on a regular basis, their corporate strategies and activities with regard to all potential and actual impacts on human rights and to make sure that all human rights are "respected." (3) However, companies are not responsible for all types of human rights violations, but "only" insofar as they have to "respect" human rights and remedy their violations. This Framework with its Guiding Principles for implementation is of utmost practical importance for companies themselves and company-watchers alike, readily demonstrable on the extraordinarily informative website of the Business & Human Rights Resource Center that has been monitoring thousands of companies (https://business-humanrights.org/en/about-us).

Notes

1 Thus corporate responsibility is understood as a core concept of corporate ethics or business ethics in a narrow sense. In this book it relates to wealth creation and human rights and thus does not cover the full range of issues of corporate ethics (see Chapter 12). However, it is a rich and understandable term, which focuses on the most important challenges of business organizations and can be extended to the full range of issues.

2 However, responsibility is briefly mentioned by Collins in his subsequent book *Good to Great* (2001).

3 More recent literature includes Brenkert (2016), who provides an overview on "Business and Human Rights," and the controversial views of Denis Arnold (2016, 2017) and Nien-hê Hsieh (2017). Deva et al. (2019) discuss past trends and propose future directions for business and human rights scholarship, several of which are addressed in this book.

4 The concept of sphere of influence was introduced into corporate social responsibility (CSR) discourse by the United Nations Global Compact and is also used by the United Nations Draft Norms (UN 2003). It is based on a model that consists of a set of concentric circles, mapping stakeholders in a corporation's value chain: with employees in the inner most circle, then moving outward to suppliers, the marketplace, the community, and the governments. It is implicitly assumed that the "influence," and thus presumably the responsibility, of a corporation declines as one moves outward from the center (UN 2008b, §§ 7–8).

16 | The Moral Status of the Business Organization

After explaining Schulz's tripartite concept of responsibility and adopting the UN Framework and Guiding Principles enhanced with several ethical explications (in Chapter 15), we now turn to the question of the subject of corporate responsibility for wealth creation and human rights. Who arguably can be held responsible in an ethical sense? To whom can "moral responsibility" be attributed with good reasons? To business organizations large and small? To business leaders and management teams? To either organizations or individuals? Or to both? This meta-ethical question[1] of the moral status is of great theoretical and practical importance, and the discussion in the literature has been filled with controversy. The answer I propose in this book is, in a nutshell, that business organizations – to the extent they are corporate actors – are also moral actors in a sense analogous to personal actors. This implies that corporate responsibility is complementary, not substitutive to personal responsibility. Take the example of the Deep Horizon oil spill that began on April 20, 2010 in the Gulf of Mexico on the BP-operated Macondo Prospect. From the ethical perspective, it would be unfair to hold Antony Hayward, CEO of BP, and his top executive team (at that time) solely responsible for the catastrophe, given BP's long-standing cost-cutting strategy, which resulted in numerous consequential casualties over many years (Lustgarten 2010; Smith et al. 2011; Kaufman & Wining 2012). While fully accounting for individual responsibilities,[2] moral responsibility of BP as a corporation can and should be acknowledged as well because it had acted as a corporate actor. Or take the example of the global financial service firm Lehman Brothers Holdings Inc. whose bankruptcy on September 15, 2008 partially caused the outbreak of the global financial crisis (Sorkin 2009; Ward 2018). There are persuasive moral reasons to hold Lehman Brothers responsible as corporate actor; however, this does not necessarily absolve Dick Fuld, its

CEO, and his top management team from their individual responsibilities.

Before discussing this question in depth, we recall the vast world of business organizations and point to some historical perspectives.

Significance of Business Organizations as Nonstate Actors

The world of business organizations is immense. Not only does it comprise an enormous variety of activities; it also contains gigantic differences in size, structure, legal form and corporate strategies. Forbes' List 2018 (2018) of the 2,000 largest publicly listed companies in sixty countries shows a total sales of USD 39.1 trillion, profits of USD 3.2 trillion, assets of USD 189 trillion and a market value of USD 56.8 trillion. Among those enterprises, we find names such as the large Chinese banks Industrial and Commercial Bank of China (ICBC), China Construction Bank, the technology corporations Apple, Samsung, Microsoft and Alphabet, and Europa's biggest enterprises HSBC Holdings, BNP Paribas, Allianz and Volkswagen. Out of these 2,000 companies, 560 come from the United States, 291 from China, 229 from Japan, dozens from EU countries and a few from developing countries.

The World Bank annually documents the number of publicly listed corporations in each country and in each region. In 2017 there were worldwide 43,036 corporations (compared to 14,779 in 1975), in the United States 4,336, in China 3,485, in Japan 3,589, in India 5,615, in the OECD 22,624 (World Bank 2018). These corporations, though, form only a small part of business enterprises. In addition, multiple types of privately held companies or close corporations in a big variety of sizes exist. Limited liability companies have considerably increased in recent years, while publicly listed companies have decreased a great deal in the United States and other developed countries (Davis 2016).

Multinational enterprises (also multinational corporations or transnational corporations) transcend the national economic area and hold facilities and other assets in at least one country outside the home country. Their offices and factories are located in different countries, led commonly from a centralized headquarter. Global multinational enterprises are global, operating not only regionally, with sales and profits in various economic areas. According to a common definition, they have at least 20 percent of sales on at least three continents.

In addition to these gigantic enterprises, there is an enormous number of micro, small and medium enterprises or MSMEs. According to a widely held definition, the micro enterprises are composed of 1–9 persons, the small of 10–49 persons and the medium of 50–250 persons. The World Bank estimates in total 365–445 million MSMEs in emerging countries (Kushnir et al. 2010). They include 25–30 million registered small and medium enterprises, 55–70 million registered micro enterprises and 285–345 million in the informal sector.

This short overview of the immense variety of business organizations points to the enormous significance of these nonstate actors. They can provide meaningful or degrading work to billions of people and produce goods and services which are useful and sustainable, or they can harm and destroy people and nature. It is therefore of paramount importance to examine how the responsibility of these business organizations is conceptualized – in economic, political and legal terms as well as in ethical terms – and how responsibility is assumed and implemented.

A Historic Perspective on Corporate Responsibility

The question of corporate responsibility arises not only in problematic business practices today; it has also been about corporate activities of the past, directed by prior generations of managers. Historically, corporations have been criticized for actively working with and enormously benefiting from repressive regimes. In the first half of the twentieth century, the German pharmaceutical company Bayer used thousands of slave workers, manufactured chemical weapons including chlorine gas and, as part of IG Farben, supplied the gas Zyklon B to the SS for the extinction of millions of prisoners (GMWatch 2009). IBM supposedly provided the Nazi regime with technology, knowing it would be used to "facilitate persecution and genocide" (Feder 2001). Even "ordinary companies" were accomplices with the Nazi regime, like Topf & Sons that built the Auschwitz ovens to cremate the gassed prisoners (Topf & Sons 2011). Another historic example of corporate complicity in criminal acts involved Agent Orange in the Vietnam War. US companies such as Monsanto, Dow Chemical and eight other companies were accused of war crimes, knowingly providing Agent Orange – one of the most toxic poisons – to be sprayed for military purposes in the Vietnam War, in violation of the 1925 Geneva Protocol banning the use of chemical and biological agents (Fawthrop 2004).

In their groundbreaking article "Historic Corporate Social Responsibility," Judith Schrempf-Stirling, Guido Palazzo and Robert Phillips (2016) theorize about the ways contemporary managers engage with these critiques and how corporate engagement with this past affects the legitimacy of current business: (1) They reflect on the theoretical basis for holding a corporation responsible for decisions made by prior generations of managers. (2) They analyze the processes by which such claims are raised and contested. (3) They identify the relevant features that render a charge of historical harm-doing more or less legitimate in the current context. And (4) they attempt to foresee how a corporation's response to such charges will affect the intensity of future narrative contests and the corporation's own legitimacy.

While harm was done by the corporation in the distant past, current leaders of the corporation, who are not responsible for the decisions in the past, have to deal with critiques raised at present which cannot but influence – positively or negatively – the legitimacy of the corporation in the future.

Given the limitation of this chapter, the four research perspectives developed by Schrempf-Stirling et al. (2016) cannot be further discussed here. But it is important to emphasize the underlying assumption that corporations are understood as *"intergenerational moral actors subject to fluctuations in socially constructed legitimacy, who are themselves participants in deliberative contests of narratives about their own past"* (p. 704; emphasis by G.E.). In other words, current corporate leaders do bear moral responsibility for decisions they make at present; however, it would be unfair to hold them responsible for corporate conduct in the past that conditions their decision making in the present. The continuity of the corporation over generations arguably justifies the assumption to conceive the corporation as a "moral actor" (located at the meso-level of analysis). It may also share responsibility with other actors at any level. To reject this assumption would overburden individuals and other actors with moral responsibility.

Concerning corporate wrongdoing in the present as well as in the past, not only responsibility but also liability is of great concern. "Liability for one's actions means that one can rightly be made to pay for the adverse effects of one's actions on others" (De George

2010, 104). This might be for legal and/or moral (that is, equity) reasons. It is based on the fact that the actor caused the damage, be it intentionally or unintentionally. Yet, even if it happened unintentionally, the actor is legally liable. Moreover, legal liability is attributed not only to individuals but also to corporations (see BP's Deepwater Horizon oil spill mentioned above). Thus, given the unequivocal affirmation of the legal liability of business organizations, one might examine if a similar affirmation can be made of their moral responsibility.

What Concepts of Business Organizations Are Compatible with Moral Actors?

As this glance at the world of business today and the historical reminder indicate, the impact of business on societies and nature is enormous and can be positive or negative. It therefore comes as no surprise that business at all levels is being held "responsible" in multiple ways, be it publicly or privately, more often by those who are being harmed than by those who benefit from it. But whoever is to be blamed or praised, today it seems to lie beyond any doubt that business is human-made. Hence there is no escape from responsibility through blaming an unfathomable "fate." This strong conviction was a force in the drive to hold countries like Germany and Japan "collectively responsible" for waging wars in the first half of the twentieth century. It is also relevant in assessing the collective responsibility of business today. As Rich argues, "the human person himself is responsible for the institutional ordering of his society and, therefore, must also accept responsibility collectively for its structural consequences on individual, personal and environmental behavior" (Rich 2006, 53).[3]

Schulz's tripartite concept of responsibility helps to clearly identify the essential components of corporate responsibility. Responsibility is not a free-standing ethical principle (like "Do not harm!"), but must be related to an actor. As actors, we include – as do the UN Guiding Principles – all business enterprises ranging from gigantic global corporations and large publicly listed companies to limited liability companies, state-owned enterprises, family businesses and medium, small and micro enterprises. Therefore, the question arises: Does it make sense – and if so, how – to expect enterprises to be ethically responsible actors and to speak of corporate responsibility in a genuine sense?

The question has been debated for decades and resulted in a large literature (Friedman 1970; Ladd 1970; Donaldson 1982; Goodpaster 1983; French 1984; Werhane 1985, 2016; Curtler 1986; Paine 2003; Velasquez 2003; Arnold 2006, 2018b; Miller 2006; De George 2010; Hess 2013; Rönnegard 2015; Orts & Smith 2017). As Lynn Paine has convincingly shown in her analysis of the evolution of the corporate personality, "in today's society, the doctrine of corporate amorality is no longer tenable" (Paine 2003, 91). Hence it is astonishing that many authors still reject or are unaware of this notion of the moral actor. Among them, one can find renowned economists like Milton Friedman (1970) and Robert Reich (2007, 12–14), along with leading business magazines like *The Economist* in its two surveys on "Corporate Social Responsibility" (*The Economist* 2005, 2008). Moreover, this notion has not been recognized in documents of the Christian churches on ethics in business and economics (see the memorandum on entrepreneurial action by the Council of the Protestant Church in Germany [Rat der EKD 2008] and the encyclical *Caritas in Veritate* [Benedict XVI 2009]). Also the *Manifesto for a Global Economic Ethic* (Küng et al. 2010) remains silent on this point.

In line with the "two-leg" approach of this book, which aims to integrate the descriptive-analytical and normative-ethical dimensions of business and economic ethics, we answer the question of corporate moral agency in two steps: First, we conceptualize the business organization in socio-economic terms as a "corporate actor" so that it is compatible with moral agency. Second, we qualify the corporate actor from the ethical perspective as a "moral actor."

To begin with the first step, we propose to use James Coleman's[4] *sociological* definition of the corporate actor, discussed extensively in his masterwork *Foundations of Social Theory* (1990). In the twentieth century corporate actors grew enormously and became powerful organizations. How can they be conceived as social systems by accounting for their power on the one hand and maintaining the relevance of personal actors on the other hand? Coleman defines the corporate actor as a purposive unit and a system of action, composed of principals and agents with rights and interests. Similar to the personal actor, the corporate actor has "control over resources and events, interests in resources and events, and the capability of taking actions to realize those interests through that control" (Coleman 1990, 542). However, different from the personal actor (who is both principal and agent in the same physical person), the corporate actor is composed of different positions held by different persons, which constitute the formal and relatively free-standing organization.[5]

To act purposively, a full-fledged corporate actor has two fundamental tasks: to collect the resources and interests of the multiple principals to create a coherent set; and to deploy the resources via the configuration of agents in a way that realizes the interests. Coleman explains:

> The most extensively developed corporate actor is one with multiple principals, object self, and multiple agents, constituting the acting self. This is the way a publicly owned corporation is conceived in modern society. The principals are the multiple owners, the shareholders of the corporations; the agents are all those employed by the corporation, from its chief executive officer to its production workers. (Coleman 1990, 421)

Thus large, well-structured, relatively free-standing and powerful business enterprises are conceived as corporate actors, which have control over resources and events, interests in resources and events and the capability of taking actions to realize those interests through that control. Given this rich socio-economic conception of the business enterprise, the question of responsibility arises unsurprisingly. It is discussed by Coleman in a tentative and descriptive way (in his chapter 21), which, though, will not be pursued further here.

Obviously, Coleman's definition differs from many economic definitions of the firm such as the firm as a production function, a nexus of contracts, a piece of property or an economic mechanism. Other than these definitions, his sociological definition is compatible with the company understood as a community of people, an agent, a provider of goods and services or a corporate citizen, which is a collective entity with a primarily (though not exclusively) economic purpose.[6]

Understanding business enterprises with relatively free-standing formal structures as corporate actors, we now ask about their *moral status*. The answer depends on how we conceive their capability of taking actions to realize their interests through their control. To be capable of taking actions means to have some space of freedom; to realize their interests through their control is acting with intention (or at least exhibiting intentional behavior) to achieve their goals; these actions have intended and unintended consequences by impacting people, society and nature; and these actions are caused by collective units, that is, corporate actors. It is therefore appropriate to define these corporate actors as *moral actors*. They are not *amoral actors* because they act with some freedom, intention and impact. And they are not *moral persons* because they are not personal actors who have a conscience and are ends in themselves; they, rather, serve purposes that are exterior to themselves. It is important to understand the attribution of a moral status and moral actions to corporate actors in an *analogous* sense to personal actors. Both types of actors have several properties in common while differing in other respects.

Hence, business enterprises as moral actors bear "corporate responsibility" and can be held responsible for their conduct in an ethical sense. They qualify as actors at the meso-level of action – as distinct from the actors at the macro (or systemic) and the micro (or individual) levels. Their responsibility is complementary, not substitutive to the responsibilities of actors at any level. Moreover, due to its bipolar nature, responsibility includes an "inner" and an "outer" side (Schulz 1972). On the one hand, the commitment of the corporate actor using its space of freedom must be embodied in its corporate culture and strategy, the inner side. On the other hand, it must express itself "in worldly relationships," that is, in corporate behavior as it impacts people, society and nature, the outer side.

Given the enormous variety of business organizations in size and power, the question arises whether the moral status of bearing responsibility can and should be attributed to all entities. The answer advanced in this book is that enterprises (like micro, small and medium enterprises), which are not corporate actors, are not moral actors either. Therefore, they cannot be held morally responsible in a genuine sense. In this case, corporate responsibility does not include the business organization as the subject of responsibility (that is, who is responsible), but only as the content of responsibility (for what is one responsible). Here the subjects are individual persons and groups (that is, at the micro level), *who* bear moral responsibility *for* the conduct of their organizations. Admittedly, it is sometimes difficult to draw the defining line between the corporate and the personal actor. But Coleman's distinction provides a reasonable and helpful orientation.

Necessary Conditions for Moral Agency of Business Organizations

In order to attribute moral agency to business organizations, it is insufficient to name them responsible actors or to expect them to behave like such actors. The attribution has to be based on sound socio-economic and ethical criteria. We contend that these criteria can be provided with Coleman's characterization of corporate actors and three uncontroversial necessary conditions of moral agency proposed by Richard De George (2010, chapter 6), Denis Arnold (2006, 2018), David Rönnegard (2015, chapter 2) and others.

According to Coleman (1990, 542), the essential properties of actors – be they personal or corporate – are (1) control over resources and events, (2) interests in resources and events and (3) the capability of taking actions to realize those interests through that control. As for corporate actors, they have their own control over and interest in resources and events and are capable of taking actions to realize those interests through that control.

Regarding the moral responsibility for an action, De George sets three conditions for the subject: (1) It is the cause of the result of the action, (2) it does the action knowingly and (3) it does the action willingly. Arnold grounds corporate moral agency on corporate intentionality as reflective commitment to future action, in line with De George's three conditions applied to the corporate actor (action, knowledge and willingness). Also Rönnegard, while rejecting the notion of *corporate* moral agency, defines the necessary conditions of moral agency in a similar way: (1) the ability to intend an action, (2) the ability to carry out an intentional action and (3) the ability to choose an intentional action autonomously.

The view advanced in this book is that these three necessary conditions of moral agency can be applied in an analogous sense to the business organization as a corporate actor, which, it should be noted, is denied by Rönnegard. The actor forms a unity that is distinct – but not separate – from the individuals of this entity. It has the collective ability to intend actions and carry them out under its control. It can reflect on its commitments and has some space of freedom to make and to change its commitments. While these properties apply to corporate actors – as they do to personal actors – their system of action, composed of positions, and their ultimate purposes outside of them differ from the individual nature of personal actors. Therefore, moral agency can be attributed to them only in an analogous sense.

For a better understanding of the moral status of the business organization as a corporate actor, it is important to dispel some common misconceptions. First, the attribution of a moral status to an actor does not imply that the actor acts in a morally good way; it only means that the actor is capable of acting morally and bearing moral responsibility. Second, individual and corporate moral responsibility do not exclude or substitute for each other; most often, they are complementary.[7] Third, if individual or corporate moral responsibility is not considered, one risks overburdening with moral blame either personal actors or corporate actors.

In conclusion, the question whether one can hold a business organization morally responsible is of paramount importance, from both a theoretical and a practical perspective. Its moral status as a moral actor must be firmly founded in order to attribute corporate responsibility in a genuine sense. Without the "anchoring" of moral responsibility in subjects (see Schulz in Chapter 15), responsibility for corporate policies and practices is groundless. This holds true for such policies and practices in the past as well as in the present and the future. To the extent that business organizations are corporate actors, the subjects of their responsibilities must be moral actors. If all responsibilities were attributed exclusively to personal actors, they would be held responsible for things they cannot control, which contradicts basic fairness. Having argued for anchoring moral responsibility at the individual (micro-) and organizational (meso-) levels, its anchoring at the systemic (macro-) level has not been addressed because it is an extremely complex problem that relates to the roles of states and international institutions (see Chapters 11 and 12), that cannot be properly dealt with in this book.

Notes

1 Meta-ethics encompasses the meaning of moral language and the nature and possibility of moral knowledge. "Meta-ethics can be described as the philosophical study of the nature, justification, rationality, truth-conditions, and status of moral codes, standards, judgments, and principles, abstracting from their specific content. Because it takes morality and moral principles as its subject, it is sometimes called 'second-order' ethics. By way of contrast, the conclusions and theories of normative ethics, or 'first-order' ethics, are themselves substantive ethical statements and theories" (Copp 2001, 1079).

2 As a sign of individual responsibility, Hayward stepped down as CEO on October 1, 2010.

3 While Rich emphasized the importance of collective responsibility, in his two volumes of business and economic ethics (2006) he did not take a position on the moral status of the corporation. He explicitly left it to his successors to "write a third volume" on the ethics of business organizations (personal note to G.E.).

4 See a short presentation of James Coleman's work in Lindenberg (2005).

5 I characterize the formal organization as relatively free-standing because the positions in this system of action are relatively independent of the persons who occupy these positions; morever, they normally outlast the occupants.

6 See Brown (2010, 209–21). Various concepts of citizenship are discussed in Crane et al. (2008).

7 See the two examples provided at the beginning of this chapter.

17 | *Mapping Corporate Responsibilities*

In Chapter 15 the ethics of business organizations was characterized as "corporate responsibility."[1] This draws on Schulz's tripartite concept of "responsibility" that distinguishes the subject (who is responsible), the contents (for what is one responsible) and the addressees (to whom is one responsible). Moreover, it adopts the notion of "corporate responsibility" elaborated in the UN Framework und UN Guiding Principles on Business and Human Rights. Chapter 16 then dealt with the question of the subject of corporate responsibility, that is, the moral status of the business organization as a moral actor. This chapter now focuses on the contents and the addressees of corporate responsibility by mapping specifically the business organization's responsibilities for wealth creation and human rights toward stakeholders, society at large and nature.

Corporate Responsibilities for Creating Natural, Economic, Human and Social Capital

To understand wealth creation in a comprehensive sense carries far-reaching consequences for corporate responsibilities. To begin with, the *substantive criteria* of the four types of capital are relevant. These can be explained with four examples.

(1) *Natural capital* consists of the natural resources minus environmental degradation. According to *The Natural Capital Declaration* (see Chapter 4), this type of capital comprises Earth's natural assets (soil, air, water, flora and fauna) and the ecosystem services resulting from them, which make human life possible. Hence the creation of wealth as natural capital signifies the improvement of Earth's natural assets of soil, air, water, flora and fauna and the reduction of their consumption and liabilities.

189

The significance of natural capital for corporate responsibility can be briefly illustrated with the Volkswagen scandal that broke in September 2015 (*Financial Times* 2015; see a more extensive discussion in Becker 2017).

Over many years Volkswagen run extensive advertising campaigns for the environment-friendly diesel-driven 2.0 liter automobiles (with EA 189 engines), which supposedly were much "cleaner" than the gasoline-driven automobiles with carbon dioxide waste gas. To prove this claim, the company pointed to the results of the test that met the very low, legally permitted limits of nitrogen oxide (NO_x) and particulate matter. (Nitrogen oxide is more toxic than carbon dioxide, causing air pollution and difficulty in breathing, and increasing the mortal danger for heart and lung patients.)

However, the U.S. Environment Protection Agency (EPA) discovered that these automobiles were equipped with built-in defeat devices to control the waste gas emissions: under test conditions of the government the automobiles respected the permitted limits, but under normal driving conditions they generated up to forty times more waste gas of nitrogen oxide. With this systematic deceit, Volkswagen deceived its customers and regulators and harmed the environment, that is, natural capital was destroyed. In addition, the destruction of natural capital led to a considerable reduction of economic, human and social capital: Volkswagen had to pay billions of dollars and euros for indemnification and penalty (economic capital; *Financial Times* 2019b); the health of thousands of persons was seriously affected (human capital); and the trust between Volkswagen and customers, investors and governments (social capital) was undermined.[2]

(2) The corporate objective of creating *economic* capital, composed of physical and financial capital, is rather undisputable; still, it should not be confused with "making money" and profit. A negative example can illustrate this: The recent scandal of the big US bank Wells Fargo (*Financial Times* 2016; Fortune.com 2016). Wells Fargo, with a net revenue of 22 billion dollars (2015), defined its code of ethics in the most ethical terms: "Integrity is not a commodity. It's the most rare and precious of personal attributes. It is the core of a person's – and a company's – reputation." Wells Fargo survived the financial crisis of 2008 better than other big banks, enjoyed an excellent reputation and expanded its customer basis considerably. Since 2008 Carrie Tolstedt had been responsible for consumer banking (that is, business with

individual customers, not with companies and other banks) and retired in July 2016 with high praise by the CEO John Stumpf; she had been "one of the bank's most important leaders and a standard-bearer of our culture and a champion for our customers." In addition to her base salary of 1.7 million dollars, she received retirement compensation of 124.6 million dollars.

In mid-September 2016 the scandal broke. The U.S. Consumer Financial Protection Bureau punished Wells Fargo with $185 million in fines as well as compensation to stung customers – so far the largest penalty the watchdog has ever imposed. Under the leadership of Ms. Tolstedt the bank opened more than 2 million unauthorized customer accounts (of which 565,000 were credit card applications). The employees were pushed to so-called sandbagging, that is, being put under pressure to open as many new accounts as possible (often of the same customers, under the banner of "cross-selling"). The bank fired 5,300 managers and employees over five years related to bad behavior. Former employees, however, accused Wells Fargo for having fired them because they did not meet the cross-selling objectives or did not execute the aggressive sales pitches.

This case is a stunning example of how a company pretended to create economic capital (that is, a broader customer basis; see Wells Fargo 2017). In actuality, it destroyed such capital in order "to make more money" and, as a result, had to pay a large fine. Moreover, human capital was diminished by ordering or condoning deceptive sales practices (in contradiction to the publicly stated corporate policy); thousands of employees were forced to act against their conscience or to lose their jobs. As a result of this customer fraud, the good reputation of the bank was damaged, the confidence in the bank undermined and hence some social capital destroyed.[3]

(3) *Human capital* stands for human beings' health and education. An excellent corporate example is Medtronic in the industry of medical devices, with its operational headquarter in Minneapolis (USA) and its principal executive office in Dublin (Ireland), counting over 86,000 employees in 150 countries (www.medtronic.com). Medtronic's mission statement was established already in the 1960s and states in the updated version:

To contribute to human welfare by application of biomedical engineering in the research, design, manufacture, and sale of instruments or appliances that *alleviate pain, restore health, and extend life.*

The former CEO Bill George made it perfectly clear: "Medtronic is *not* in the business to maximize shareholder value. We *are* in business to maximize value to the patients we serve" (emphasis in original, Murphy & Enderle 2003). First are the customers, then come the employees and only third are the shareholders (George 2003, 153–61). The Integrated Performance Report 2018, established, like the previous reports since 2014, according to the Sustainability Reporting Guidelines of the Global Reporting Initiative (GRI), demonstrates Medtronic's successful achievement of its mission: Innovation through product engineering; quality and trust to transform lives; creating fairness in health care; recognizing personal worth of employees; and maintaining good citizenship. Without exaggeration, one can affirm that Medtronic with its focus on human health has achieved a considerable level of human capital and thereby remarkably increased economic, natural and social capital as well.[4]

(4) *Social capital* – as trust relations according to Robert Putnam – indicates the level of trust between human beings and organizations. An outstanding example for the creation of social capital is the micro-credit movement founded by Muhammad Yunus in the mid-1970s in Bangladesh (Yunus 1999, 2004, 2007, 2018; Enderle 2004). It is important to focus on the original Grameen model that starkly differs from many profit-maximizing micro-credit organizations with disastrous consequences for the poor (Ledgerwood 2013; Bateman 2014; Chiu 2014, 2017). The core idea of the Grameen model came out of the experience that the poor are trustworthy and do not necessarily use micro-credits for consumption (for example, to buy rice), rather they invest them for productive purposes (for instance, to purchase a cow in order to produce and sell milk). Against the opposition of the banks and the government, Yunus championed relatively modest interest rates. He developed a communitarian model in which representatives of a few families in a village (Grameen means rural) met in order to get individual loans while supporting each other in the use and repayment of the loans. It was particularly surprising that, in a Muslim country especially, women engaged in Grameen projects because they were able to deal with micro-credits in a productive manner – much more diligently than men. As the poor were treated as creditworthy and, at the same time, were trained in careful dealing with money, the payback quotas were extraordinarily high, that is, 95 percent (see also the story

---

Box 17.1 Corporate responsibility for creating wealth

Negative examples:

- Destroying *natural capital*: Volkswagen scandal
- Destroying *economic capital*: Wells Fargo scandal

Positive examples:

- Creating *human capital*: Medtronic
- Creating *social capital*: Grameen Bank

---

of Aleya in Chapter 7). The Grameen example shows that the creation of social capital with the poor, supported by appropriate economic organizations, brings about "real freedoms" to the poor as Amartya Sen (1999) in his human capability approach proposes. As a consequence, also human capital gets advanced and economic capital increases (see Box 17.1).

Corporate Responsibilities for Creating Private and Public Wealth

As explained in Part I of this book (particularly in Chapter 5), the wealth of a society, ranging from the local up to the global level, is understood as *a combination of private and public wealth* – not just as an aggregation of private wealth. This means that the creation of private wealth depends on the availability of public wealth, and, in turn, the creation of public wealth is dependent on the availability of private wealth. Thus private and public wealth cannot be separated strictly from each other. Consequently, the market institution and the motivation of self-interest – powerful drivers for creating private wealth – can only play a limited – though indispensable – role in creating wealth in the comprehensive sense. Collective actors (like the state and local communities) and other-regarding motivations are necessary as well.

This mutual dependence of creating private and public wealth implies for corporate responsibility that business enterprises not only have to create private wealth, but they *should also contribute to the creation of public wealth*. Moreover, self-regarding motivations of enterprises need to be complemented with other-regarding motivations. Like the substantive criteria of wealth discussed above, these formal criteria of private and public wealth are fundamental to determine the contents of corporate responsibility.

To illustrate this public aspect of corporate responsibility, we refer to the well-known challenge for the public and private sector to build and maintain infrastructure projects. In the fall 2016 Lawrence Summers (2016) criticized Donald Trump's investment plans for infrastructure projects. They would support only projects that generate profit for the private sector. By advancing this type of projects, many of the highest return infrastructure investments – such as improving roads, repairing 60,000 structurally deficient bridges, upgrading schools or modernizing the air traffic control system – would be excluded because they do not generate a direct commercial return.

This example shows that Trump's investment plans are questionable for two reasons: The government abstains from assuming its public role as creator of public wealth and delegates its role to the private sector, which, in turn, is not supposed to create public wealth. However, if wealth creation in the comprehensive sense is taken seriously, the government as collective actor has to engage in creating public wealth and business enterprises have to go beyond their exclusive pursuit of self-interest and take responsibility to contribute to the creation of public wealth. Obviously, creating public wealth includes both creating "public goods" and avoiding "public bads."

Contributing to public wealth creation has its limits. Corporate responsibility cannot and should not replace the public duty of government at all levels of society. Business enterprises and governments are supposed to play complementary roles. As the UN Framework for Business and Human Rights attributes different, but complementary roles to states and businesses (that is, "the two pillars") for securing human rights, a similar "division of labor" is proposed in this book for the creation of wealth in a comprehensive sense. It allows for a wide range of possible combinations. But it excludes both extremes: on the one hand, that businesses should be the main creators of public wealth and, on the other hand, that they bear no responsibility at all to contribute to the creation of public wealth.

Further Corporate Responsibilities for Creating Wealth in a Comprehensive Sense

In addition to the two features of wealth creation mentioned above, the comprehensive conception of wealth creation encompasses five more features relevant for corporate responsibility. To begin with, a comprehensive understanding of wealth creation cannot limit itself to the *productive* dimension of its processes – a shortsightedness of many scholars and practitioners. Rather, it also has to account for its *distributive* dimension that permeates the original endowments of resources, the processes and the outcomes of wealth creation (see Chapter 6). If the distributive dimension is not understood and accounted for, the productive dimension cannot be properly understood either and far-reaching negative consequences follow in economic and ethical terms: misallocation of resources, unawareness of differentiated economic impact of corporate policies, failure in achieving long-term wealth, insensitivity to ethical demands of fair wages and many other implications. To illustrate the importance of the distributive dimension of wealth creation at the meso-level, Chapter 19 addresses key aspects of income inequality in business organizations.

As for the *material and spiritual* aspects, the fourth feature of wealth creation, several examples and conceptual clarifications are provided in Chapter 7. Konosuke Matsushita – with his philosophy *Not for Bread Alone* – wanted Matsushita Electronic to create peace and prosperity. More specifically, Robert Giacalone and Carole Jurkiewicz define workplace spirituality as *"aspects of the workplace, either in the individual, the group, or the organization, that promote individual feelings of satisfaction through transcendence*. To elaborate, that the process of work facilitates employees' sense of being connected to a nonphysical force beyond themselves that provides feelings of completeness and joy"* (Giacalone & Jurkiewicz 2010, 13; emphasis by the authors). Practical applications of workplace spirituality can take a large variety of forms: spiritual needs and well-being in end-of-life care; spiritual distress, self-consciousness and growth in crisis and disaster management (for example, in the case of the 2017 Hurricane Maria in Puerto Rico); and spiritual intelligence and transcendence in the self-discovery in the IT-workplace (Giacalone & Jurkiewicz 2010, 255–333). Joan Marques and colleagues (2007) conducted several studies among business executives, middle, lower and non-managerial workers to find out "what [spirituality in the workplace] is, why it matters, [and] how to make it work for you." And Marilyn Byrd, in her edited volume, provides "a philosophical and justice perspective" on the spirituality at work (2016).

While these approaches are very valuable and address a growing need in the workplace, they tend to transcend the economics of the workplace without paying sufficient attention to changing the economics from within. Sen's ethics-related approach to economics (see Chapter 1) and the comprehensive conception of wealth creation can strengthen the economic critique of the model of maximizing shareholder value without diminishing the spiritual aspect, that is having "a connection to something greater than ourselves, whatever you might call it; and a sense of meaning and purpose that guides our lives" (Judy Neal in Marques et al. 2007, ix).

The fifth feature of wealth creation defines sustainable wealth in terms of *human capabilities*. Applied to corporate responsibility, Sen's capability approach offers a better understanding in several respects (Enderle 2013b, González-Cantón et al. 2018). It overcomes "value-free" economics by incorporating human motivations and the judgment of social achievements. It goes beyond exclusively instrumental rationality by respecting human capabilities for their intrinsic values. And it is particularly sensitive to poverty and distribution. By taking each person as an end and focusing on real opportunities or substantial freedoms, it is decisively people-centered. This manifests itself in, at least, four ways: (1) There are multiple and interdependent functionings and capabilities. The functioning of working in a company may generate the capabilities of connecting with other people and being well respected in the community. Moreover, it can create the capability to be loyal to the company's mission and the functioning of being promoted. (2) In the company's dialogue with stakeholders, relevant capabilities may be determined for employees in terms of health and training, for customers in terms of safe products, for investors in terms of transparency and for the community in terms of keeping jobs. (3) Capabilities and human rights are closely connected. They share a common motivation and contribute to something that neither can provide alone. The human rights approach links the human development approach to the idea that others have duties to facilitate and enhance human development (human rights as entitlements to capabilities), and human development helps to augment the reach of the human rights approach (capabilities as potential contents of human rights). Moreover, capabilities can be easily related to the UN Guiding Principles on Business and Human Rights (UN 2011; see Chapter 11). Although the Principles do not mention the capability approach, they prominently refer to "human rights and fundamental freedoms" (General Principles [a], p. 1). (4) Several well-thought-out metrics for economic, social and environmental performance are today available that cover a fairly comprehensive range of issues through which business organizations affect people. It is suggested that GRI sustainability reporting, ISO 26000 and other metrics may benefit in their organizational perspectives from the capability approach, similarly to the Stiglitz-Sen-Fitoussi Report (Report 2009) that consistently focuses on people and the quality of life from a broad, societal perspective.

An outstanding example of sustainable wealth creation in terms of human capabilities can be found in the *Unilever Sustainable Living Plan (USLP)*. Under the leadership of former Unilever CEO Paul Polman, USLP was instituted in 2010, focuses on the total value chain – from farm to fork – and has three major goals, with sub-goals under each: (1) Improving health and well-being for more than one million people, (2) reducing environmental impact by one-half and (3) enhancing livelihoods of millions. An extensive discussion of this corporate initiative can be found in the case study by Patrick Murphy and Caitlin Murphy (2018).

Creating means *making something new and better,* the sixth feature of wealth creation, which goes far beyond acquiring and possessing wealth. As explained in Chapter 9, innovation is the successful application of ideas beyond the ordinary that can lead to gradual change or great disruption. It is about making something new, which has ethical implications. It requires curiosity and a risk-taking attitude. Corporate responsibility requires ethical innovation at the organizational level, which can take multiple forms of products, services, processes, strategies, and business models. Distinct from imagination and invention, innovation transforms new human thinking into new practical doing, making and behaving. It makes things new and feasible in economic and financial terms. But it is not necessarily better in ethical terms (whence there can be ethical and unethical innovations). Therefore, innovation needs ethical qualification in order to become creative activity, which makes things not only new, but also better from the ethical perspective. Thus corporate responsibility for wealth creation is about *ethical* innovation.

To illustrate how a small enterprise can live up to this responsibility, the case of Rohner Textil AG is briefly presented, based on the case studies in Gorman et al. (2003) and Enderle (2004). Founded in 1947 as a family-owned, joint-stock company, the Swiss company produces Climatex Lifecycle compostable upholstery fabric for home and office. It is "all about climatizing and regenerative textiles" (www .climatex.com). In the mid-1980s the small dye-works with thirty employees faced increasing competitive pressure and rising ecological expectations and regulations. The management realized that "either economics or ecology" was not an option and thus developed a strategy to combine both. It took the vision, commitment and perseverance of the management to pursue this goal step by step over the years, despite skepticism and hostility in the textile industry. Two partnerships with a big chemical transnational corporation and a nongovernmental organization turned out to be crucial: from Ciba-Geigy, Rohner Textil AG acquired the right to use sixteen biodegradable dyes with which almost all color variations are possible, except black; Rohner Textil AG also cooperated with the independent environmental institute EPEA in Hamburg, Germany. Its head, Dr. Michael Braungart, and the American designer and architect William McDonough developed a measurable design tool for environmentally sound products and production, the "Index of Sustainability" (www.epea.com). Climatex® is an innovative technology for sustainable materials. The textiles balance temperature, regulate moisture and are durable. climatex® products promote health and well-being. They can be separated homogeneously, recycled in entirety and thus return to their natural and technical cycles. climatex® is Cradle to Cradle certified. In sum, with a clear vision, a long-lasting commitment and smart collaboration with like-minded partners, Rohner Textil AG succeeded in putting corporate responsibility for ethical innovation into practice.

The seventh feature of wealth creation requires *both self-regarding and other-regarding motivations*. As Sen's ethics-related approach to economics argues, motivations deserve full attention at all levels of economic activity. This holds particularly true with regard to the creation of wealth understood as a combination of private and public wealth. In Chapter 10, the motivation of self-interest was critically assessed, especially in its extreme assumption of the "economic man," while its important role to produce private goods and create private wealth was acknowledged. However, when it comes to creating public wealth, the motivation of self-interest is utterly insufficient, for economic and non-economic reasons alike. Other-regarding motivations are indispensable to create wealth in a comprehensive sense. Having recalled the need for both self-regarding and other-regarding motivations in general, how does it apply to the motivations relevant to business organizations? If its purpose were only the creation of private wealth, self-regarding motivations – or, in short, self-interest – would suffice. If, however, the business organization is also responsible for contributing to the creation of public wealth, it needs also other-regarding motivations, such as a commitment to corporate citizenship, an obligation to give back to society and a sense of solidarity. While these motivations are essential for business operations in the national context, they are even more imperative for creating urgently needed public wealth in the global context. However, these public goals cannot be achieved as long as business organizations are focusing exclusively on their self-interest and do not contribute to the creation of public wealth from the local to the global levels.

Corporate Responsibilities for Respecting Human Rights

Today's understanding of human rights is presented and extensively discussed in Part II of this book. Chapter 11 delineates all thirty internationally recognized human rights. Chapter 12 argues for human rights as minimal ethical requirements. Chapter 13 considers cost-benefit implications of human rights. And Chapter 14 qualifies human rights as ethically demanded global public goods. In applying these broad perspectives to corporate responsibility, Chapter 15 discusses the UN Framework (2008) and the UN Guiding Principles on Business and Human Rights (2011) and elaborates some key ethical features of this approach. It is fair to say that this now well established approach makes a groundbreaking and very helpful contribution to the clarification of corporate responsibility with regard to human rights. It, therefore, serves as a solid foundation for the approach proposed in this book.

As summarized in Chapter 15, corporate responsibility for respecting human rights includes three main components: (1) Business enterprises have to "respect" all internationally recognized human rights worldwide, independently of states' abilities and/or willingness to fulfil their own human rights obligations. This means, they must not cause directly or be involved as accomplices directly or indirectly in human rights violations. (2) In order to perceive and fulfill these responsibilities, the enterprises have to exercise "due diligence" (that is, to be committed) to examine, on a regular basis, their corporate strategies and activities with regard to all potential and actual impacts on human rights and to make sure that all human rights are "respected." (3) However, enterprises are not responsible for all types of human rights violations, but "only" insofar as they have to "respect" human rights and remedy their violations.

Adverse business impact on human rights can be illustrated with the following examples (UN 2012, 17). (1) *Direct causation* occurs when customers are discriminated against by a restaurant due to race and when factory workers are exposed to hazardous working conditions without adequate safety equipment. (2) Business *contributes* to adverse human rights impacts by providing data about internet service users to a government that uses the data to trace and prosecute political dissidents contrary to human rights; and by targeting children with high-sugar foods and drinks, causing child obesity. (3) Although business does *not contribute* to adverse human rights impact, it is *directly linked* to the affected persons through its operations, products or services, for example, by providing financial loans to an enterprise for business activities that, in breach of agreed standards, result in the eviction of families; and when the supplier subcontracts embroidery on a retail company's clothing products to child laborers in homes, counter to contractual obligations (see Box 17.2).

Addressees of Corporate Responsibility

Having explained the contents of corporate responsibility, we now turn to its addressees, that is, the instances or authorities *to whom* business enterprises are supposed to be responsible in an ethical sense. As noticed in Chapter 1, three views, broadly speaking, can be distinguished about the addressees. Free-market economists claim that business executives as the "agents" (that is, individuals, not business organizations) are solely responsible to the shareholders (as the "principals") for maximizing shareholder value. The proponents of the stakeholder approach with either an instrumental or a normative

---

Box 17.2 Corporate responsibility for respecting human rights

No adverse human rights impact by:

- *Direct causation:* Customers are discriminated against by a restaurant due to race. Factory workers are exposed to hazardous working conditions without adequate safety equipment.
- *Contribution:* Providing data about internet service users to a government that uses the data to trace and prosecute political dissidents contrary to human rights. Targeting children with high-sugar foods and drinks, causing child obesity.
- *No contribution, but direct linkage through the company's operations, products or services:* Providing financial loans to an enterprise for business activities that, in breach of agreed standards, result in the eviction of families. When the supplier subcontracts embroidery on a retail company's clothing products to child laborers in homes, counter to contractual obligations.

---

perspective conceive the business organization as a corporate or even moral actor that must consider the interests of multiple stakeholders (not only shareholders but also customers, employees and others) and even be responsible to them in an ethical sense. The third view agrees with the stakeholder approach in general; however, it determines the contents of corporate responsibility more specifically (as outlined in this chapter) and adds to the affected stakeholders broader addressees such as the society at large, future generations and nature, embracing a resolutely sustainable perspective.

When asking which of the three views is proposed in this book, it probably does not come as a surprise that the comprehensive conception of wealth creation and human rights supports the third view. What are the main arguments? The tripartite conception of corporate responsibility qualifies its *subjects*, that is business enterprises, as corporate and moral actors which bear responsibility, in addition and complementarity to individuals or moral persons (see Chapter 16). The prevalent agency model of maximizing shareholder value, though, rejects this moral status of the business organization and consequently cannot respond to any addressee. And even if only the individual agent is considered, he or she cannot be held responsible by the principal for things other than shareholder value maximization (with Friedman's caveat of "engaging in open and free competition and without deception and fraud"; Friedman 1970, 282). If the *contents* of wealth creation and human rights are taken seriously, they cannot be simply reduced to a financial amount for which the enterprise or the agent is responsible to the owners of the shares, who, properly speaking, are not the owners of the enterprise (as argued in Bower & Paine 2017).

The creation and destruction of wealth have a much larger impact on multiple stakeholders, societies and nature, and thus the *addressees* of corporate responsibility cannot be limited to the shareowners. In the scandals of Volkswagen and Wells Fargo (destroying natural and economic capital on a large scale), the instances (or addressees) who required accountability were not only the shareholders and investors of these corporations (after the scandals broke), but also customers, employees, environmental organizations, communities and other entities – in addition, of course, to the judiciary institutions. Medtronic's responsibility for "alleviating pain, restoring health, and extending life" – that is, creating human capital – is directed towards patients, doctors and hospitals. Microcredits of the Grameen Bank can function well because trust – that is, social capital – is put into impoverished individuals and groups who respond by creating economic and human capital.

With regard to the creation of private and public wealth, the addressees can vary a great deal. Private wealth creation has to respond not only to the owners and other stakeholders of the enterprise, but also to the legal demands and social expectations of society. As for the creation of public wealth such as infrastructure projects and a fair and effective rule of law, the main addressees are public authorities and institutions based on the ethical foundation of human rights and well-being.

While it is not always easy to identify the addressees for wealth creation, it is most often straightforward to determine the addressees of corporate responsibility in the case of adverse human rights impacts. Enterprises causing racial discrimination are responsible for their policies towards the affected persons in the first place. Corporations contributing to childhood obesity by targeting high-sugar foods and drinks at children violate the right to health of the children to whom they are responsible. Licensees turning a blind eye on child labor in the supply chain bear responsibility for this exploitation towards the abused young people. In each case the addressees of corporate responsibility are clearly identifiable, based on the three criteria of the UN Guiding Principles. This, however, does not exclude additional addressees (like families, communities and institutional arrangements) who may rightly demand enterprises to live up to their responsibilities.

In sum, by impacting real persons, human rights violations can be understood as violations of the Golden Rule that balances self- and other-regarding motivations: "Treat the others as you want to be treated by them!" Or, do not violate the human rights of others as you do not want to have your human rights violated by them! It seems that the time has come for "rediscovering the Golden Rule for a globalizing world" (Enderle 2008) and re-evaluating this oldest moral principle in human history for today.

Notes

1 Please note that responsibility in the singular indicates the tripartite concept of responsibility including its subject, contents and addressees while responsibilities in the plural stands for specific contents of responsibility.

2 Further case studies about the creation and destruction of natural capital in China can be found in Enderle and Niu (2012): positive examples: Baosteel and Haworth; negative examples: Apple's supply chain and ConocoPhillips's oil spill.

3 The Investigation Report by Wells Fargo (Wells Fargo 2017) provides a sober analysis of the sales practice failures and requires a thorough reform and strict accountability. Yet the FT Big Read in the *Financial Times* (2019a) goes far beyond this report.

4 This does not mean that Medtronic has a perfect record. After Bill George left, the company faced serious problems with paying physicians for collaboration. In 2010, all internal policies and procedures around compensation and collaboration with US physicians were renewed and strengthened, and guiding principles were established to preserve the integrity of physician–patient relationships and to remain transparent about compensation and policies. See www.medtronic.com/us-en/health care-professionals/services/physician-collaboration/physician-payment-guidelines.html.

18 | Corporate Governance for Wealth Creation and Human Rights

Corporate governance, understood as the authoritative direction and control of the company, has to serve the purpose of the company. As explained in this book, the purpose of the company or business organization is to create wealth in the comprehensive sense and to respect human rights. Consequently, corporate governance of primarily economic organizations involves both an economic and an ethical dimension (to "walk on two legs"): it takes seriously the seven features of wealth creation as well as the UN Guiding Principles on Business and Human Rights.

In line with the tripartite concept of responsibility (see Chapter 15), corporate governance's responsibility can be analyzed with the following three questions: (1) Regarding the subject: who is responsible? (2) Regarding the contents: for what is the subject responsible? (3) Regarding the addressees: towards whom is the subject responsible?

As for the first question, the subject of responsibility is determined as "the board" in the sense used by the G20/OECD Principles of Corporate Governance (2015). The Principles are intended to guide any board structure, which may vary within and among countries. In countries with two-tier boards (that separate the supervisory function and the management function into different bodies), the Principles apply to the "supervisory board" composed of non-executive board members and the "management board" composed entirely of (key) executives. They also apply to the "unitary" boards, which bring together executive and non-executive board members in the same body, and to additional statutory bodies for audit purposes (p. 51). While the Principles focus on publicly traded companies, both financial and nonfinancial, they are also meant to be a useful tool to improve corporate governance for "all [other] companies, including smaller and unlisted companies" (p. 9).

With regard to the second and third questions, the contents and the addressees of corporate responsibility have been mapped extensively in Chapter 17. They are equally relevant to the board and thus define its responsibilities in terms of wealth creation and human rights. They distinguish themselves by their relatively specific economic nature and their relatively concrete ethical demands. What the contents and the addressees mean in even more specific and concrete terms will be exemplified in Chapter 19 with regard to income inequality in business organizations and society and in Chapter 20 with regard to worker participation in the global supply chains.

A Brief Overview of Different Conceptions of Corporate Governance

Corporate governance for wealth creation and human rights emphasizes a new perspective that can be placed in the context of the discussion about corporate governance in the last twenty-plus years.[1] In the 1990s corporate governance became the subject of a few important reports and publications, which, after the Enron and WorldCom scandals (2001–02) and the global financial crisis (2008–09), attracted a great deal of attention from policy makers, business leaders, media and scholars.

In the United Kingdom, in the wake of a series of corporate scandals, the Cadbury Report was published in 1992 (Cadbury Report 1992; Boyd 1996). It defines corporate governance as "the system by which companies are directed and controlled" (Cadbury Report 1992, 2.5) and proposes a code of best practices by focusing on the financial aspects with the broader intention of promoting good corporate governance as a whole (2.1). Sir Adrian Cadbury was instrumental in advancing a holistic conception of corporate governance internationally over many years. As he writes:

corporate governance is concerned with holding the balance between economic and social goals and between individual and communal goals. The corporate governance framework is there to encourage the efficient use of resources and equally to require accountability for the stewardship of those resources. The aim is to align as nearly as possible the interests of individuals, corporations and society. (Cadbury 2003)

In South Africa, after the abolition of the apartheid-regime, the King I Report on Corporate Governance was promulgated in 1994 to address the enormous challenges of racial integration from a business perspective (IOD 1994). The King II Report (IOD 2002) proposed an inclusive stakeholder approach (referred to as a "participative corporate governance system"; Rossouw 2006, 259). The King III Report (IOD 2009) expanded the reach to all forms of business and shifted its focus from "comply or explain" to "apply or explain." And the King IV Report (IOD 2016) aimed to address three shifts in the corporate world: (1) From financial capitalism to inclusive capitalism. (2) From short-term capital markets to long-term, sustainable markets. (3) From siloed reporting to integrated reporting. Moreover, it proposed to move from "apply or explain" to "apply and explain."

The Organisation for Economic Cooperation and Development (OECD) promulgated its Principles of Corporate Governance in 1999, defining corporate governance that "involves a set of relationships between a company's management, its board, its shareholders and other stakeholders ... [it] also provides the structure through which the objectives of the company are set, and the means of attaining those objectives and monitoring performance are determined" (OECD 1999, 11). Greater shareholder rights were advocated, but the stakeholder view of corporate governance was also acknowledged (if not endorsed; see the critique of Emmons & Schmid 2000, 63). The revised OECD Principles of 2004 (OECD 2004) reiterated, by and large, the main points of the 1999 document. In addition, they introduced a new first principle "ensuring the basis for an effective corporate governance framework," which emphasizes the importance of exercising the ownership rights by all shareholders and requires that the stakeholders should be able to freely communicate their concerns about illegal or unethical practices to the board.

After extensive consultations with all G20 countries, experts from key international institutions (Basel Committee, Financial Stability Boards, World Bank Group) and Regional Corporate Governance Roundtables in Latin America, Asia, the Middle East and North Africa, the G20/OECD Principles of Corporate Governance were endorsed in 2015 (G20/OECD 2015). They are "intended to help policy makers evaluate and improve the legal, regulatory, and institutional framework for corporate governance, with a view to support economic efficiency, sustainable growth and financial stability" (G20/OECD 2015, 9). They constitute "the international reference point and ... an effective tool for implementation" of corporate governance

(Angel Gurría, OECD Secretary-General in G20/OECD 2015, 3). With their six principles explained on sixty-one pages, they likely form the most comprehensive and detailed framework for corporate governance to date.

The crucial role of corporate governance is also emphasized in the UN Principles for Responsible Investment, launched in 2006 (www .unpri.org). They assess the responsibility of investment with the help of three ESG factors, namely the environmental, social, and governance factors. Although these factors are broadly defined and need some specification, they are highly relevant not only for assessing investment objects but also relevant for the self-evaluation of the board's governance performance.

In addition to these pioneering documents, four scholarly publications are briefly presented to indicate the wide range of different scientific approaches. In their influential article of 1997 "A Survey of Corporate Governance," Andrei Shleifer and Robert Vishny define corporate governance as an agency problem, based on the separation of management and finance. It emphasizes that "the opportunities for managers to abscond with financiers' funds, or to squander them on pet projects, are plentiful and well-documented." Therefore, "[t]he fundamental question of corporate governance is how to assure financiers that they get a return on their financial investment" (Shleifer & Vishny 1997, 773). The answer, in a nutshell, lies in establishing "mechanisms," namely "economic and legal institutions," which set the appropriate incentive systems to address this agency problem. While this approach undoubtedly deals with an important problem, it drastically limits corporate governance to this problem. It ignores the broader range of problems addressed in the Cadbury and King reports, the OECD Principles and multiple scholarly contributions (see below): the balance between economic and social goals, the role of stakeholders other than shareholders, the well-being of the company as a whole, and the long-term, sustainable markets, to name a few.

The widely received book *Corporate Governance* by Robert Monks and Nell Minow was published first in 1995 and ran into four more editions (2001, 2004, 2008, 2011). It also speaks of "mechanisms for directing corporate behavior," but it defines the purpose of the corporation in a much broader sense (Monks & Minow 2008, 12 ff.). The key players of corporate governance are the shareholders, directors, and management, while other stakeholders can only play an instrumental role to support these three key players. In their view, "'stakeholder' language, in legislation or in corporate charters, can camouflage neglect, whether intentional or unintentional, of the rights of shareholders" (48).

Martin Hilb has elaborated the concept of a "New Corporate Governance" enriched by long-standing practical board experiences since the 1990s. The sixth edition of the German version was issued in 2016 (Hilb 2016), while the book also appeared in several other languages (English, Vietnamese, Spanish, Chinese, Portuguese, Japanese and French). He supports the view "that the board of directors should both direct and control the firm" and therefore defines "New Corporate Governance" as a system "by which companies are strategically directed, *integratively* managed and holistically controlled in an entrepreneurial and ethical way and in a manner appropriate to each particular context" (Hilb 2008, 9f.; emphasis by the author). In contrast to the traditional approach, Hilb's new approach is decisively practice-oriented: (1) The implementation has to be appropriate to the specific context of the firm. (2) Strategic development is a central function of the supervisory board. (3) Selection, appraisal, compensation and development of the supervisory and management boards have to be integrated and targeted. (4) The results must be holistically monitored from the perspectives of shareholders, clients, employees and the public. Moreover, "a further cornerstone" of Hilb's definition of corporate governance is "an entrepreneurial and ethical orientation," which, however, has not been developed explicitly.

Against the backdrop of these previously presented notions of corporate governance, it is noteworthy that most of them do not articulate the distinct ethical character of corporate governance. Definitions, based on agency theory and transaction theory, even exclude, at least implicitly, the normative-ethical dimension, as demonstrated in a fine article by Thomas Donaldson (2012).[2] The task of explicitly addressing the ethical character of corporate governance has been taken up by Deon Rossouw and other scholars, who placed it on the agenda of the Third World Congress of the International Society of Business, Economics, and Ethics (ISBEE) in 2004 and published their contributions in 2006 (Roussow & Sison 2006), followed by further publications (Sison 2008; Roussow 2009a, 2009b, 2009c).

To describe and explain the ethical dimension of corporate governance is not easy, particularly from a global perspective. Therefore,

Rossouw (2009a) proposes three crucial distinctions, which can help, in a first step, to map out the ethical dimension:

(1) *The ethics of governance and the governance of ethics:* The ethics of corporate governance refers to the ethical values that underpin and guide a corporate governance regime on the regulatory or the enterprise level (Rossouw 2009c, 6 ff.). These values might be articulated openly and explicitly, or they might be invisible and not mentioned at all. *In any case, they exist and shape the regime.* If not articulated, they can be uncovered by asking, in whose interests ought companies to be run? Or, what are the objectives of a corporate governance regime? Then these interests and objectives can be assessed for how fair, responsible, or socially benevolent they are.

In contrast, the governance of ethics deals with the question how companies are required or recommended to manage their own ethical affairs. It is always presented in an explicit manner and concerns only one (that is, the ethical) aspect including *codes of ethics, rules of conduct, ethics auditing, etc.* Such requirements and expectations can originate from both the external and the enterprise levels of corporate governance.

(2) *External and internal corporate governance:* External corporate governance is by definition located outside of the corporation either in regulatory institutions (such as laws, professional standards, and listing requirements), or societal norms (such as social values, practices, and conventions), or in the market itself (such as corporate take-overs and acquisitions). That is at the macro-level of analysis.

Internal corporate governance refers to the direction and control exerted by a board and executive managers over the performance of a company; it means to steer the strategic direction and ensure that the company adheres to formal and informal standards of corporate behavior in a given context. Within the bounds of legal and social norms, the board and executive managers have considerable discretion to exercise internal corporate governance. That is at the meso- and micro-levels of the analysis.

(3) *Shareholder and stakeholder orientations in corporate governance:* This distinction is based on the question of whose interests the

corporate governance models prioritize in the exercise of corporate direction and control. Companies might be governed in the best interest of shareholders, either by deliberately excluding the interests of other stakeholder groups or by assuming that the focus on shareholders will benefit best all other stakeholders, though indirectly. In contrast, the stakeholder-oriented model means that corporate direction and control need to be exercised in the interest of all legitimate stakeholders, recognized in their own rights and not only used as mere vehicles for creating shareholder value.

These distinctions have been successfully applied to empirical investigations into corporate governance models in different regions around the world. Based particularly on the ethics of governance (that is, the explicit or implicit underpinning value system), the requirements and expectations at the regulatory and enterprise level, and the distinction of shareholder and stakeholder orientation, the study discovered quite different models: prevalent in Africa is the "inclusive" model, in Asia-Pacific the "expansive" model, in Continental Europe the "participatory" model and in North America the "shareholder-oriented" model (Roussow 2009c with numerous references). It is noteworthy that, from a global perspective, these results demonstrate a stark *divergence* rather than a convergence (postulated by various authors), due to context-specific factors such as the views of the corporation's role in society, the socio-cultural context, and some forms of ownership (like family ownership and the impact of the state).

It is noteworthy that the North American shareholder-oriented model was recently changed by the prestigious Business Roundtable[3] toward a stakeholder-oriented model, which affirms that "each of our stakeholders [customers, employees, suppliers, communities, and shareholders] is essential. We commit to deliver value to all of them, for the future success of our companies, our communities and our country" (Business Roundtable 2019).

Contributions to a New Perspective of Corporate Governance

Having briefly presented a selected number of pioneering reports and scholarly works, we may now ask how wealth creation and human rights can contribute to a new perspective of corporate governance. The comprehensive conception of wealth creation expands the narrow focus on financial capital used in many practical and theoretical approaches to corporate governance (like Shleifer and Vishny) and holds the board responsible for creating natural, economic, human and social capital, supported by an appropriate legal, regulatory and institutional framework in line with the G20/OECD Principles of Corporate Governance. If the production of financial capital is the exclusive objective, then environmental concerns, healthy and educated people, and trust relations among economic and social actors are not respected in their own right and suffer. Moreover, intergenerational sustainability cannot be achieved.

Because the wealth of a society, ranging from the local up to the global level, constitutes a combination of private and public wealth, the responsibility of the board cannot be limited to the creation of private wealth. It also has to contribute to the creation of public wealth, which can be done in multiple ways according to the specific context of the firm (Hilb). While the Cadbury and King Reports emphasize this public responsibility, the OECD Principles do not require this kind of responsibility, with the exception of Principle #5 on disclosure and transparency, a clearly stated public good. Furthermore, the scholarly works mentioned above (Shleifer and Vishny; Monks and Minow; Hilb) abstain from demanding public responsibility, unless the public interest counts as a stakeholder (which is criticized in Chapter 17).

A major contentious point in the practical and theoretical discussions of corporate governance has been to determine to which stakeholders the board is supposed to be responsible. Along with Shleifer and Vishny and Monks and Minow, mainstream economics and finance and a multitude of practitioners contend that the responsibility pertains only to the shareholders; other stakeholders such as employees, customers and suppliers would play, at best, an instrumental role to advance the interests of the shareholders. However, the range of stakeholders beyond the shareholder supremacy has broadened in the course of the last twenty-plus years. The Caux Round Table Principles of Business promulgated the stakeholder-oriented model in 1994 (including also competitors as one of six stakeholders; Caux Round Table 1994). The Cadbury and King Reports as well as the OECD Principles (most explicitly the Principles #4 of 2015) have affirmed the important role of several stakeholders for corporate governance. Moreover, Hilb's concept of a "new corporate governance" and

Rossouw and others' empirical findings in various regions of the world argue for and corroborate the stakeholder-orientation, respectively (see also Business Roundtable 2019 mentioned above). As explained in Chapter 17, the book agrees with the stakeholder approach in general; however, it determines the contents of corporate responsibilities – and also for the board – more specifically and adds to the affected stakeholders broader addressees such as society at large, future generations, and nature.

As the productive and distributive dimensions of wealth creation are intrinsically interrelated, corporate governance has to pay equal attention to the distributive side of directing and controlling the company. Aggregate growth numbers of revenues, expenditures and profits do not provide an adequate account of the company's creation of wealth. It is noteworthy that the G20/OECD Principles of 2015 want not only to "support investment as a powerful driver of growth" but also promote "inclusiveness" by "addressing the rights of these stakeholders [that is, millions of households holding their savings in the stock market and more than 200 million jobs provided by publicly listed companies] and their ability to participate in corporate wealth creation" (Gurría in G20/OECD 2015, 3). An important task of the board is to determine the pay policy of the company including CEO and board member compensation. Not surprisingly, the board has to deal with multiple ethical, economic, social and other challenges, which are discussed, to some extent, in Chapter 19.

If wealth creation is conceived in the comprehensive sense as proposed in this book, it cannot be just a material matter, but necessarily involves a spiritual dimension as well. As discussed in Chapter 7, spirituality relates to an ultimate reality and can be summarized as "the experience of a transformative connection" (Judy Neal 2013). Corporate governance has to radiate this spirit that can be inspired by religious or non-religious traditions. To serve on the board is not just a "job"; rather, it should be understood as a noble vocation or calling. To illustrate what this can mean, Catholic Social Teaching has offered "a reflection" (Vocation 2018). It is a kind of vade-mecum for business men and women to engage with the contemporary economic and financial world in light of the principles of human dignity and the common good.[4] Challenged by a greater meaning in life, board members (as any business men and women) are supposed to live up to this calling.

Creating sustainable wealth in terms of human capabilities puts people center stage (see Chapter 8). Based on the intergenerational definition of sustainability by the World Commission on Environment and Development, it substantiates "the needs" of the present generation and "the ability" of future generations to meet their own needs, and requires intergenerational justice: that the needs of the present generation be met without detriment to future generations. Sustainability in this sense should be an essential benchmark for corporate governance. This means, first of all, that short-termism is not acceptable from the economic as well as the ethical perspective. Then, focusing on real opportunities and substantial freedoms of people manifests itself in at least four ways: (a) by looking for multiple functionings and capabilities and building on their synergies, (b) by strengthening the relevant capabilities in stakeholder-dialogues, (c) by understanding the relations between capabilities and human rights and enforcing their links and (d) by using appropriate metrics such as GRI sustainability and ISO 26000 reporting with a view to direct and control corporate performance.

Creating has been defined in Chapter 9 as making something new and better. It is about making (not only thinking) and making better (not only new); in other words, it is about ethical innovation that is relevant at all levels of decision-making and action. At the meso-level, it not only pertains to the company's products and services, but also to its production processes, organization, culture and identity, and it is made feasible and successful in economic and financial terms. The role of corporate governance is to instigate, support and advance ethical innovation. The initiative may come from employees at any level, from outside the company, or from individual board members. The board needs to be open-minded, conscious of its ethical values, familiar with the initiative's potentials and limits and wise in its decision-making. To mention a timely example, the governance of digitalization presents major challenges today, full of tempting opportunities and uncertain risks. How to address these challenges at the board level is a question whose time has come. It is discussed, for instance, from multiple perspectives in *Governance of Digitalization. The Role of Boards of Directors and Top Management Teams in Digital Value Creation* (Hilb 2017). With the help of Hilb's framework (see above), four sets of recommendations are proposed: (1) Providing strategic directions for digitalization, (2) Controlling outcomes of digitalization, (3)

Promoting the culture for digital transformation, and (4) adapting the digital business approach to the context.

Dealing with Trade-offs

In addition to the contributions of wealth creation to corporate governance, the thirty internationally recognized human rights provide clear ethical guidance for the board. In contrast to a large part of the literature on corporate governance that does not address ethical issues in an explicit fashion (including Hilb's *Governance of Digitalization* [2017]), the respect for human rights (see Chapter 12) sets explicit ethical standards that specify in relatively concrete terms what Rossouw outlines above in broader terms. However, these are only minimal ethical standards, which involve both a great opportunity and a tough challenge: a great opportunity because, beyond these minima, the board has a wide space of freedom to choose its ethical standards; and a tough challenge because the board may face difficult trade-offs when trying to respect all human rights, given the limited available resources. For example, the fulfillment of the right to health may conflict with the fulfillment of the right to enjoy just and favorable conditions of work. However, these trade-offs of rights are substantially reduced, if not eliminated, when the three criteria of respect according to the UN Guiding Principles on Business and Human Rights are applied (that is, direct impact, indirect impact, and complicity of the company; see Chapter 15). Moreover, when the fulfillment of conflicting rights does not seem possible within limited available resources, it might be necessary to reallocate corporate resources to make this fulfillment possible.

Trade-offs can also arise with regard to wealth creation in the comprehensive sense. Should the company create more natural capital at the expense of economic capital? Should economic capital be increased to the detriment of social capital? Or should the company expand its contributions to public wealth by forgoing private wealth? These few questions indicate that, indeed, trade-offs may appear and thus need to be addressed. However, it is noteworthy that often they look like trade-offs at first glance, but, at a closer look, they are revealed to not exist. Recall the corporate examples for creating or destroying natural, economic, human and social capital (Chapter 17). Volkswagen intended to create economic capital; but, in fact, it destroyed natural, human and social capital, and finally economic capital as well. Wells Fargo pretended to create economic capital (by broadening the customer base); however, it actually reduced human and social capital and ended up with less economic capital as well. On the other hand, positive examples can also show "win-win" – not "trade-off" – situations: Medtronic's focus on creating healthy people (that is, human capital) significantly helps to increase economic and social capital. The Grameen Bank's emphasis on trust relations with poor, mostly female, borrowers has been a major reason for its economic success and educational impact.

Still, trade-offs between creating one or another type of capital can, and do, occur. Frequent examples are trade-offs between natural and economic capital. It is not always possible to achieve "eco-efficiency" (that is, combining ecological and economic efficiency; see Chapter 2). An increase of natural capital can require high economic costs, that is, a decrease of economic capital.

To address this issue, the triple distinction of "the balanced concept of the firm" can help by differentiating three levels of ethical claims (see Chapter 12): minimal ethical requirements, social obligations beyond the minimum, and aspirations for ethical ideals (De George 1993). Accordingly, the creation of each type of capital can be divided into these three levels: the minimal, the social obligation and the aspirational level. While trade-offs between any type of capital at the minimal level are not acceptable (as it is the case with human rights), they are allowed at the second and third levels. It is then up to the judgment of the board to decide the mix of wealth creation in terms of natural, economic, human and social capital.

Similar considerations also apply to the mix of creating private and public wealth. At the minimal level, no trade-offs are permissible; for example, legal and regulatory obligations to contribute to the creation of public wealth (say, the construction of infrastructure) are binding. Beyond the minimal requirements, the board may decide the extent to which the company should contribute to creating public wealth in terms of one or more types of capital. It goes beyond saying that genuine public wealth (not disguised private wealth) must be created (see Summers's critique of Donald Trump's investment plans for infrastructure projects in Chapter 17).

A further discussion about applying "the balanced concept of the firm" to the board's decisions of creating wealth and respecting human rights goes beyond the scope of this book. What matters for now is that internal corporate governance (supported by external corporate governance; see Rossouw 2009a) needs both clear minimal ethical standards and good judgment and wisdom to deal with the trade-offs beyond the minima in a responsible manner.[5]

Notes

1 The noun "governance" and the verb "to govern" stem from the Latin verb "gubernare," that is, "to steer." The Merriam-Webster's Collegiate Dictionary defines "govern" (verb) as "to exercise continuous sovereign authority over something, *especially:* to control and direct the making and administration of policy." www.merriam-webster.com/dictionary/govern.

2 It should be noted that the Business Ethics Quarterly had published a special issue on corporate governance in January 2001, shortly before the Enron scandal erupted.

3 "About Us: Business Roundtable is an association of chief executive officers of America's leading companies working to promote a thriving US economy and expanded opportunity for all Americans through sound public policy." www.businessroundtable.org/about-us.

4 This document shares many concerns, views and proposals of this book, among others the ascending methodology of "seeing, judging, and acting" (similar to the "action-oriented" approach to business and economic ethics), the importance and problems of globalization, sustainability and financialization (see Chapter 2), the principles of human dignity and solidarity with the poor. Unfortunately, human rights are not mentioned at all (with one exception in No. 20), although they are concrete expressions of human dignity and promulgated in the Encyclical *Pacem in Terris* (John XXIII 1963) and confirmed by the Second Vatican Council (1965). Further, the concept of wealth is rather narrow, and its creation refers only to production and does not include a distributive dimension.

5 These difficult situations are often called "ethical dilemmas," in which no possible option has a clear and satisfactory ethical solution. Nonetheless, the pressure of making a decision cannot be avoided and thus demands ethical scrutiny and reasoning. With regard to the ethics in finance and banking, Paul Dembinski diligently applies this approach to ethical dilemmas in his book *Ethics and Responsibility in Finance* (2017).

19 | *A Case in Point: Corporate Responsibility for Less Income Inequality*

Introduction

In the wake of the Great Recession, inequality of income and wealth has attracted much attention in public debates and scholarly discussions. While the financial crisis and its aftermath hit large segments of the population in many countries, surprisingly, small segments were spared or even experienced an increase in their share of income and wealth. Moreover, it became manifest that increasing inequality has actually been a long-term trend since the 1980s. These developments are now documented in many publications; see, for instance: Frank (2007), Wilkinson & Pickett (2009), Piketty (2014, 2015), Wolf (2014), Atkinson (2015), Stiglitz (2015), Foreign Affairs (2016), King (2016), Boushey et al. (2017), Atkinson (2019).

It is noteworthy that these inequality concerns relate primarily to inequality of income and wealth within and between countries, the main unit of analysis being countries. However, there is much less literature on income inequality within organizations in general and within business organizations in particular.[1] As Andrew Hill (2016) writes, opening up corporate pay data to the public seems to open a Pandora's box that would cause many companies excessive disruption and emotional upheaval (see also Colella et al. 2007). Or, less demanding, but still potentially revelatory is the recent rule of the U.S. Securities and Exchange Commission that requires public companies to disclose the ratio of the compensation of their chief executive officer (CEO) to the median compensation of their employees, mandated by the Dodd-Frank Wall Street Reform and Consumer Protection Act (2015).

Indeed, concrete examples illustrate the extreme disparity of pay in numerous US corporations. A single mother working at Walmart earned $9 an hour and was reliant on the US government to pay her $294 a month in food stamps (which were spent at Walmart; Whipp &

Fleming 2016) while Doug McMillon, CEO of Walmart, was paid $22.4 million in 2016 (Fortune 2017). Another example is the pay ratio between Greg Wasson, CEO of Walgreens (in 2014), and the median employee. While the median employee pay was $28,700, Wasson's compensation package (including base salary, bonuses, stocks and awards) amounted to $16.7 million, that is, 582 times more (Chicago Magazine 2015).

Furthermore, except for a few recent articles (Davis & Cobb 2010; Cobb 2016; Tsui et al. 2016, 2018), little recent literature exists on the important question of how income inequality in organizations actually impacts – and should impact – income inequality within countries and worldwide. Cobb (2016) theorized that the power of executives and stakeholders influences the criteria firms use to hire and reward employees and their executives. The pay policies in turn shape societal-level income inequality. Cobb offered no data to support his conjecture. Tsui et al. (2016) provided statistics on the relationship between the Gini coefficient of income inequality for twenty-three OECD countries and the ratio of CEO pay to average employee pay in these same twenty-three countries for each of the four years from 2011 to 2014. The lagged correlation coefficients (national Gini coefficient lags CEO-employee pay ratio by one or more years) ranged from 0.63 to 0.71, all significant at less than 0.01 level. These data support the observation by economists (for example, Atkinson 2015; Stiglitz 2015) that earned income is the major contributor of society-level income inequality. Regarding the literature of business ethics, income inequality in companies has not been a topic in many textbooks (Velasquez 2006; Crane & Matten 2010; De George 2010; Wicks et al. 2010; Painter-Morland & Ten Bos 2011; DesJardins 2014) and has been addressed only recently (Beal & Astakhova 2017; Bapuji et al. 2018). Tsui et al. (2016, 2018, 2019) call for more research in understanding how organizational pay policies may contribute to inequality both inside the organization and in the society and in considering the possibility and desirability of reducing the extremely high level of income inequality in corporations.

This chapter is a response to this call. It aims to explore two questions: First, how should we define corporate responsibility for less income inequality *in business organizations*? And second, how should we define corporate responsibility for less income inequality *in society at large*?[2]

Corporate Responsibility for Less Income Inequality in Business Organizations

As explained in Chapter 15, the concept of responsibility has become a key concept in contemporary ethical thinking – both in practical life and in scholarship. As a relational concept, it is "anchored" in one or more actors (*who* is responsible?), relates to an authority or addressee *to whom* one is responsible and concerns a very concrete matter *for which* one is responsible. As moral actors, we include – as the UN Guiding Principles do – all business enterprises, located at the meso- and micro-levels of action. They bear "corporate responsibility" and can be held responsible for their conduct in an ethical sense. While Chapters 16, 17 and 18 extensively discussed the tripartite concept of responsibility applied to business enterprises, this chapter focuses on the contents of corporate responsibility with regard to the precise question: How much less income inequality are business enterprises responsible for? To answer this question, we first clarify the exact basis of inequality and the notion of "less" income inequality.

The basis of inequality under investigation is the *income or earnings in monetary and non-monetary terms*, which the individuals of the company receive for their *work*, be they workers, employees or leaders. These payments are made by the employer and can include monetary benefits (for example, wages, premiums for pension funds, shares) as well as in-kind benefits (for example, child care); hence, they are not provided by sources outside the employing organization like food stamps granted by the government or charitable contributions by philanthropic civil organizations. Earning income means having a job and an entitlement, which is different from consumption. Discussing the difference between income and consumption as basis of inequality, Atkinson concludes "to continue to focus on income as an indicator of potential control over resources. The use of income is indeed recognition that the use of resources [that is, income] goes beyond consumption" (Atkinson 2015: 35). This holds true at the lower and upper ends of the distribution of income. The minimum-rights approach to poverty – as distinct from the standard-of-living approach – conceives the disposal of resources as a matter for individual decisions (including about saving), and high income conveys power that extends beyond consumption. It goes without saying that income and job are only two, though crucial, components of human well-being. Many more components are relevant, pointed out in the OECD well-being framework discussed in Chapter 4.

Related to income as the basis is the question of the *unit* for which the income is earned. Is it the individual person who actually works in the organization? Or is it the family which may include a spouse and children? Or is it the (broader) household that may have additional members such as grown-up children and other adult relatives or friends? This question of the unit is particularly important for low-income earners and definitions of minimum and living wages, which will be discussed below.

A further clarification concerns the notion of "less" income inequality. To begin with, the claim does not require no income inequality at all, as if income equality were the goal. What we propose is to focus on the *direction towards* less income inequality. Thereby, less can be qualified in different ways. Under one definition, less can pertain to the whole distribution of income in the organization and affect all levels of income, which can be measured by the commonly used Gini coefficient or other coefficients (see Lüthi 1980).

Another way to define "less" is to divide the whole income distribution into segments and look at the potential of each segment to reduce the overall inequality. In the low-income segment, less inequality can be achieved by raising the lowest incomes to the (legally required) minimum-wage level or even to the (higher) living-wage level and by increasing the minimum wage to the living wage, assuming the living wage as the ethically required minimal income. Similarly, income inequality in the organization can be reduced by decreasing the top incomes down to the lower level which is ethically acceptable. A third way of achieving less income inequality can focus on the segment between the living wage and the acceptable top income level, reducing the inequality within this range of incomes. Additional ways discussed in the literature concentrate on the ratio between a bottom and a top segment, for example, the lowest 20 percent and the top 20 percent or the low 99 percent and the top 1 percent.

Among these different ways we suggest choosing as benchmarks the living wage at the lower end and the "acceptable" top income at the higher end, which may be called "a decent, arguable and feasible proposition" that can be supported by strong arguments. If one takes the entire income distribution as basis and measures its inequality with the Gini coefficient (for instance), it is hard to argue that a certain value (for example, 0.3) should be achieved. No easier would be the argument for reducing the ratio between the bottom and the top to a certain number: claiming, for instance, that Greg Wasson's compensation package should be no more than 50 (instead of 582) times of the median employee pay of Walgreens.

Furthermore, it seems very difficult to provide a rationale to reduce the range of incomes *between* the living wage and the "acceptable" top income by a certain amount in relative or absolute terms. This range is strongly shaped by the dispersion of earnings which, to a large extent, depends on supply and demand on the labor markets (influenced, in turn, by the economic and social context). To the extent that the dispersion of earnings reflects the distribution of acquired skills of workers, less income inequality would disrespect the well-deserved dispersion of earnings.

Moreover, focusing on the minimum wage instead of the living wage might be a first step to reduce income inequality in the company. But it is insufficient and might be misleading. The minimum wage is normally set by the legislature, often at a very low level and behind the times, and does not necessarily meet the needs of income workers adequately. It is the outcome of political bargaining which often lacks economic and ethical reasoning. Since its actual strength lies in the argument for a living wage, one might better argue for a living wage directly.

Let's now turn to our "decent, well arguable and feasible proposition" with the living wage at the lower end and the "acceptable" top income at the higher end of the distribution. For both benchmarks, we will examine important ethical and economic aspects.

Corporate Responsibility for Paying at Least Living Wages

As a first approximation, the living wage can be defined as "the amount of money a full-time employee needs to either afford the basic necessities in life or exceed the poverty threshold. It is based on the principle that people working full-time should make enough money to financially support their families" (Collins 2018). The living wage is an old demand and has raised a great deal of controversy up to the present time.

The contentious issues fall in three groups. The first set of questions concerns *the kind of claims* a full-time worker may have for a living wage. A clear answer can be found in the Universal Declaration of

Human Rights 1948, which states in Article 23.3: "Everyone who works has the right to just and favorable remuneration ensuring for himself and his family an existence worthy of human dignity, and supplemented, if necessary, by other means of social protection." A second group of questions relates to *the addressees* of this right claim. Is it the employer who is responsible for paying a living wage or is it the government (at the local, regional or state level) which bears this responsibility? Or do the private and public sectors share this obligation and, if so, in what ways? The third set of questions regards *the substantive content* of the claim: How should the living wage be conceptualized and measured? To what unit should it relate: to the family, the household or the individual?

A brief historic retrospection shows that the living wage became a "social question" with the Industrial Revolution, although under different terms. Adam Smith advocated "liberal wages" which are higher than the bare wage minimum of the individual worker (Smith 1976: 98–99; see also Stabile 1997). More than 100 years later, Pope Leo XIII (1891) published the encyclical *Rerum Novarum: On Capital and Labor*, in which he addressed the problem of fair wages (Leo 1891, No. 43–46). A few years later appeared two influential publications, which masterfully discussed the living wage for a country and the responsibility of business: *Industrial democracy* by Sidney and Beatrice Webb (1897) which advanced the doctrine of the living wage for Great Britain and defended it in economic terms; and *A Living Wage: Its Ethical and Economic Aspects* by John A. Ryan, in the United States (1912). Since the 1900s discussions about the living wage have taken many turns from the insistence in the "economic law of supply and demand in the labor markets" to the social movement for living wages in the United States and the promotion of the United Nations Guidelines on Business and Human Rights (2011). Donald Stabile (2008) offers an informative history of the ups and downs in economic thought from Plato and Aristotle to Adam Smith, Arthur Okun and Amartya Sen. Jerold Waltman (2004) updated and expanded Ryan's work. Andrea Werner and Ming Lim (2016) present a masterly review and research agenda on the ethics of the living wage, referring also to the few articles on living wage questions in business ethics journals (McMahon 1985; Arnold & Bowie 2003, 2007; Zwolinski 2007; Karnes 2009; Preiss 2014). Moreover, the literature on business and human rights has increased considerably in recent years (see Part II).

We now attempt to make the ethical *and* the economic cases that companies should pay at least a living wage to all their employees. Against the deterministic economic law of supply and demand in the labor markets, it is assumed (as an empirical fact) that business organizations and their leaders in the free-enterprise system do have some space of freedom and power to decide on the low wages of their employees. Hence they bear ethical responsibility for these decisions – recalling the principle: with (great) power comes (great) responsibility.

The ethical case of corporate responsibility for a living wage can be grounded in the *human right* enshrined in Article 23.3 of the Universal Declaration of Human Rights mentioned above: "Everyone who works has the right to just and favorable remuneration ensuring for himself and his family an existence worthy of human dignity ..." While this declaration of 1948 did not directly call upon business to respect human rights, it has been directly applied in 2011 to business with the UN Guiding Principles on Business and Human Rights. These principles state that companies are responsible for their *direct adverse impact on human rights*:

The responsibility to respect human rights requires that business enterprises:

(a) Avoid causing or contributing to adverse human rights impacts through their own activities, and address such impacts when they occur;
(b) Seek to prevent or mitigate adverse human rights impacts that are directly linked to their operations, products or services by their business relationships, even if they have not contributed to those impacts. (UN 2011, #13)

Therefore, because companies with their pay policy have a direct impact on each employee, they are ethically responsible to pay just and favorable remuneration that ensures for each employee and his family an existence worthy of human dignity. In addition, with moral imagination and entrepreneurial spirit, most companies do also have the capacity to honor this right, if not immediately, then in the longer term. Innovation should help improve the quality of jobs without reducing their quantity – a clear opportunity for "creating wealth" (which means making new and better things; see Chapter 9). In short, corporate responsibility is about self-commitment originating from freedom in the concrete challenge of paying living wages (see the definition of responsibility in Chapter 15).

This right to a living wage is based on the employees' personal dignity and their right to a decent livelihood as citizens and not merely as productive forces. Personal dignity means to be capable of living a decent life and having the means for subsistence and decency not only for the employee herself but also for her family with one or several children until they are grown-up adults. The living wage is relative to the socio-economic standards of the community in which the employee lives and necessarily varies in time and space. Although it is not easy to determine the precise living wage, it can be done within a certain range of imprecision (see, for example, the Alice Report 2018[3]). Moreover, it must be done if the ethical and economic reasons for a living wage are taken seriously.

Complementary to the ethical arguments, strong *economic* reasons in both micro- and macroeconomic terms can be advanced to support corporate responsibility for paying living wages (related to the meso-level). Some considerations go back to Adam Smith, while some have been developed since then. According to Smith, and supported by many subsequent scholars, if the employees are recognized and paid as valuable collaborators, most of them are better motivated for work and become more productive. Employers may pay and benefit from "efficiency wages," which are set at above the market clearing rate in order to encourage workers to increase their productivity (implying that the price system in the labor market may not work under these circumstances). If their basic human capabilities are enhanced (Sen 1999), companies may benefit in various ways: through stronger identification of the employees with the corporate mission, improved self-esteem, health and skills, more proactive behavior and willingness to cooperate, and other advantages. Forward-looking companies understand their educational role in facing globalization and technological change.

Extending Donald Stabile's (2008) history of economic thought, there are three sets of arguments for a living wage that are of micro- and macro-economic relevance: sustainability, capability and externality. *Sustainability* requires that the labor force should not be depleted, but rather renewed and strengthened. Parasitic trades and businesses which do not pay living wages take more from nature, people and society than they give back and hence are unsustainable.

The *capability* argument takes employees seriously not merely as productive forces but as human beings, supporting thus the arguments about "efficiency wages" mentioned above. Wages should enable them to improve their abilities as members of both the organization and society. To the extent that wages have a positive correlation with employee productivity, higher wages pay for themselves through higher productivity (Akerlof & Yellen 1988).

The *externality* argument claims that not paying living wages causes net negative externalities, meaning it hurts third parties who are not involved in the supply and demand of wages. One can argue that the earner of less than a living wage does not get the resources necessary for a decent survival. If this lack of resources is not to hurt the earner herself, support has to come from other persons (for example, family members) and institutions (for example, government or charities) and can take the form of private and/or public goods. In any case, it is normally not the employer who bears these costs.

Against all these arguments in favor of a living wage, one may object that this proposition, though decent and well argued, is not feasible. To raise very low wages to the level of living wages is too expensive for companies, due to three types of reasons: competitive pressure from the labor market, insufficient productivity of low-wage earners and allocation of revenues for more important corporate expenses. If they are forced by law to do so, they may have to lay off people who then need to be supported by government or charity organizations. To respond to these difficulties, several considerations should be noted: (1) Many companies do have sufficient space of freedom to pay for this kind of pay rise.[4] (2) The expenses of such a pay rise are normally not enormous in relation to the corporate balance-sheet when using moral imagination (see, for example, Ciulla 2015). (3) If the pay rise is a heavy burden for the company, it can be staggered and introduced over a longer period of time. (4) To cover the expenses of this increase of wages, a redistribution of wages within the company is possible; that is, through the reduction of top wages to an "ethically acceptable" level (see below).

To conclude, our discussion of corporate responsibility for paying at least living wages has focused on developed countries. It goes without saying that the challenge of a living wage is not limited to these countries. With globalization and the increasing interconnectedness of economies and societies, the struggle for living wages has also become an urgent matter in the global economy in general and in global supply chains in particular (see Chapter 20). Therefore, much work in research on living wages in international business remains to be done.

Corporate Responsibility for Ethically Acceptable Top Incomes

Having dealt with the living wage as the required floor of the income distribution in the business organization, we now turn to the more difficult question of identifying and justifying the ethically acceptable ceiling of top incomes (which stands here for CEO pay) in the organization. This step is necessary if our proposition aims to reduce the income inequality in the organization. If a ceiling is not set, it is possible, even with a fixed floor, that inequality increases. For top incomes may continue to grow even with an established living wage level.

As Randall Thomas and Jennifer Hill (2012, 1) note, executive compensation has been brought again to center stage and onto the regulatory agenda, due to recent corporate scandals and crises, including the global financial crisis. Moreover, Atkinson observes that "the explosion of very high salaries occurred in some developed countries but not others. This suggests that institutional differences between countries rather than general and a priori universal causes such as technological change played a central role" (Atkinson 2015, 315).

Thomas and Hill (2012) offer a history and explanations of executive compensation. This chapter focuses on the question of how and to what extent executive compensation should not exceed an ethically acceptable ceiling.

In the following we concentrate on the United States to provide a concrete understanding of the dollar amounts of CEO pay (including base salary, bonuses, stock options and other pay; see Kolb 2012; Pozen & Kothari 2017):

Across all companies [based on the S&P 500], the average CEO pay was $13.8 million per year [in 2014], the average median worker pay was about $77,800 and the average ratio of CEO pay to median worker pay was 204. In other words, on average, CEOs earn around 204 times what his or her median worker earns. (Chamberlain 2015)

David Zaslav, 2014 CEO of Discovery Comm., ranked number 1 with $156,077,914 (median employee pay: $80,000; ratio: 1,951). In contrast, for example, W. Craig Jelinek, CEO of Costco Wholesale, made $5.6 million (median employee pay: $30,555; ratio: 184) and many CEOs of small- and medium-sized companies earn less than $1 million.

There are several ethical and economic arguments that strongly support a drastic reduction of executive compensation while leaving open the question as to how much in absolute and relative terms this reduction should be (see Moriarty 2005, 2009).

A first ethical consideration concerns the understanding of the business organization. If it is conceived as a community of persons (see Chapter 16), human relations – be they direct or indirect – exist between persons. Expectations for solidarity and mutual respect arise and – if met – are a strong motivational force for collaboration and the attitude of "being in the same boat." This is not the case if the organization is essentially understood as a piece of property, a production function or a nexus of contracts.

Given the extremely wide dispersion of income, a sense of fairness impels one to ask how the various stakeholders of the company, particularly employees and shareholders, should be rewarded in proportion to their respective contributions to the company's performance (see also Ghoshal 2005). Respect for human dignity also requires that every employee earns at least a living wage. What appears to be clear is that limit*less* executive compensation is not ethically acceptable while the incomes of employees and shareholders are limited.

Consequently, we may ask on what grounds executive compensation can arguably be limited and who has the authority to impose such limitations. Standard arguments in the literature are the exercise of power, the forces of the market and performance for pay based on merit. According to Thomas and Hill (2012),

Managerial power theorists argue that American CEOs dominate friendly boards of directors comprised of their loyal subordinates and largely passive outsiders. These compliant directors and their well-paid, amenable compensation consultants will . . . make little attempt to negotiate the CEO's pay in a manner that forcefully protects the shareholders' interest. Rather, they will prefer to rely on industry surveys of pay levels, which have the (un)intended consequence of continuously ratcheting up executive pay levels. (p. 1)

In other words, American CEOs are so powerful that their pay can be limited only by themselves. A second school of thought advocates the optimal contracting theory, which explains executive compensation and its limitation by optimal contracting:

Executive compensation contracts are designed to maximize shareholder value net of contracting costs and transaction costs. Thus ... executive contracts minimize agency costs and the costs of any residual divergence of interests between a principal and agent. Contracts reflect the underlying US corporate governance system, which although imperfect may in fact be extremely good given the existence of information costs, transaction costs, and the existing legal and regulatory system. (pp. 1–2)

In this view the limitation of executive compensation is based on the agency theory that accounts for information and transaction costs and the legal and regulatory framework. To the extent that agency theory is theoretically sound, costs are accurately accounted for and the framework reflects the preferences of the citizens, then executive pay is explained at whatever level it is set.

A third school of thought argues that executive compensation is grounded on corporate performance. As performance has increased in the preceding year, the executive should get a correspondingly higher pay, and if it has decreased, the pay should be lowered accordingly. Often the pay package has been endowed with stock options or other forms of equity-based compensation. However, the linking of these forms of compensation to corporate value has proved that stock options have little downside risk and can allow executives to exploit their informational advantages over shareholders.

These three sets of arguments can explain, to some extent, the current situation of executive compensation in the United States and therefore help design effective measures to limit excessive pay. However, they also have serious theoretical flaws and often are not validated by empirical studies (see Tsui et al. 2018). The power argument may explain (part of) the status-quo of executive compensation; but it cannot justify it in normative terms. One can also assume that the CEOs have the freedom to reduce their compensation, when they are free to determine their current high compensation. If top executives, boards of directors, shareholders or other stakeholders are not able or willing to contain the explosion of high salaries, it is the role of government to step in and set limitations. The agency theory has proven deficient, if not dangerous, in the global financial crisis (Bower & Paine 2017) and cannot justify the status quo. As for pay for performance, it is not based on theoretically and practically sound merits of executives, and, if proposed, it should be applied consistently in both up- and downturns of performance. However, research has shown no correlation between CEO pay and firm performance (Bebchuk & Fried 2006; Martin 2011; Marshall & Lee 2016). Even during the period of 1980 to 2010, executive compensation increased four times while corporate earnings declined slightly (Martin 2011).

In conclusion, we argue for a drastic reduction of executive compensation in the United States. This proposition is based on the undeniable fact that executives do have a relatively large space of freedom in their decision-making. They can use it and are ethically responsible for their actions. The arguments for the status quo are hardly convincing, while ethical considerations strongly support such reduction. Gains from these cuts can be used for internal redistribution of income in the company, research on innovation, educational programs for employees and other productivity and motivation enhancing policies. Far from being harmful to the organization, these and other measures are quite effective in enhancing the productivity of the organization.

Having argued for a drastic reduction of executive compensation, we are still left with the question of how much this reduction should be in absolute and relative terms. Unfortunately, given the current state of literature, this question remains unanswered – and I do not offer an answer either – even if we do not seek a precise amount and rather accept only a certain range of pay as the ceiling of executive compensation (for example, of $5–7 million). Nevertheless, several recommendations may help to move toward practical solutions (see Atkinson 2015: 133–54, 179–204): (1) Strengthening and expanding the transparency of top incomes in business organizations (already initiated in the Dodd-Frank Act). (2) Giving a say to the shareowners with regard to executive pay. (3) Establishing voluntary pay codes in companies. (4) Adopting a pay limit in the public sector. (5) Promoting "a national conversation" about the distribution of income, the distribution of the gains from a growing economy and the extent to which those in the middle and below are being left behind.

Having considered corporate responsibility for living wages and executive compensation within the boundaries of the business organization, we now ask what companies should contribute to society at large with regard to the challenges of living wages and executive compensation.

Corporate Responsibility for Less Income Inequality in Society

As mentioned in the introduction, so far little literature exists on the important question of how income inequality in organizations actually impacts and should impact income inequality within countries and worldwide. However, we can assume with good reason that such a relationship exists. Earned income is the major contributor of society-level income inequality (see Atkinson 2015; Stiglitz 2015) and there is a strong correlation between the Gini coefficient of income inequality for twenty-three OECD countries and the ratio of CEO pay to average pay in these same twenty-three countries for each year from 2011 to 2014 (Tsui et al. 2016).[5]

With our focus on the normative-ethical dimension of this relationship, we now ask how corporate responsibility should be defined for less income inequality in society at large. The answer – in a nutshell – is twofold: First, the ethical responsibility of the business organization consists in setting a good example by reducing income inequality as proposed above within its own boundaries. Second, corporate responsibility goes beyond "keeping one's house in order" and requires acting responsibly as a "corporate citizen" in society. While wealth, well-being and public goods and bads are important to adequately assess the economic situation of income earners, our perspective is limited here on inequality of income alone.

Setting a Credible Example and Supporting Initiatives in Society to Reduce Income Inequality

Before placing ethical demands on others, one has to ask oneself what responsibilities one has to bear oneself. Similarly, the ethical responsibility of a business organization is, first of all, a challenge for the organization itself that wants to act in a proactive manner, irrespective of its competitive environment. As explained above, corporate responsibility for less income inequality requires paying at least living wages and establishing ethically acceptable top incomes. By living up to these standards, the company makes an important contribution to the reduction of income inequality not only in its own organization but also in society. In addition, it sets a credible example for other companies and proves that such a policy is feasible.

While fully recognizing this contribution, corporate responsibility, however, demands more for several reasons. In order to implement those standards nationally and internationally, pioneering conduct by individual companies – even if they are numerous – will not be sufficient. What is needed is a level playing field, which prevents good companies from getting punished and encourages them to maintain income inequality reduction plans. Because living wages vary in space and time, they have to be determined in a scientific manner according to the relevant circumstances. More difficult is the determination of the ethically acceptable ceiling of top incomes, which needs a certain consensus in society that lies beyond the control of companies. Even more manifest are the limitations of what companies can contribute when looking at the broader context of wealth, well-being and public goods and bads.

Still, despite multiple economic, social, legal and other constraints, companies in a free enterprise system do have some space of freedom to make contributions to society beyond the profit rationale. But they have to use their freedom, and they should not be satisfied with reactive attitudes and behavior.

These contributions should help to establish "a decent, arguable and feasible policy," nationally and internationally, with two main objectives: securing living wages and establishing ethically acceptable top incomes.

In view of the developments of income inequality in the last thirty-plus years, it would be naïve to assume that these two objectives could be achieved in societies without strong legislation. The establishment of both a floor and a ceiling of income distribution has faced and will face fierce opposition from many circles in society. Therefore, Atkinson (2015, 153f.) is certainly right that "a national conversation" about the distribution of income is necessary. All social groups should be included: organizations in business and the economy, in politics and in civil society. So business organizations, too, have to play an indispensable and constructive role.

However, this conversation must not falter and fizzle out. Much is at stake. It needs persistent struggle for consensus, legal commitment and clear orientation. The two ethical guidelines elaborated in this chapter point to appropriate legislation which has to be supported by companies: first, to establish a law that guarantees a living wage to all employees in private and public organizations; and, second, to enact a strong progressive income tax that discourages businesses from paying incomes to top executives beyond the ethically acceptable ceiling.

On the long way to such legislation, many initiatives can be undertaken in the meantime, some of them mentioned above: not obstructing the efforts of raising the minimum wage in many cities and countries; supporting Oxfam's initiative for a living wage in global supply chains; strengthening and expanding the transparency of top incomes in business organizations; giving a say to shareowners with regard to executive pay; establishing voluntary pay codes in companies; and adopting a pay limit in the public sector.

Conclusion

Nationally and internationally, we are facing an urgent concern about increasing income inequality in our societies, manifested sometimes by passionate expressions of helplessness and anger, followed sometimes by a call for tough laws. Unfortunately, income inequality is an extremely complex problem that cannot be solved with some simple measures and without the active involvement of many social actors, including business organizations.

As argued in this chapter, less income inequality can be achieved within companies by granting living wages and drastically reducing top incomes, supported by strong economic and ethical arguments. Moreover, as "good corporate citizens," companies can support legislation for a living wage and an ethically acceptable ceiling of executive pay. Because such legislation has a long way to go, still many initiatives can be taken with no further ado and a wide range of research opportunities is opening up.

Notes

1 Organizational theory has rarely focused directly on income distribution within organizations, although they deal with fairness issues extensively. The literature on "organizational justice" (as part of organizational theory) deals with fairness perceptions within companies that generate attitudes and behaviors of employees (see Greenberg 1987). However, it addresses explicitly neither underlying empirical pay dispersion nor social justice in a normative-ethical sense.

2 Thus the chapter also helps clarify the Sustainable Development Goal #10: *Reduced Inequality*.

3 A recent initiative to improve the lives of vulnerable, low-income households in the United States is the United Way ALICE Project. **Alice** stands for **Asset Limited, Income Constrained, Employed** and is a way of defining and understanding the men and women who work hard, earn above the federal poverty level, but not enough to afford a basic household budget of housing, child care, food, transportation, and health care. According to the Alice Report (2018), in 2016 the survival household budget in St. Joseph County, Indiana (population: 269,141) was $19,716 for a single adult and $54,564 for a family (one infant and one pre-kindergarten child), compared to the US poverty rates of $12,140 and $25,100, respectively. Out of the 97,071 households, there were 16 percent under the poverty rate plus 27 percent under the survival budget; only 57 percent of all households had a survival budget and more.

4 Two examples may illustrate the discretionary power companies have to set pay policies and pay practices. After the scandal of fourteen suicides of workers broke in 2010, Foxconn doubled the wages of workers (Forbes 2012; Lei Guo et al. 2012). Walmart and Costco operate in the same industry. Even though they cater to different market segments, their employees perform essentially the same work, stocking shelves or checking out customers. Walmart uses many part-time employees with no benefits; Costco employs mostly fulltime workers with full benefits (see Tsui et al. 2018). Moreover, the minimum wages at Walmart and Costco have differed substantially, even after the minimum wage increase at Walmart to USD 11.00 (in January 2018) and at Costco to USD 14.00 (in June 2018) (Nassauer 2018).

5 This strong correlation suggests that income inequalities *between* firms and industries might not have a major influence on the overall income inequality in society at large.

20 | A Case in Point: How Can Universities Promote Corporate Responsibility in Their Supply Chains? The Experience of the University of Notre Dame

Introduction: Setting the Stage

Universities[1] are not only institutions of higher education; they also constitute powerful economic actors as employers of hundreds or thousands of employees, as collectors of millions of dollars of tuition fees, as investors in buildings, equipment and pension plans, as organizers of multiple sports programs and – not the least – as buyers of products and services for their own use and for sale to their customers. A special category of products is the clothes, sportswear, memorabilia and many other goods which carry – often conspicuously – the trademark of the university. Not only does the trademark indicate the name of the university, but it also represents the brand and reputation of the institution. Customers buy and use these licensed products with pride and often with the feeling of being valuable members of the institution's "family." Depending on the size and public recognition of the institution and the success of its most famous sports teams, the gross annual retail sales of trademark licensed products can amount to over 60 million dollars.

How proud can the customers be when they learn under what conditions these licensed products actually are manufactured? What responsibility does the university bear to make sure that these goods are produced under fair and humane conditions rather than in sweat-shops? This chapter looks at the supply chain of the licensed products that carry the trademark of universities. It argues that these institutions have a moral obligation to promote corporate responsibility in the supply chain, and it proposes ways to achieve this promotion. To illustrate the development of a responsible policy, the chapter explains the experience of the University of Notre Dame and discusses, in more general terms, the challenges and opportunities for universities when dealing with these kinds of supply chain problems.

The question of corporate responsibility in supply chains has been an issue since business organizations began to rely on others' resources. Should a business organization be responsible for the decisions and actions of its suppliers? Since the 1990s, the world has become ever more interconnected through increased globalization (see Enderle 2005; Radin 2018), which has resulted in supply chains stretching around the globe. The increased complexity makes the management of the supply chains highly challenging for corporations (Quinn 2017; Kryder 2018).

Therefore, it has not come as a surprise that multinational enterprises have been criticized for multiple irresponsibilities in their supply chains, ranging from using child and forced labor to polluting water and air. One might recall the Nike scandal in the early 1990s when the sportswear company bought their products from sweatshops in China and Indonesia (Locke 2002), or the suicides of young Chinese workers who were producing iPads for Apple in 2010 at Foxconn (Guo et al. 2012), or the collapse of the Rana Plaza factory building in 2013 in Bangladesh that killed over 1,100 workers (Labowitz & Baumann-Pauly 2014).

Early on, the intensified process of globalization was applauded by many business people, economists, policy makers and media gurus. But critical voices were also raised against the downsides of globalization, pointing to the disruption of labor markets, violations of human rights, environmental degradation, the lack of fair and strong global institutions, the reckless power play of global corporations, and other issues. As for North America, the negotiations for a trade agreement between Canada, Mexico and the United States resulted in NAFTA – the North American Free Trade Agreement – that went into effect in 1994. On the request of President Clinton, it included side agreements on labor cooperation (NAALC) and environmental cooperation (NAAEC). Although these side agreements were not followed up with strong implementation policies, they signaled, at least, the awareness of lawmakers about two sensitive areas of concern brought along with globalization.

The awareness of labor and environmental challenges also led in 1996, at the initiation of the U.S. Department of Labor, to the Fashion Industry Forum, with 300 apparel company representatives (see Schein 2018). It aimed to raise awareness of labor and human rights violations against persons employed in manufacturing clothing. As a result, the Apparel Industry Partnership (AIP) was formed, that consisted of representatives of labor unions and consumer advocacy, human rights, and religious groups, with the goal to improve conditions and eliminate abuse of adults and children in the garment industry, regardless of location. In 1999, AIP formed the Fair Labor Association (FLA) as a 501(c) (3) nonprofit organization in order to recruit additional companies for membership, monitor compliance, and publicize the compliance with the code of conduct (www.fairlabor.org).

Another initiative of monitoring labor rights in the supply chain is the Worker Rights Consortium (WRC), founded in April 2000 by university administrators, students, and international labor rights experts in North America (see Roy 2018b). It conducts investigations of working conditions in factories around the world with the goal to protect the rights of workers producing apparel and products bearing university names and logos. The independent nonprofit organization began with the support of forty-four universities and by 2020 has reached 157 higher educational affiliates in the United States and Canada (www.workersrights.org).

To put these initiatives into a global context, it is worth mentioning that in 2000 the United Nations launched the UN Global Compact for companies around the world to align strategies and operations with universal principles on human rights, labor, environment and (since 2004) anti-corruption, and to take actions that advance societal goals (www.unglobalcompact.org). It became the world's largest corporate sustainability initiative and was followed by several other UN initiatives such as the UN Principles for Responsible Investing in 2006 (www.unpri .org) and the UN Principles for Responsible Management Education in 2007 (www.unprme.org). Of particular importance for our discussion on corporate responsibility in supply chains are the UN Guiding Principles on Business and Human Rights, unanimously endorsed by the UN Human Rights Office in 2011 (discussed in Chapter 15).

The Experience of the University of Notre Dame: In Search of the Right Policy

The following case study presents the experience of the University of Notre Dame in its search for the right policy regarding its supply chains of Notre Dame-licensed products. The narrative is based, to a large extent, on the two reports of the University of Notre Dame's Worker Participation Committee (WPC) in 2015 and 2018 (WPC

2015, 2018). It also reflects the author's personal view, as he was involved in the WPC's search over five years and learned a great deal about the intricacies and ethical challenges of supply chains.

The Enthusiastic Beginning and Its Failed Outcome

As described in the previous section, due to accelerated globalization, the 1990s brought about rising awareness of ethical issues in supply chains and produced multiple initiatives for addressing these issues. The University of Notre Dame was participating actively in this movement. As the Review of the Freedom of Association Policy 2015 proudly states, "Notre Dame has always been at the forefront of efforts to improve wages and working conditions at foreign factories that manufacture Notre Dame licensed products. In 1997, Notre Dame was the first university to adopt a labor code of conduct for licensees. It was a founding member of the Fair Labor Association and is a member of the Worker Rights Consortium" (WPC 2015, 5).

As a Catholic university, Notre Dame wanted to live up to Catholic Social Teaching that, since Pope Leo XIII's encyclical *Rerum Novarum* in 1891 (Leo XIII 1891), has taken a stand on "social questions" as they have arisen over the years and provided guidance to address these questions. As a consequence, in 1999, President Fr. Edward A. Malloy, C.S.C., appointed a Task Force on Anti-Sweatshop Initiatives. In its report, the task force noted that "Catholic Social Teaching … has long recognized the rights of workers throughout the world to form labor unions and engage in collective bargaining with their employers" and proposed a Freedom of Association (FOA) Policy that was the "most effective and efficient way to give voice to these commitments" (WPC 2015, 5). The Policy included three recommendations:

1. Products bearing the name or other trademarks of the University shall be manufactured only by workers who enjoy the legal rights to freely associate, form labor unions, and collectively bargain with their employers concerning wages, hours, working conditions or other terms and conditions of employment.
2. A system of limited public disclosure, which would only require disclosure of factory locations to the University and its designated monitors.
3. The creation of a regional pilot monitoring program (WPC 2015, 5).

The FOA Policy was adopted by Notre Dame in 2001. With its clear focus on legal rights of freedom of association and collective bargaining, it states that Notre Dame licensed products cannot be manufactured in countries without these rights. In other words, the decisive criterion for choosing factories are the relevant laws of the countries where factories are located rather than practices at individual factories. However, in reality, such practices might not live up to or might even squarely violate these national laws, while in countries without similar rights-protecting laws, factory practices might be much better in terms of worker participation and collective bargaining. Thus, based on this country criterion, the FOA Policy excludes the factories of a number of countries including China and ten other countries (Afghanistan, Equatorial Guinea, Iran, Laos, Oman, Qatar, Saudi Arabia, Somalia, Turkmenistan and United Arab Emirates). Not surprisingly, this exclusion became a critical point in later discussions about the revision of the FOA Policy by the WPC and was rejected by some committee members as a kind of discrimination.

The FOA Policy was announced as a strong and consequent commitment to Catholic Social Teaching. Convinced of its trailblazer role, Notre Dame was hoping that other universities would follow suit and adopt similar policies. However, none did. Moreover, as the task force itself admitted, "lobbying by licensees [would be] unlikely to have much of an impact upon the policies of governments as large and powerful as the Chinese government" (WPC 2015, 6). Unfortunately, the FOA Policy generated meager results and was not supervised by a standing committee. It was unclear whether and how workers' freedom of association had been respected in factories where Notre Dame licensed products were manufactured (only one specific case of assessment could be found). And no positive impact on worker rights could be assumed in countries in which the University did not allow manufacturing of licensed products.

Despite these sobering results, Notre Dame kept its membership with the FLA and WRC. In 2013 the Executive Vice President John F. Affleck-Graves was approached by the FLA with the request to review Notre Dame's FOA Policy. This was the starting point of a new search for Notre Dame's policy regarding the supply chains of its licensed products.

A Pilot Project on Worker Participation with Verité

The status of the FOA Policy in 2013 was unsatisfactory for several reasons. First, after twelve years, the policy impact was difficult to assess so that the policy could hardly be said to have achieved its goal. Second, Notre Dame was unable to build a coalition with other universities to advance worker rights to free association and collective bargaining. Third, Notre Dame's attitude toward China appeared somewhat inconsistent: while the FOA Policy prohibited the manufacture of Notre Dame licensed products in China, the University had expanded relationships in China in recent years on multiple levels, including the number of Notre Dame undergraduate and graduate students who visit China, the number of Chinese students who come to study at Notre Dame, the opening of a university office in Beijing, investments held by the endowment and the many non-licensed products that the University purchases from China annually (WPC 2015, 6). Fourth, in order to get a more accurate grasp of workers' involvement in factories' decision making in countries with and without national legislation on FOA and collective bargaining (CB), a new concept of worker participation seemed to be necessary that would allow for empirical studies in factories around the world. Fifth, the University's commitment to Catholic Social Teaching could not content itself with the unsatisfactory situation of the FOA Policy.

For these reasons, in 2013 John Affleck-Graves invited a committee to review the current policy and to determine whether any changes to the policy should be recommended, specifically with regard to production in China. Under his leadership, the Worker Participation Committee (WPC) included two (subsequently five) student representatives, four professors, two personnel of the Licensing Department and eight (subsequently ten) personnel of the University's administration.

The committee considered two approaches to address the policy issue: a factory-centric approach and a country-centric approach, and recommended that the University conduct *a pilot program in China* to determine whether workers' rights have improved to the extent that factories meet and can sustain an acceptable standard of performance. By targeting workers' rights at the factory level, the focus was placed on *worker participation defined as a process by which factory management actively involves and/or engages employees/workers in business management and decision making*. In addition to assessing factories in China, this focus allowed comparison of factories across the world, independent of national legislation on freedom of association and collective bargaining.

Because the assessment of worker participation in factories requires a great deal of expertise, the University considered several specialized organizations and eventually engaged Verité, a global, independent, nonprofit organization. This nongovernmental organization provides consulting, training, research and assessment services worldwide, is based in Amherst, Massachusetts, and has offices in Shanghai. Since its inception in 1995, it has partnered with hundreds of multinational brands, suppliers, and international institutions to improve working conditions and social and environmental performances (www.verite.org).

In a first step, the committee selected six factories in China nominated by five Notre Dame licensees in order to better understand the status of worker participation in China. The factories included two plants producing headwear, three producing apparel and one producing a variety of non-apparel products (for example, tailgate tents, chairs and soft sided coolers). Their sizes ranged from 80 to more than 3,000 workers.

The committee worked with Verité to develop a solid and detailed assessment tool with seventy-one criteria (formulated in English and Chinese) against which all factories were measured as well as an agreed upon standard of acceptable performance against those criteria. The tool focused on worker participation and the ways in which line workers and management experience these rights and protections, thereby targeting three fundamental aspects: communication, consultation and participation in decision making (which will be specified below).

Verité next administered an online self-assessment of management and then conducted onsite assessments at each of the six factories, including individual interviews with managers and workers. As a result, Verité determined that two factories met the committee's standards; two required additional improvements to meet the standards; and the remaining two needed substantially more capacity building to reach an acceptable level. In addition, seven committee members visited four of the six factories in China and confirmed the results of the Verité assessments.

After a campus-wide conversation and dialogue on the proposed pilot program, University President Fr. John I. Jenkins, C.S.C., approved the recommendations of the WPC in September 2015. Based on the experience in the six Chinese factories, the pilot project was refined with an assessment tool of eighty criteria, continued with follow-up assessments of the Chinese factories and extended to eight factories in Bangladesh, El Salvador, Guatemala and India – all countries with the *de jure* right of freedom of association and collective bargaining, in which the University currently allows production.

As a result, three of the four Chinese factories showed sufficient improvement against their corrective action plan and, along with the first two factories, which met the standards right away, began production for twelve months. The eight factories outside China are plants producing apparel (4), infant, toddler and youth apparel (2), headwear (1) and wallets (1), and employing 42 to 2,100 workers. Their assessments used the same method as in China, namely a series of online assessments followed by a factory visit and in-depth on-site audit by Verité. Like in the investigation in China, upon receipt of Verité's assessments, a subcommittee of the WPC conducted an on-site visit of four factories in El Salvador and Guatemala to evaluate the working conditions at the factories, which confirmed the WPC's confidence in Verité and the assessment tool.

Based on Verité's work, the WPC was able to compare the performance of all of the pilot factories. The results revealed that some of the factories located in China performed better on the assessed criteria than many of the factories located in other countries: three Chinese factories met 79–85 percent and three met 52–62 percent of the criteria, while two factories in El Salvador and one in Guatemala met 61–77 percent and the remaining five factories ranged from 20 to 47 percent

Verité provided the WPC with the following conclusions about the pilot program overall (WPC 2018, 19):

- All factories in China demonstrated improvement from the 2014 assessments.
- Improvement was sufficient at several key suppliers to proceed with sourcing decisions, although on a pilot basis only.
- Performance of factories outside China varied, and although only audited once, some would not have met the University criteria developed for this project (based on the presence of several zero tolerance issues).
- Suppliers in China can achieve continuous improvement on freedom of association and worker participation at the factory-level, although this requires time and management commitment.

Expanding the Assessment Process to a Broader Scale

The pilot program about worker participation was an important step forward in the search for Notre Dame's Policy of Freedom of Association. But it was limited in two ways: it focused only on some core worker rights without considering a broader range of social and environmental responsibilities of the factories producing Notre Dame licensed products, and it assessed only fourteen factories without regarding all or at least a majority of the factories from which Notre Dame gets its licensed products.

Given these two limitations, the WPC looked for a second assessment partner. Notre Dame's licensing program currently has 189 licensees and 561 licensees contracted factories. They are located in thirty-five countries, 55 percent within the United States and 45 percent overseas. Fifteen percent of the factories are owned by the licensees and 85 percent are independently owned or operated. Because Verité had neither the capacity nor the interest in significantly expanding its work to cover all of the factories and, moreover, because of the cost to conduct such detailed assessment in all factories, the WPC explored other approaches and vendors capable of implementing the assessment process on a broader scale.

After consultation with other universities, the choice fell to Sumerra, which was invited to present its approach to the WPC in spring 2017. Sumerra (a short name of "summa terra," that is, the whole earth) is a global for-profit organization that provides supply chain management, compliance management and consulting services worldwide. It is based in Portland, Oregon, with offices in Hong Kong, Bangalore and Dhaka. Sumerra has partnered with multinational brands, organizations, licensees and factories who are striving to improve working conditions and promote their fair treatment of workers (www .sumerra.com).

As extensive conversations with Sumerra's CEO Jason Roberts in August 2017 showed, Sumerra offered several services crucial for the expansion of Notre Dame's pilot program: (1) It has a multi-pronged assessment platform that includes licensees by using a pre-survey, and factories by employing specialized audit organizations. (2) The pre-survey and the auditing questions evaluate a wide range of human rights and environmental concerns. (3) Universities can choose to use the portions of the platform that are most appropriate for their needs.

(4) Schools that partner with Sumerra receive access to the assessment results of any licensee and factory that uses its platform. As a result, licensees that Notre Dame has in common with other schools do not need to conduct additional assessments. (5) At the time of the WPC's initial meeting with Sumerra, 46 percent of Notre Dame's current licensees had already completed the Sumerra licensee survey at the request of another school.

Given the WPC's strong emphasis on worker participation, the WPC conducted a thorough review of Sumerra's assessment instruments in order to make sure that Notre Dame's long-standing concerns about worker rights are fully taken into account while other social and environmental concerns are addressed as well.

As mentioned above, Verité's revised assessment tool for worker participation comprehends eighty criteria with five compliance levels: zero-tolerance, minimum, good, better and best. It distinguishes two types of worker organizations: unions and worker representation bodies. And the active involvement of these organizations and workers can take three forms:

- Worker grievance system – policies/procedures, implementation, effectiveness.
- Worker feedback system – policies/procedures, implementation, effectiveness.
- Worker participation – policies/procedures, implementation, effectiveness.

In contrast, Sumerra's assessment tool focuses on a wide range of ten topics, including a factory profile and a pre-survey (to be filled out by the licensee) and a semi-announced audit of the factory. The ten topics of the assessment data contain 409 provisions: employment relations (87 provisions), nondiscrimination (14), child labor (8), forced labor (14), harassment and abuse (18), hours of work (23), compensation and benefits (32), freedom of association (27), health and safety (94) and environment (92). The audit consists of:

- References (topics, definitions, observations, documents, interviews).
- Assessment data on ten topics and evaluated in five categories (performance, audit finding and legal / code of conduct violation, auditor comments (confidential), root cause analysis, recommendations / corrective action.

- Interviews (with workers).
- Scorecard: non-compliance defined with five categories: zero tolerance, critical-high risk immediate action / critical-high risk /
  significant-medium risk / minor-low risk.
- Executive summary.

Moreover, Sumerra's assessment tool distinguishes – like Verité's – two
types of worker organizations: union and legal alternatives of worker
associations (or worker organizations).

Comparing Verité's with Sumerra's assessment tool, the Criteria
Subcommittee of the WPC determined that there was substantial convergence between the zero-tolerance and minimum criteria identified by
Verité and Sumerra (regarding the provisions of employment relations
[87] and freedom of association [27]). Both tools include a large number
of criteria related to three areas of concern and based on Verité's tool:

- *Factory respects and honors workers' rights to freedom of association and collective bargaining:* 3 zero-tolerance (Z), 4 minimum
  (M), 3 good (G). All Z and M are met.
- *Factory refrains from any acts of interference with the operation of union
  or worker participation bodies (which serve the function of unions):* 3
  zero-tolerance, 6 minimum, 1 good, 6 better. All Z and M are met.
- *Grievance system (confidential internal complaint system):* 8 minimum, 6 good. All M are met.

Not included in Sumerra's tool are two minimum criteria of Verité:
encouraging worker feedback systems and worker participation
systems; and Factory maintains complete documentation of worker
grievance, feedback and participation activities and outcomes.

Given this convergence, the Criteria Subcommittee suggested adding
these few missing criteria and some other changes to supplement the
Sumerra tool. Summera expressed a strong willingness to incorporate
all of the requested suggestions in order to provide an enhanced
assessment tool suitable for all factories in countries with and without
de jure legislation on FOA and CB.

*Drawing on the strength of the UN Framework for Business and
Human Rights, the UN Guiding Principles and its Interpretive Guide*

When Notre Dame set up the Freedom of Association Policy in
2001, it was right after the promulgation of the UN Global Compact

in 2000. However, it took many more years at the international level to establish the UN Framework for Business and Human Rights (UN 2008a, 2008b), the UN Guiding Principles (UN 2011) and the Interpretive Guide (UN 2012a). Thanks to these developments, the WPC could benefit in its own search for an appropriate Notre Dame policy and strengthen and expand its approach to become more suitable for building up an alliance with other like-minded universities.

Because the UN Framework and UN Guiding Principles (in short, UNGP) were discussed extensively in Chapter 15, we only recall the key assumptions here:

(1) The "duty" of the state to "protect" human rights and "remedy" violations of human rights;
(2) The "responsibility" of business enterprises to "respect" human rights and "remedy" violations of human rights;
(3) The business enterprise conceived as moral actor that bears moral responsibility, independent of the state's duty;
(4) The business enterprise's adverse human rights impact based on the criteria of causation, contribution, and direct linkages without contribution;
(5) The business enterprise's responsibility for human rights due diligence;
(6) All business enterprises are included and all internationally recognized human rights are relevant.

Recommendations for Notre Dame's Policy of Promoting Corporate Responsibility in Its Supply Chains of Notre Dame Licensed Products

Since Notre Dame adopted a labor code of conduct for licensees in 1997, the University has experienced many ups and downs in its search – inspired by Catholic Social Teaching – for a consistent, effective and persuasive policy for Notre Dame licensed products. It is fair to say that the search has made remarkable progress, although it has not reached its completion yet. Several key factors have contributed to this progress: the continuous engagement of the Worker Participation Committee over five years, collaboration with the specialized organizations of Verité and Sumerra to assess worker participation and corporate responsibility in the supply chain and the development and worldwide expansion of the UN Framework and Guiding Principles on Business and Human Rights.

The results of Notre Dame's search process can be summarized as follows:

(1) The original focus on a single issue, that is the freedom of association, has been expanded to a *comprehensive approach to "corporate responsibility"* – understood as the policy commitment of the business organization (licensee, factory) to act ethically with regard to all economic, social and environmental aspects of corporate performance that come under the control of licensees and/or factories.

(2) Corporate responsibility includes respecting *all human rights* according to the UN Framework and Guiding Principles on Business and Human Rights.

(3) The University of Notre Dame is committed to its *mission* inspired by Catholic Social Teaching and *promotes* corporate responsibility in the supply chains of its licensed products.

(4) Notre Dame's licensees and factories have their respective spaces of freedom and are supposed to take responsibility, *independent* of the duties of the countries' governments. This implies – among other things – that the treatment of the workers at the factory level has precedence over the country's legislation of freedom of association and collective bargaining.

(5) The *enhanced assessment tool* developed in collaboration with Verité and Sumerra is a relatively comprehensive, effective and reliable instrument to evaluate the performance of corporate responsibility. Relatively reliable means that the assessment results express at least 80 percent of actual corporate performance.

(6) Given the complexity and changing nature of the supply chains, a *Standing Committee* should be set up to supervise and guide the progress of Notre Dame's policy.

(7) The University should help to build up an *alliance with like-minded organizations* to respect human rights and promote corporate responsibility in the supply chains in accordance with the UN Guiding Principles on Business and Human Rights.

While recognizing these important results, some limitations of this policy may be noted. First, the focus on Notre Dame licensed products does not include all the other products and services Notre Dame purchases for its operations. Second, the policy covers only Notre Dame licensed products manufactured abroad, that is 45 percent; 55 percent are produced domestically. Third, the supply chain of Notre Dame licensed products reaches only the first tier, that is the factories in which the final products are made, but not the second, third and other tiers that supply intermediate goods and raw materials for these final products.

In April 2018 the WPC drafted its Final Report and Recommendations, conducted a campus-wide conversation and submitted the document to President Fr. John I. Jenkins, C.S.C. In October he approved it with the following five recommendations (WPC 2018, 5, 21–22; explanations on pp. 22–32):

(1) A Standing Committee[2] should be established to monitor the University's progress toward the goals outlined below and consider additional aspirational goals to advance its commitment to workers' rights, as well as other human rights and the values of Catholic Social Teaching to promote corporate responsibility.

(2) The University should expand its review of licensees and factories to include a broader range of human rights issues. These assessment tools should be reviewed annually to ensure they address the broad spectrum of human rights concerns as required by the University's Licensing Code of Conduct.

(3) In countries that recognize freedom of association by law, every licensee should be required to participate in the Sumerra assessment process to evaluate their organization's current corporate responsibility program and the level of knowledge of manufacturing practices within their contracted factories. These factories would be under the ongoing oversight of the Standing Committee.

(4) In countries that do not recognize freedom of association by law, the University should consider, within its discretion, a limited exemption[3] to manufacture products in those countries only after the factory has successfully completed both the Sumerra assessment and a more in-depth audit by Verité. These factories would also be under the ongoing oversight of the Standing Committee.

(5) The University should cultivate partnerships with other organizations to advance respect for workers' rights and other human rights and to promote corporate responsibility in the supply chain.

As the narrative of Notre Dame's experience shows, these recommendations represent a successful completion of a long search process for a policy that is solidly based and well thought-out. One can only hope that it will bear multiple fruits.

Reflections on and beyond the Notre Dame Experience
As briefly described in the introduction, with the accelerated globalization in the 1990s the ethical challenges in supply chains have increased enormously and become ever more complex and urgent. At the same time, these developments have provoked heated public debates, thorough and far-reaching investigations and a vast variety of practical initiatives. Compared to the early 1990s, today we are in a clearly better – though still unsatisfactory – position to understand and address the ethical challenges in international supply chains.

Looking back to the Notre Dame experience, what can we learn about "promoting corporate responsibility in the supply chain" in more general terms that might be helpful to other like-minded universities? And what are important research questions which remain to be scrutinized?

Suggestions to Other Universities

The Notre Dame experience of twenty-plus years shows that the questions of "why," "what" and "how" to promote corporate responsibility in the supply chain are connected; however, they need to be treated severally and, in the process, they will reinforce each other.

First, the *"why"-question* has to be stated clearly from the beginning and answered at least in a broad and positive way. The mission statement of the university might provide necessary guidance throughout the process of policy formation and implementation. If such guidance is not available or too general, the institution needs to set up a task force in order to determine the mission in a way that is specific enough to direct the policy search. It is crucial for success that the mission be clearly stated and embraced with full support by the leadership of the university.

Second, with regard to the *"what"-question*, the goals and limitations of the supply chain policy are to be clearly identified and determined, basically following the UN Framework and Guiding Principles on Business and Human Rights. This approach includes four characteristics:

(1) The policy is about "corporate responsibility," that is, the ethics of business enterprises (see Chapter 15).
(2) The policy is factory-centered, not country-centered, which means that the factory is held responsible for what it can control, independently of the country's legislation and the "duty of the state."
(3) The policy does not focus on just one or a few single issues, instead, it is holistic and concerns basically all economic, social and environmental aspects of the factory's performance.
(4) The policy requires minimal performance standards, which consist of potentially all human rights according to the UN Guiding Principles.

An additional fifth characteristic of the policy – not mentioned by the UN approach – is its developmental purpose, which means enabling better factory performance in economic, social and environmental terms. Its emphasis obviously goes beyond controlling and policing factories. While this purpose concerns primarily the factories, the licensees and the universities as the buyers of the final products have to engage in this developmental task as well.

For a better understanding of this policy to promote corporate responsibility in the supply chain, three limitations should be mentioned. They are assumed and recognized here – as they are in the Notre Dame experience; however, obviously, they are not fixed forever and can be changed. First, the supply chains under consideration include only the first tier, that is the factories in which the final products are made, but not the second, third or other tiers that supply intermediate goods and raw materials for these final goods. Second, this policy covers only products manufactured abroad and does not include those made domestically. Third, this policy is restricted to the products which are licensed by the university and does not relate to all the other products and services the university purchases for its operations.

With these limitations, the proposed policy is clearly focused and feasible and does not require a complete change of the university's entire supply chain policy. Nonetheless, it is a significant change that expresses the university's commitment to its mission. It represents a step forward that might be followed by further steps in the future, and it creates the opportunity to gather experiences of what corporate responsibility in the supply chain specifically means.

Third, not less important than the *why*- and the *what* question is the *"how"-question*, that is, the method of implementing the policy of promoting corporate responsibility in the supply chain. An effective and efficient implementation fulfills at least five requirements:

(1) The university collaborates with licensees, factories and specialized organizations in supply chain management and assessment, based on an agreed upon consensus about policy goals.

(2) To evaluate actual factory performance, the university relies on assessment tools of high quality, which are material, consistent and relatively comprehensive.

(3) A Standing Committee, established by the university, monitors the progress of the policy, makes appropriate changes, and shares its experience with students, faculty and staff.

(4) The university helps to build an alliance of like-minded universities, based on the UN Framework and the UN Guiding Principles and using the same assessment tools.

(5) While the university is committed to self-regulation within the proposed framework, it also wisely supports and uses pressures from outside (such as consumer initiatives, ethical investing and legal proposals), which help promote corporate responsibility in the supply chain.

Research Opportunities

To widen these reflections, several research opportunities are presented. The first set of questions concerns the *economic implications* of the policy proposal. Simply put, does "corporate responsibility" in the supply chain "pay" (see Chapter 13)? What are the costs of compliance with social and environmental standards at the levels of "minimum" and "good" – for example, of labor rights such as minimal wage and grievance mechanisms or substantial energy reduction and air pollution treatment? Are there also economic benefits involved? How many? What are acceptable balances of costs and benefits? Alternatively, what results do economic cost-benefit analyses yield, if the factory does *not* comply with those social and environmental standards at the "minimum" and "good" levels?

Regarding the distribution of costs and benefits of "corporate responsibility" across the supply chain, who bears the costs and who gets the benefits? How are they distributed between the factories (first, second, third and other tiers), the licensees, the sellers of the final products, and the consumers? What is a "fair" distribution, and based on what criteria?

To investigate these questions, one can use the *conceptual* framework of "corporate responsibility" proposed in Chapter 15, along with further conceptual developments. *Theoretical* explorations would gain from new approaches to understand the buyer–supplier relationship not as a principal–agent relationship, but as a relationship in which suppliers are conceived as stewards of buyers (see Assländer et al. 2016). Many research ideas about the limits of economic analysis and global labor justice and the limits of choice and the ethics of sweatshops can be found in Preiss (2014) and Kates (2015), respectively. That cultural differences do not necessarily conflict with labor rights, but can support each other is demonstrated in the stimulating article "Confucian Ethics and Labor Rights" (Kim 2014), which opens innovative ways of implementing human rights in different cultures.

Empirical studies may focus on particular industries (such as the apparel, toy or electronics industries) and compare supply chains in which standards of corporate responsibility are respected with those in which they are violated; see, for example, Lin-Hi and Blumberg (2017) showing that corporations' buying behavior is decisive in order for industry self-regulation to become an appropriate means of improving labor standards in the Chinese toy industry; or Oka (2018) that analyzes the effectiveness of "brand advocacy" in Cambodia's garment industry. Moreover, it would be interesting to find out if, how and why these two types of supply chains differ in terms of distribution patterns of costs and benefits between the different actors. As for the management of social issues in management, see the literature review by Yawar and Seuring (2017).

Given the controversial discussion in Notre Dame's Worker Participation Committee on the exclusion of Chinese factories from its supply chains of Notre Dame-licensed products (see pages 238 and 247), several articles help better understand the critical issues of *business and human rights in China*, a second fruitful area of research. Whelan and Muthuri (2017) investigate human rights pressures on

Chinese state-owned enterprises stemming from transnational, national and intra-organizational forces. Dawkins (2012) emphasizes the importance of collective bargaining and freedom of association while criticizing Zwolinski (2007) and Powell and Zwolinski (2012) for being "conspicuously silent" on these issues (Kates 2015, 207, note 16). Still, the question remains whether Chinese factories with a decent level of worker participation should be barred from participating in supply chains. Would such denial amount to a kind of _discrimination_ because those factories are located in a country whose national legislation does not allow freedom of association and collective bargaining? What are the ethical (and economic) arguments in support of and against such denial?

Another controversial issue discussed in the WPC concerns the _reliability of the assessment tools_ developed and used by special organizations for supply chain management (see Locke 2013). Critical MIT studies question Nike's longstanding audit approach (Locke et al. 2006; Locke & Romis 2007). And newer investigations have shown that even elaborated auditing schemes have been "ineffective when confronted with sophisticated deception methods that some suppliers employ" (Locke et al. 2009, quoted in Assländer et al. 2016, 661–62). However, recent conversations with leaders of specialized organizations like Sumerra suggest that the quality of assessment tools has improved substantially in the last several years. It is therefore important to investigate the information content and the reliability of the assessment tools currently in use and, if necessary, to raise them to an acceptable level (see Searcy & Ahi 2014). In addition, one may analyze the structure and distribution of the _assessment costs_ and develop fair schemes to charge factories, licensees, sellers and consumers.

As the UN Framework and the UN Guiding Principles on Business and Human Rights affirm the important and independent role of the (moral) responsibility of business enterprises to "respect human rights," the question arises as to what role the state (or government) should play to secure human rights. The answer – according to this framework – is that the state has "the duty to protect" its citizens against human rights violations and, along with business enterprises, to respect human rights and remedy human rights violations. While this "division of labor" is conceptually clear, although not undisputed (see, for example, Wettstein 2012, 753–54), it still opens a large number of research questions regarding the legal incentives for

enterprises to respect human rights and remedy human rights violations nationally and internationally.

Three perspectives seem particularly promising. In the wake of the
promulgation of the UN Guiding Principles by the UN Human Rights
Council in 2011, states were invited to set up their own "National
Action Plans on Business and Human Rights," and as of now more
than thirty countries have developed or are in the process of developing
such plans, while non-state initiatives are pushing for such plans in at
least fifteen countries (Morris et al. 2018). While these plans vary a
great deal, they provide a wide field of research questions about their
stated and ignored objectives, their rationales, their implementation
strategies, their assessments and their proposed changes resulting from
past achievements and failures.

An interesting example of incorporating the UN Guiding Principles
into national legislation for global corporations was a "petition" to the
Swiss National Council in 2012, signed by 135,000 citizens. It provoked many public debates, was discussed in the national legislative
body and finally defeated. In 2015 the "Responsible Business
Initiative" was launched and debated in the parliament again. The
National Council accepted a compromise in June 2018 while the
Council of States was still undecided in the summer of 2019 (https://
konzern-initiative.ch). In the fall of 2020 the Swiss people will vote on
this initiative. Research questions may address the potential impact of
this legislation on different constituencies: the improvement of
working conditions and environmental performance in the supply
chain; the competitiveness of global corporations and their willingness
to stay located in Switzerland; the reputation of Switzerland and its
global corporations in the world community; and the potentially pioneering role of this initiative for other countries.

With regard to international legislation about human rights, the
European Union developed a range of human rights conditionality into
"an autonomous instrument of foreign policy and cooperation for
development" that can be included in its international agreements
(Violini & Rangone 2020). A case in point are the currently ongoing
negotiations on a Free Trade Agreement (FTA) between the EU and
Vietnam. While the European Commission twice refused to integrate
human rights in the FTA draft, the European Ombudsman – on the
demand of two NGOs, the International Federation for Human Rights
and the Vietnam Committee on Human Rights – found

maladministration of the Commission in both cases and forwarded the issue to the complicated EU process of ratification, which at that time was not been settled yet (see Cassel & Ramasastry 2016; Jennings 2017; Carrillo & Batalli 2018). On June 30, 2019 the European Union signed a landmark free trade deal with Vietnam. Vu and Phuong Nguyen write, "it still needs the approval of the European Parliament, which is not a given as some lawmakers are concerned about Vietnam's human rights record" (2019). On March 30, 2020 the Council of the European Union gave final green light to the European Union Vietnam Free Trade Agreement (EVFTA). This includes commitments to implement ILO core standards and UN conventions relating for example to the fight against climate change or the protection of biodiversity (Council of the EU 2020). On June 8, 2020 Vietnam's National Assembly ratified the EVFTA that took effect in July 2020 (Nguyen 2020).

Research may investigate the likely impact of the agreement on promoting corporate responsibility among different types of companies in Vietnam; how the human rights requirements are perceived by business leaders of national, European and other enterprises, by worker representatives, civil society and government – as an intrusion of a foreign power, as an additional cost factor or as support of the development of the country; and how these negotiations can help develop a "National Human Rights Action Plan" for Vietnam.

Conclusion

As stated in the introduction, universities are not only institutions of higher education, they also constitute powerful economic actors and sell licensed products carrying their names and their reputation. Inspired by its mission and Catholic Social Teaching, the University of Notre Dame has engaged, over many years, in the search of a policy of freedom of association and ended up with a policy of promoting corporate responsibility in the supply chains of its licensed products. This experience was not only a great learning process for Notre Dame. It also offers policy suggestions to other like-minded universities, in line with the UN Guiding Principles on Business and Human Rights, and opens a wide range of fascinating research opportunities on corporate responsibility in the supply chains. Finally, this endeavor to care for human rights and the environment in international supply chains may lead, in a quest for consistency, the university to demonstrate the same level of serious concern at home as well. Not only business enterprises, but also other non-state actors can learn from the UN Guiding Principles on Business and Human Rights (see Kirchschläger 2017).

Notes

1 In this chapter the term "university" stands for universities and colleges.
2 The Standing Committee was named Trademark Licensing and Human Rights Committee and began its work in January 2019.
3 This "limited exemption" can be interpreted in two ways. It can mean that factories in countries without recognized freedom of association by law have to meet *higher* standards of worker participation than factories in countries with *de jure* freedom of association. Or it can mean that the *same* standards are applied to *all* factories across the world while the *validity* of the assessment has to be ensured by an audit of Verité in uncertain cases. The first interpretation implies a discrimination of Chinese factories and factories of other countries without *de jure* freedom of association. The second interpretation (which the author supports) neither implies discrimination nor expresses a lack of trust in Sumerra's enhanced assessment tool; rather, it reduces the somewhat uncertain validity of the assessment results.

Epilogue

Creating wealth and respecting human rights seem to be an odd couple, the first evoking a rush for money and the second admonishing restraint for politics. And, applied to business enterprises, this couple brings forth an unusual creature: corporate responsibility. In this book I have undertaken to combine these three ideas in the hope that this creation will be well received by scholars, practitioners and a broader interested audience.

The question of the purpose of business is an old and widely debated topic. It has often been answered by asserting that the purpose is about making money or maximizing shareholder value, period. Milton Friedman's famous article about "the business of business is business" (1970) has dominated the debate for decades, despite the robust critique of many scholars, business people and activists. More recently, the "purpose-first movement," which pursues something beyond profit and "[encourages] companies to have a clear mission, consider their communities and steer their innovative impulses to good ends" (Edgecliffe-Johnson 2019), has revived the questioning of business's purpose. Business is seen as embedded in society and cannot help but deal with societal issues. As a consequence, the literature on business and society has become an important area of research (see, for example, the Special Issue "Focusing on Fields" of *Business & Society*, 58[7], Mitnick 2019).

While business undoubtedly is embedded in society, one tends to overlook that businesses as economic organizations form only part of the economy and the economic system. In fact, the economy is the primary interface between "business" and "society." Therefore, the way the purpose of the economy is defined also determines the purpose of business.

In this book I proposed to define the purpose of the economy and hence of business as the creation of wealth in the comprehensive sense. This view relates to Adam Smith's inquiry of the "wealth of nations"

256

(Smith 1776/1976) and, at the same time, significantly extends beyond it. The substantive contents of wealth include not only economic capital, but also natural capital (that is, all relations of economic activities with nature), human capital (that is, healthy and educated people) and social capital (that is, trust relations between economic actors). These four types of capital are necessary conditions for the sustainability of human well-being over time (as defined by the OECD framework for well-being, [OECD 2013a]). Moreover, the wealth of a community, a city, a country, a continent, the planet Earth is conceived as a combination of private and public wealth; two forms of goods and wealth – private and public – whereby either can be "good" or "bad" from the ethical perspective.

What are the proportions of private and public wealth in a social entity? They obviously vary. Extreme proportions like 90 to 10 percent or 10 to 90 percent are hardly realistic. If we assume the proportion lies somewhere in between, both forms of wealth turn out to be immensely important and consequential. The market institution, powerful in producing private goods but failing in producing public goods, can only play a limited role in the economy (which is often wrongly called "the marketplace"). In turn, collective actors such as governments and communities can be effective in producing public goods, but likely fail in producing private goods. As regards the motivations for creating wealth in the comprehensive sense, both self-regarding and other-regarding motivations are indispensable.

Along with the focus on wealth creation from the economic perspective as an ethics-related approach in the sense of Amartya Sen, this book defines the thirty internationally recognized human rights as the ethical perspective for wealth creation. These human rights are understood as minimal ethical requirements relevant for corporate responsibility in accordance with the UN Guiding Principles on Business and Human Rights. They are minimal ethical requirements (which, undoubtedly, are quite demanding for many business enterprises). They cover only one, though a very important, part of the ethics of business organizations and thus leave room for a wide range of ethical norms and values beyond these minima. It is fair to say that they express a relatively undisputed worldwide consensus without any comparable alternative ethical standards and are deemed necessary for business enterprises operating in the global and pluralistic context.

Throughout the book the focus is placed on joint objectives of wealth creation and human rights, first from the macro-perspective and then applied to the business enterprises. This approach aims to be relevant for any economic, political and cultural system. It intends to provide guidance for corporate responsibility in any country and culture. It develops a universal vision for corporate responsibility in any context.

Thereby – as one might have noticed – the questions of appropriate institutions and cultures, collective values and the common good do not take center stage here. No discussion is offered to determine the relationship between the market and the state (or government) and to explain the concepts and roles of collective values and the common good. This obvious silence does not mean that these questions are not important. It only indicates my view that we should focus first on a deep and comprehensive conception of wealth creation and a well-founded understanding of human rights and their relevance for corporate responsibility in the global and pluralistic context. Many examples were used to illustrate this vision. In addition, two case studies were presented to show in very specific terms what corporate responsibility entails for less income inequality and how universities can promote corporate responsibility in their global supply chains for trademark licensed products.

Having emphasized the focus – and hopefully the strength – of this book, it also becomes clear that this book has its limitations. While it is well-founded and provides basic guidelines for corporate responsibility, it does not address more specific challenges, which wealth creation and human rights pose in different countries, cultures and industries. How can wealth creation be specified and promoted in informal economies in sub-Saharan Africa? What does creating natural capital mean for companies in the Amazons? What kind of public wealth can and should domestic and foreign firms provide in countries afflicted by gangs and war? Facing the challenges of financialization, how can and should investment banks create wealth in a genuine sense? What are the responsibilities of Chinese enterprises for human rights in the extractive industry, domestically and internationally? How can and should global corporations respect human rights in the digital age?

These questions show that corporate responsibility for wealth creation and human rights extends far beyond the focus and the scope of this book. What I have discussed in these twenty chapters is only a beginning. The book invites further investigations and conversations from multiple geographic and cultural perspectives in order to promote and strengthen the commitment of business enterprises to both wealth creation and human rights.

Bibliography

Acemoglu, D., & Robinson, J. A. 2012. *Why Nations Fail: The Origins of Power, Prosperity and Poverty*. New York: Crown.

Adams, C. A. 2015. The International Integrated Reporting Council: A call to action. *Critical Perspectives on Accounting*, 27, 23–28.

Adler, M. 2012. *Well-Being and Fair Distribution: Beyond Cost-Benefit Analysis*. Oxford: Oxford University Press.

Akerlof, G. A., & Yellen, J. L. 1988. Fairness and unemployment. *American Economic Review*, 78, 44–49.

Alice Report. 2018. Indiana. www.iuw.org/alice, accessed on October 25, 2019.

Allenby, B. R., & Sarewitz, D. 2011. *The Techno-Human Condition*. Cambridge, MA: MIT Press.

Amnesty International. 2009. *Freedom: Stories Celebrating the Universal Declaration of Human Rights*. New York: Broadway Paperbacks.

Amnesty International and The Prince of Wales Leadership Forum (AI and PWLF). 2000. *Human Rights – Is It Any of Your Business?* London: Amnesty International UK and The Prince of Wales Leadership Forum.

Argandona, A. 2018. Capitalism. In Kolb 2018, 370–79.

Aristotle. 1980. *The Nichomachean Ethics*. Translated by R. Ross. Revised edition. Book 1, Section 5. Oxford: Oxford University Press.

Arnold, D. G. 2006. Corporate moral agency. *Midwest Studies in Philosophy*, XXX, 279–91.

  2016. Corporations and human rights obligations. *Business and Human Rights Journal*, 1(2), 255–75.

  2017. On the division of moral labour for human rights between states and corporations: A reply to Hsieh. *Business and Human Rights Journal*, 2(2), 311–16.

  2018a. Human rights. In Kolb 2018, 1762–67.

  2018b. Corporate moral agency. In Kolb 2018, 713–17.

Arnold, D. G., & Bowie, N. 2003. Sweatshops and respect for persons. *Business Ethics Quarterly*, 13, 221–42.

  2007. Respect for workers in global supply chains: Advancing the debate over sweatshops. *Business Ethics Quarterly*, 17, 135–45.

Arrow, K. J. 1963. *Social Choice and Individual Values.* New Haven: Yale University Press.

Arrow, K., Dasgupta, P., & Mäler, K.-G. 2003. Evaluating projects and assessing sustainable development in imperfect economies. *Environmental and Resource Economics*, 26(4), 647–85.

Arruda, M. C., & Enderle, G. (eds.). 2004. *Improving Globalization.* Rio de Janeiro: Editora FGV.

Assländer, M. S., Roloff, J., & Nayir, D. Z. 2016. Suppliers as stewards? Managing social standards in first- and second-tier suppliers. *Journal of Business Ethics*, 139, 661–83.

Atkinson, A. B. 2015. *Inequality: What Can Be Done?* Cambridge, MA: Harvard University Press.

2019. *Measuring Poverty around the World.* Edited by J. Micklewright & A. Brandolini. With afterwords by F. Bourguignon & N. Stern. Princeton and Oxford: Princeton University Press.

Atkinson, R. D., & Ezell, S. J. 2012. *Innovation Economics: The Race for Global Advantage.* New Haven, CT: Yale University Press.

Audi, R. 2009. *Business Ethics and Ethical Business.* New York: Oxford University Press.

Auer, A. 2016. *Autonome Moral und christlicher Glaube. Mit dem Nachtrag zur Rezeption der Autonomievorstellung in der katholisch-theologischen Ethik von 1984 und mit einem einleitenden Essay von Dietmar Mieth.* Darmstadt: Wissenschaftliche Buchgesellschaft.

Avery. C. L. 2000. *Business and Human Rights in a Time of Change.* London: Amnesty International UK, February.

Ayios, A., Jeurissen, R., Manning, P., & Spence, L. J. 2014. Social capital: A review from an ethics perspective. *Business Ethics: A European Review*, 23(1), 108–24.

Baker, L. 2019. With Trump sitting nearby, Macron calls nationalism a betrayal. November 11. www.reuters.com/article/us-ww1-centenary-macron-nationalism/with-trump-sitting-nearby-macron-calls-national ism-a-betrayal-idUSKCN1NG0IH, accessed on October 27, 2019.

Balch. O. 2009a. Access all areas. *Ethical Corporation*, April, 12–16.

Balch, O. 2009b. Shell shocked and in the dock. *Ethical Corporation*, June, 12–16.

Bandelj, N., & Wherry, F. F. (eds.). 2011. *The Cultural Wealth of Nations.* Stanford: Stanford University Press.

Bapuji, H., Husted, B. W., Lu, J., & Mir, R. (guest eds.). 2018. Special issue: Business, society, and economic inequality. *Business & Society*, 57(6), 983–1285.

Barney, G. O., Blewett, J., & Barney, K. R. 1993. *Global 2000 Revisit(ed.), What Shall We Do? The Critical Issues of the 21st Century.* Arlington, VA: Millennium Institute.

Bartkus, V. O., & Davis, J. H. (eds.). 2009. *Social Capital: Reaching Out, Reaching In.* Cheltenham: Edward Elgar.

Bateman, M. 2014. The rise and fall of Muhammad Yunus and the micro-credit model. International Development Studies: Working Paper Series #001. Saint Mary's University.

Baumann-Pauly, D., & Nolan, J. (eds.). 2016. *Business and Human Rights. From Principles to Practice.* New York: Routledge.

Baumann-Pauly, D., & Posner, M. 2016. Making the business case for human rights: An assessment. In Baumann-Pauly & Nolan 2016, 11–21.

BBC. 2018. Myanmar Rohingya. What we need to know about the crisis. April 24. www.bbc.com/news/world-asia-41566561.

Beal, B. D., & Astakhova, M. 2017. Management and income inequality: A review and conceptual framework. *Journal of Business Ethics*, 142, 11–23.

Bebchuk, L. A., & Fried, J. M. 2006. Pay without performance: Overview of the issue. *Academy of Management Perspectives*, February, 5–24.

Becker, G. K. 2017. Paying the price: Lessons from the Volkswagen emissions scandal for moral leadership. *The Journal of the Macau Ricci Institute*, 9, 15–28.

Becker, G. S. 1964. *Human Capital: A Theoretical and Empirical Analysis, with Special Reference to Education.* New York: National Bureau of Economic Research.

Becker, L. C., & Becker, C. B. (eds.). 2001. *Encyclopedia of Ethics.* Second edition. New York: Routledge.

Behrman, J. R., & Taubman, P. 1994. Human capital. In D. Greenwald (ed.), *The McGraw-Hill Encyclopedia of Economics.* Second edition. New York: McGraw-Hill, 493–95.

Bekink, M. J. 2016. Thinking long-term: Investment strategies and responsibility. In Baumann-Pauly & Nolan 2016, 225–35.

Benedict, X. V. I. 2009. *Caritas in Veritate.* www.vatican.va/holy_father/benedict_xvi/encyclicals/ documents/hf_ben-xvi_enc_20090629_caritas-in-veritate_en.html.

Beschorner, T., & Kolmar, M. 2015. Moral capabilities and institutional innovation – An extended transaction cost approach. In Enderle & Murphy 2015, 47–71.

Bergen, D. 2018. Germany's tortured conscience. Review of *Then they came for me* by M. D. Hockenos. *The Wall Street Journal*, December 8–9, C8.

Betz, H. D., Browning, D. S., Janowski, B., & Jüngel, E. (eds.). 2012. *Religion Past & Present: Encyclopedia of Theology and Religion.* Volume XII. Leiden, NL: Brill.

Bhagwati, J. 2004. *In Defense of Globalization*. New York: Oxford University Press. With a new afterword 2007.

Bird, R. C., Cahoy, D. R., & Prenkert, J. D. (eds.). 2014. *Law, Business and Human Rights: Bridging the Gap*. Cheltenham: Edward Elgar.

Black, J., Hashimzade, N., & Myles, G. 2009. *A Dictionary of Economics*. Third edition. Oxford: Oxford University Press.

Bobbert, M., & Mieth, D. 2015. *Das Proprium der christlichen Ethik: Zur moralischen Perspektive der Religion*. Luzern, CH: Edition Exodus.

Bornstein, D. 1996. *The Price of a Dream: The Story of the Grameen Bank and the Idea That Is Helping the Poor to Change Their Lives*. Chicago, IL: University of Chicago Press.

Boukaert, L., & Zsolnai, L. (eds.). 2011. *The Palgrave Handbook of Spirituality and Business*. New York: Palgrave Macmillan.

Bourdieu, P. 1986. In J. G. Richardson. 1986. *Handbook of Theory and Research for the Sociology of Education*. Westport, CT: Greenwood Press.

Bourguignon, F. 2015. *The Globalization of Inequality*. Princeton, NJ: Princeton University Press.

2019. Growth, inequality and poverty reduction. In Atkinson 2019, 218–31.

Boushey, H., DeLong, J. B., & Steinbaum, M. (eds.). 2017. *AFTER PIKETTY: The Agenda for Economics and Inequality*. Cambridge, MA: Harvard University Press.

Bower, J. L., & Paine, L. S. 2017. The error at the heart of corporate leadership. Most CEOs and boards believe their main duty is to maximize shareholder value. It's not. *Harvard Business Review*, May–June, 50–60.

Boyd, C. 1996. Ethics and corporate governance: The issues raised by the Cadbury report in the United Kingdom. *Journal of Business Ethics*, 15, 167-182.

Braybrooke, D., & Mohanan, A. P. 2001. Common Good. In Becker, L.C., & Becker, C.B. (eds). 2001. *Encyclopedia of ethics*. Second edition. New York: Routledge, 262–66.

Brenkert, G. G. 2009. Google, human rights, and moral compromise. *Journal of Business Ethics*, 85(4), 453–78.

2015. Business, moral innovation and ethics. In Enderle & Murphy 2015, 25–46.

2016. Business and human rights: An overview. *Business and Human Rights Journal*, 1(2), 277–306.

Brenkert, G. G., & Beauchamp, T. L. 2010. *The Oxford Handbook of Business Ethics*. New York: Oxford University Press.

Brent, R. J. 1998. *Cost-Benefit Analysis for Developing Countries*. Cheltenham: Edward Elgar.

2018. *Advanced Introduction to Cost-Benefit Analysis*. Cheltenham: Edward Elgar.

Brieskorn, N. (Hg.). 1997. *Globale Solidarität: Die verschiedenen Kulturen und die Eine Welt*. Stuttgart: Kohlhammer.

Brown, M. 2010. *Civilizing the Economy*. Cambridge: Cambridge University Press.

Bruni, L., Comim, F., & Pugno, M. (eds.). 2008. *Capabilities and Happiness*. New York: Oxford University Press.

Buhmann, K. 2017. Chinese human rights guidance on minerals sourcing: Building soft power. *Journal of Current Chinese Affairs*, 2(1), 135–54.

Burke, R. 2010. *Decolonization and the Evolution of International Human Rights*. Philadelphia: University of Pennsylvania Press.

Business and Human Rights Research Center (BHRRC). http://tinyurl.com/hb54fe9.

Business Leaders Initiative on Human Rights (BLIHR). 2009. *Policy Report 4*. www.blihr.org.

Business Roundtable. 2019. Statement on the purpose of a corporation. https://opportunity.businessroundtable.org/wp-content/uploads/2019/08/Business-Roundtable-Statement-on-the-Purpose-of-a-Corporation-with-Signatures.pdf

Byrd, M. Y. (ed.). 2016. *Spirituality in the Workplace: A Philosophical and Justice Perspective*. San Francisco, CA: Jossey-Bass.

Cadbury, S. A. 2003. Corporate Governance and Development. Foreword by Sir Adrian Cadbury. *Global Corporate Governance Forum*. Washington, D.C.: World Bank.

Cadbury Report. 1992. *Report of the Committee on the Financial Aspects of Corporate Governance*. London: GEE Professional Publishing Ltd.

Cameron, P. D., & Stanley, M. C. 2016. *Oil, Gas, and Mining: A Sourcebook for Understanding the Extractive Industries*. Washington, DC: World Bank Group.

Campbell, T., & Miller, S. (eds.). 2004. *Human Rights and the Moral Responsibilities of Corporate and Public Sector Organisations*. Dordrecht: Kluwer Academic Publishers.

Carrillo, H., & Batalli, L. 2018. European values or European Profit? A case study of the EU's responsibility to protect human rights in the Free Trade Agreement with Vietnam. Research paper in the MBA Course "International Business Ethics" in the Mendoza College of Business, University of Notre Dame, April.

Carroll, A. B. 2008. A history of corporate social responsibility: Concepts and practices. In Crane, A., Matten, D., McWilliams, A., Moon, J., & Siegel, D. S. (eds). 2008. *The Oxford Handbook of Corporate Social Responsibility*. New York: Oxford University Press, 19–46.

Carroll, A. B., Lipartito, K. L., Post, J. E., Werhane, P. H., & Goodpaster, K. E. (executive eds.). 2012. *Corporate Responsibility: The American Experience*. Cambridge: Cambridge University Press.

Cassel, D., & Ramasastry, A. 2016. White Paper: Options for a treaty on business and human rights. *University of Notre Dame Journal of International & Comparative Law*, September. Class materials for Transnational Corporations and Human Rights, spring semester 2018.

Caux Round Table. 1994. Caux Round Table Principles for Responsible Business. New edition 2009, updated in 2010. www.cauxroundtable.org.

CCCMC. 2015. *Chinese Due Diligence Guidelines for Responsible Mineral Supply Chains*. Beijing: The China Chamber of Commerce of Metals, Minerals and Chemicals. https://mneguidelines.oecd.org/chinese-due-diligence-guidelines-for-responsible-mineral-supply-chains.htm, accessed on December 16, 2018.

Chabrak, N., Craig, R., & Daidj, N. 2016. Financialization and the employee suicide crisis at France Telecom. *Journal of Business Ethics*, 139, 501–15.

Chamberlain, A. 2015. www.glassdoor.com/research/ceo-pay-ratio, accessed on October 27, 2017.

Chatterji, M., & Zsolnai, L. (eds.). 2016. *Ethical Leadership: Indian and European Spiritual Approaches*. New York: Palgrave Macmillan.

Chicago Magazine. 2015. October. chicagomag.com/ceopay, accessed on February 5, 2017.

Chiu, T. K. 2014. Putting responsible finance to work for Citi microfinance. *Journal of Business Ethics*, 119, 219–34.

2017. Factors influencing microfinance engagements by formal financial institutions. *Journal of Business Ethics*, 143(3), 565–87.

Ciulla, J. B. 2015. Drops in the pond: Leaders, morality, and imagination. In Enderle & Murphy 2015, 119–36.

Ciulla, J. B., & Scharding, T. K. (eds.). 2019. *Ethical Business Leadership in Troubling Times*. Cheltenham: Edward Elgar.

Cobb, J. A. 2016. How firms shape income inequality: Stakeholder power, executive decision making, and the structure of employment relationships. *Academy of Management Review*, 41(2), 324–48.

Cohen, S. S., & Boyd, G. (eds.). 2000. *Corporate Governance and Globalization: Long Range Planning Issues*. Cheltenham: Edward Elgar.

Colella, A., Paetzold, R. L., Zardkoohi, A., & Wesson, M. J. 2007. Exposing pay secrecy. *Academy of Management Review*, 32, 55–71.

Coleman, J. S. 1990. *Foundations of Social Theory*. Cambridge, MA: Belknap Press of Harvard University Press.

2000. Social capital in the creation of human capital. In Dasgupta & Seragedin 2000, 40–58.

Collier, P. 2010. *The Plundered Planet: Why We Must – and How We Can – Manage Nature for Global Prosperity*. New York: Oxford University Press.

Collins, D. 2018. Living wage. In Kolb 2018, 2102–05.

Collins, J. C. 2001. *Good to Great: Why Some Companies Make the Leap ... and Others Don't*. New York: HarperBusiness.

Collins, J., & Porras, J. I. 1994. *Built to Last: Successful Habits of Visionary Companies*. New York: HarperBusiness.

Copp, D. 2001. Metaethics. In Becker & Becker 2001, 1079–87.

Corporate Responsibility Magazine. www.3blassociation.com/insights/magazines.

Cortina, A. 2013. Sen's capabilities, poverty and economic welfare. In Luetge 2013, 659–741.

Council of the European Union (Council of the EU). 2020. Press Release of 30 March. https://trade.ec.europa.eu/doclib/press/index.cfm?id=1437, accessed on July 19, 2020

Cragg, W. 2010. Business and human rights: A principle and value-based analysis. In G. G. Brenkert & T. L. Beauchamp (eds.), *The Oxford Handbook of Business Ethics*. Oxford: Oxford University Press, 267–304.

Crane, A., & Matten, D. 2010. *Business Ethics: Managing Corporate Citizenship and Sustainability in the Age of Globalization*. Third edition. Oxford: Oxford University Press.

Crane, A., Matten, D., & J. Moon. 2008. *Corporations and Citizenship*. Cambridge: Cambridge University Press.

Crane, A., McWilliams, A., Matten, D., Moon, J., & Siegel, D. S. (eds.). 2008. *The Oxford Handbook of Corporate Social Responsibility*. New York: Oxford University Press.

Curran, C. E., & McCormick, R. A. (eds.). 1980. *Readings in Moral Theology No. 2: The Distinctiveness of Christian Ethics*. New York: Paulist Press.

Curtler, H. (ed.). 1986. *Shame, Responsibility and the Corporation*. New York: Haven.

Cushen, J. 2013. Financialization in the workplace: Hegemonic narratives, performative interventions and the angry knowledge worker. *Accounting, Organizations and Society*, 38, 314–31.

Dasgupta, P. 2003. Social capital and economic performance: Analytics. In E. Ostrom & T. K. Ahn (eds.), *Foundations of Social Capital*. Cheltenham: Edward Elgar.

Dasgupta, P., & Mäler, K. G. 2000. Net national product, wealth, and social well-being. *Environmental and Development Economics* 5, 69–93.

Dasgupta, P., & Mäler, K. G. (eds.). 2004. *The Economics of Non-convex Ecosystems*. Dordrecht: Kluwer Academic Publishers.

Dasgupta, P., & Serageldin, I. (eds.). 2000. *Social Capital: A Multifaceted Perspective*. Washington, DC: World Bank.

Davis, G. 2016. Post-corporate: The disappearing corporation in the new economy. www.thirdway.org/reports/post-corporate-the -disappearing-corporation-in-the-new-economy.

Davis, G. F., & Cobb, J. A. 2010. Corporations and economic inequality around the world: The paradox of hierarchy. *Research in Organizational Behavior*, 30, 35–53.

Davis, P. 2011. John Ruggie: A common focus for human rights. *The Ethical Corporation*, February, 43.

Dawkins, C. E. 2012. Labor relations: Corporate citizenship, labor unions, and freedom of association. *Business Ethics Quarterly*, 22, 473–500.

De George, R. T. 1987. The status of business ethics: Past and future. *Journal of Business Ethics*, 6, 201–11.

  1993. *Competing with Integrity in International Business*. New York: Oxford.

  2010. *Business Ethics*. Seventh edition. Upper Saddle River, NJ: Prentice Hall.

Dees, J. G., Emerson, J., & Economy, P. 2001. *Enterprising Nonprofits: A Toolkit for Social Entrepreneurs*. New York: Wiley.

Dembinski, P. H. 2009. *Finance: Servant or Deceiver? Financialization at the Crossroad*. New York: Palgrave Macmillan.

  2017. *Ethics and Responsibility in Finance*. New York: Routledge.

DesJardins, J. 2014. *An Introduction to Business Ethics*. Fifth edition. New York: McGraw-Hill.

Deva, S., Ramasastry, A., Wettstein, F., & Santoro, M. 2019. Editorial: Business and human rights scholarship: Past trends and future directions. *Business and Human Rights Journal*, 4(2), 201–12.

Dodd-Frank Wall Street Reform and Consumer Protection Act. 2015. www .sec.gov/news/pressrelease/2015-160.html, accessed on January 30, 2017.

Dodgson, M., Gann, D., & Salter, A. 2008. *The Management of Technological Innovation, Strategy and Practice*. New York: Oxford University Press.

Dodgson, M., & Gann, D. 2010. *Innovation: A Very Short Introduction*. New York: Oxford University Press.

Donaldson, T. 1982. *Corporations and Morality*. Englewood Cliffs, NJ: Prentice Hall.

  2001. The ethical wealth of nations. *Journal of Business Ethics*, 31, 25–36.

2012. The impossibility theorem for corporate governance. In Crane et al. 2008.

Dumas, J., Bernardi, C. Guthrie, J., & Demartini, P. 2016. Integrated reporting: A structural literature review. *Accounting Forum*, 40(3), 166–85.

Dutt, A. K. 1990. *Growth, Distribution and Uneven Development*. Cambridge: Cambridge University Press.

Eatwell, J., Milgate, M., & Newman, P. (eds.). 1987. *The New Palgrave: A Dictionary of Economics*. 4 volumes. New York: Stockton.

(eds.). 1989. *The New Palgrave: General Equilibrium*. New York: Norton.

Ebeling, H. 1984. Betroffenheit, Mitleid und Vernunft. In K. O. Apel et al. (Hg.). 1984. *Praktische Philosophie/Ethik: Dialoge*. Band 2, 147–68.

Edgecliffe-Johnson, A. 2019. Beyond the bottom line. For 50 years, companies were told to put shareholders first. Now even their largest investors are challenging that consensus. But can we trust CEOs to decide what is best for society? *Financial Times*, January 5.

Emmons, W. R., & Schmid, F. A. 2000. Corporate governance and corporate performance. In Cohen & Boyd 2000, 59–94.

Emunds, B. 2014. *Politische Wirtschaftsethik globaler Finanzmärkte*. Wiesbaden: Springer.

Enderle, G. 1982. *Die Auswirkungen der Weltwirtschaftskrise der dreissiger Jahre auf die personelle Einkommens- und Vermögensverteilung - Methodische und theoretische Probleme, Ergebnisse einer Fallstudie* [*The Impact of the Great Depression in the Thirties on the Personal Distribution of Income and Wealth – Methodological and Theoretical Problems – Results of a Case Study*]. Freiburg/Schweiz: Universitätsverlag.

1987. *Sicherung des Existenzminimums im nationalen und internationalen Kontext – eine wirtschaftsethische Studie* [*Securing the Minimal Standard of Living in the National and International Context – A Business Ethics Perspective*]. Bern/Stuttgart: Haupt.

1989. Das Armutsproblem als Paradigma der Wirtschaftsethik [The problem of poverty as paradigm of business ethics]. In P. Eicher (Hg.). 1989. *Neue Summe Theologie*, Band 2. Freiburg: Herder, 342–73.

1993. *Handlungsorientierte Wirtschaftsethik. Grundlagen und Anwendungen* [*Action-Oriented Business Ethics. Foundations and Applications*]. Bern: Haupt.

1995. An outsider's view of the East Asian miracle: Lessons and questions. In S. Stewart & G. Donleavy (eds.), *Whose Business Values? Some Asian and Cross-Cultural Perspectives*. Hong Kong: Hong Kong University Press, 87–120.

1996. A comparison of business ethics in North America and continental Europe. *Business Ethics: A European Review*, 5(1), 117–22.

1997. In search of a common ethical ground: Corporate environmental responsibility from the perspective of Christian environmental stewardship. *Journal of Business Ethics*, 16(2), 173–81.

1998. Business ethics as a goal-rights-system. In E. Morscher, O. Neumaier, & P. Simons (eds.), *Applied Ethics in a Troubled World*. Dordrecht: Kluwer Academic Publishers, 151–66.

Enderle, G. (ed.). 1999. *International Business Ethics: Challenges and Approaches*. Notre Dame: University of Notre Dame Press.

2000. Whose ethos for public goods in a global economy? An exploration in international business ethics. *Business Ethics Quarterly*, 10(1), 131–44.

2003a. Business ethics. In N. Bunnin & E. P. Tsui-James. 2003. *The Blackwell Companion to Philosophy*. Second edition. Oxford: Blackwell Publishers, 531–51.

2003b. Special section: Religious resources for business ethics in Latin America. *Latin American Business Review*, 4(4), 87–134.

2004. Global competition and corporate responsibilities of small and medium-sized enterprises. *Business Ethics: A European Review*, 13(1), 51–63.

2005. Globalization. In P. H. Werhane & R. E. Freeman (eds.), *Blackwell Encyclopedic Dictionary of Business Ethics*. Second edition. Oxford: Blackwell, 215–18.

2006. Corporate responsibility in the CSR debate. In J. Wieland, J. M. Reder, & T. Karcher (eds.), *Unternehmensethik im Spannungsfeld der Kulturen und Religionen*. Stuttgart: Kohlhammer, 108–24.

2007. The ethics of conviction versus the ethics of responsibility: A false antithesis for business ethics. *Journal of Human Values*, 13(2), 83–94.

2008. Rediscovering the golden rule in a globalizing world. In Tze-wan Kwan (ed.), *Responsibility and Commitment: Eighteen Essays in Honor of Gerhold K. Becker*. Waldkirch: Edition Gorz, 1–15.

2009. A rich concept of wealth creation beyond profit maximization and adding value. *Journal of Business Ethics*, 84, Supplement 3, 281–95.

2010a. Wealth creation in China and some lessons for development ethics. *Journal of Business Ethics*, 96(1), 1–15.

2010b. Clarifying the terms of business ethics and corporate social responsibility. *Business Ethics Quarterly*, 20(4), 730–32.

2011a. What is long-term wealth creation and investing? In A. Tencati & F. Perrini (eds.), *Business Ethics and Corporate Sustainability*. Cheltenham: Edward Elgar, 114–31.

2011b. Three major challenges for business and economic ethics in the next ten years: Wealth creation, human rights, and active involvement of the world's religions. *Business and Professional Ethics Journal*, 30(3–4), 231–52.

Enderle, G., & Niu, Q. 2012. Discerning ethical challenges for marketing in China. *Asian Journal of Business Ethics*, 1(2), 143–62. Also in Murphy & Sherry 2013, 281–305.

2013a. Defining goodness in business and economics. In V. Hösle (ed.), *Dimensions of Goodness*. Notre Dame, IN: University of Notre Dame, 281–302.

2013b. The capability approach as guidance for corporate ethics. In Luetge 2013, 675–91.

2013c. Wealth creation in China from a Christian perspective. *Qing Feng*, n.s. 12, 119–36.

2014a. The option for the poor and business ethics. In D. Groody & G. Gutierrez (ed.), *The Preferential Option for the Poor beyond Theology*. Notre Dame, IN: University of Notre Dame Press, 28–46.

2014b. Some ethical explications of the UN framework for business and human rights. In O. F. Williams (ed.), *Sustainable Development: The UN Millennium Development Goals, the UN Global Compact, and the Common Good*. Notre Dame, IN: University of Notre Dame Press, 163–83.

2015a. Exploring and conceptualizing international business ethics. *Journal of Business Ethics*, 127(4), 723–35.

2015b. Business and the greater good as a combination of private and public wealth. In K. Ims & L. J. Tyles Petersen (eds.), *Business and the Greater Good: Rethinking Business Ethics in an Age of Crisis*. Cheltenham: Edward Elgar Publishing, 64–80.

2015c. Ethical innovation in business and the economy: A challenge that cannot be postponed. In Enderle & Murphy 2015, 1–22.

2018a. Manifesto for a global economic ethic. In Kolb 2018, 2159–61.

2018b. Interfaith declaration of international business ethics. In Kolb 2018, 1883–85.

2018c. Economic systems. In Kolb 2018, 1028–34.

2018d. How can business ethics strengthen the social cohesion of a society? *Journal of Business Ethics*, 150(3), 619–29.

2018e. Corporate responsibility for less income inequality. *Review of Social Economy*, 76(4), 399–421.

Enderle, G., Homann, K., Honecker, M., Kerber, W., & Steinmann, H. eds. 1993. *Lexikon der Wirtschaftsethik*. Freiburg: Herder.

Enderle, G., & Murphy, P. E. (eds.). 2015. *Ethical Innovation in Business and the Economy*. Cheltenham: Edward Elgar.

Enderle, G., & Niu, Q. 2012. Discerning ethical challenges for marketing in China. *Asian Journal of Business Ethics*, 1(2), 143–62. Also in Murphy, P. E., & Sherry, J. F. (eds.). 2013. *Marketing and the Common Good. Essays from Notre Dame on Societal Impact.* Abingdon, Oxon: Routledge, 281–305.

Enderle, G., & Tavis, L. A. 1998. A balanced concept of the firm and the measurement of its long-term planning and performance. *Journal of Business Ethics*, 17, 1121–44.

Epstein, G. A. (ed.). 2005. *Financialization and the World Economy.* Cheltenham: Edward Elgar.

Etinson, A. 2018. *Human Rights: Moral or Political?* Oxford: Oxford University Press.

Fawthrop, T. 2004. Vietnam's war against agent orange. *BBC News*, June 14: http://news.bbc.co.uk/2/hi/health/3798581.stm, accessed on October 27, 2019.

Feder, B. J. 2001. Lawsuit says I.B.M. aided the Nazis in technology. *New York Times*, February 11. www.nytimes.com/2001/01/11/world/law suit-says-ibm-aided-the-nazis-in-technology.html.

Financial Times. 2015. Volkswagen emission test cheating rocks Europe's car manufacturers. Volkswagen makes a monumental blunder. VW woes cast doubts over chief's place in driving seat. September 11, pp. 1, 8, 15.

2016. Record fines for Wells after staff set up secret accounts to hit goals. Fake account put focus on Wells Fargo Culture. Wells Fargo caves in and dispenses with chief. Wells to scrap branch sales targets. The high cost of Wells Fargo's sales practices. Wells scandal stiffens resolve to end board inertia. John Stumpf – The Labrador of Main Street. Wells Fargo scandals turns attention to pay. Wells chief savaged in Congress over fake accounts. September 9, 12, 14, 14, 14, 15, 17, 19, 21.

2018. Macron attempts to reset Beijing trade ties. By L. Hornby & A. S. Chassany, January 10.

2019a. Repairing a damaged brand. By R. Armstrong & L. Noonan, January 15.

2019b. Volkswagen and 400,000 diesel drivers set to lock horns in German court battle. By J. Miller, September 30.

Forbes. 2012. Apple's Foxconn to double the wages again. www.forbes.com/sites/timworstall/2012/05/28/apples-foxconn-to-double-wages-again/#23ddcad15d16, accessed on October 23, 2017.

Forbes Global. 2000. Ranking 2018. www.forbes.com/global2000/list/

Foreign Affairs. 2016. Inequality. What causes it. Why it matters. What can be done. 95(1), 1–44.

2019. Autocracy now. 98(5), 10–54.

Fort, T. M. (ed.). 2011. *Peace through Commerce: A Multisectoral Approach*. New York: Springer.

Fortune.com. 2016. Wells Fargo exec who headed phony accounts unite collected $125 million. September 9. http://fortune.com/2016/09/12/wells-fargo-cfpb-carrie-tolstedt

Fortune. 2017. Walmart CEO Dough McMillon got a solid raise last year. April 21.

Francis. 2015. *Laudato Si' – On Care for Our Common Home*. Encyclical letter. http://w2.vatican.va/content/francesco/en/encyclicals/documents/papa-francesco_20150524_enciclica-laudato-si.html

Frangieh, C. G., & Yaacoub, H. K. 2017. A systematic literature review of responsible leadership. Challenges, outcomes and practices. *Journal of Global Responsibility*, 8(2), 281–99.

Frank, R. H. 2007. *Falling Behind: How Rising Inequality Harms the Middle Class*. Berkeley, CA: University of California Press.

Frankl, V. 1984. *Man's Search for Meaning: An Introduction to Logotherapy*. Third edition. New York: Simon and Schuster.

Freeman, C., & Soete, L. 1997. *The Economics of Industrial Innovation*. London: Pinter.

Freeman, R. E. 1984. *Strategic Management: A Stakeholder Approach*. Boston: Pitman.

Frederick, R. E. (ed.). 1999. *A Companion to Business Ethics*. Malden, MA: Blackwell.

French, P. A. 1984. *Collective and Corporate Responsibility*. New York: Columbia University Press.

Friedman, B. M. 2005. *The Moral Consequences of Economic Growth*. New York: Knopf.

Friedman, M. 1970. The social responsibility of business is to increase its profit. *The New York Times Sunday Magazine*, September 13.

Friedman, T. L. 2000. *The Lexus and the Olive Tree*. New York: Anchor Books.

Fukuda-Parr, S. 2004. Justice, not charity in development: Today's human rights priorities. In Arruda & Enderle 2004, 105–14.

G20/OECD. 2015. *G20/OECD Principles of Corporate Governance*. Paris: OECD.

George, B. 2003. *Authentic Leadership: Rediscovering the Secrets to Creating Lasting Value*. San Francisco, CA: Jossey-Bass.

Gewirth, A. 1978. *Reason and Morality*. Chicago, IL: University of Chicago Press.

  1982. *Human Rights: Essays on Justification and Application*. Chicago, IL: University of Chicago Press.

  1984. The epistemology of human rights. *Social Philosophy and Policy*, 1 (2), 1–24.

1996. *The Community of Rights.* Chicago: University of Chicago Press.

2007. Duties to fulfill the human rights of the poor. In Pogge 2007, 219–36.

Ghoshal, S. 2005. Bad management theories are destroying good management practices. *Academy of Management Learning and Education*, 4 (1), 75–91.

Giacalone, R. A., & Jurkiewicz, C. L. (eds.). 2010. *Handbook of Workplace Spirituality and Organizational Performance.* Second edition. Armonk, NY: M. E. Sharpe. First edition 2003.

GMWatch. 2009. Bayer: A history. February 1. www.gmwatch.org/en/gm-firms/11153-bayer-a-history.

Golding, M. P. 1984. The primacy of welfare rights. *Social Philosophy and Policy*, 1(2), 119–36.

González-Cantón, C., Boulos, S., & Sánchez-Garrido, P. 2018. Exploring the link between human rights, the capability approach and corporate responsibility. *Journal of Business Ethics*, DOI 10.1007/s10551-018-3801-x.

Goodpaster, K. E. 1983. The concept of corporate responsibility. *Journal of Business Ethics*, 2, 1–22.

2001. Business ethics. In Becker & Becker 2001, 170–75. First edition 1992.

Gorman, M. E., Mehalik, M. M., & Werhane, P. H. 2003. *Ethical and Environmental Challenges to Engineering.* Englewood Cliffs, NJ: Prentice Hall. Case Study: Rohner Textil AG, 109–45.

Götzmann, N. 2017. Human rights impact assessment of business activities: Key criteria for establishing a meaningful practice. *Business and Human Rights Journal*, 2(1), 87–110.

Gräb-Schmidt, E. 2012. III. Philosophy of religion. IV. Fundamental theology. V. Dogmatic. VI. Ethics. 226–28.

Greenberg, J. 1987. A taxonomy of organizational justice theories. *Academy of Management Review*, 12, 9–22.

Grethlein, C. 2012. Practical theology. In Betz et al. 2012, 228–29.

Gröschl, S., & Bendl, R. (eds.). 2015. *Managing Religious Diversity in the Workplace. Examples from Around the World.* Farnham: Gower.

Grunberg, I., & Stern, M. A. (eds.). 1999a. *Global Public Goods: International Cooperation in the 21st century.* Published for the United Nations Development Programme (UNDP). New York: Oxford University Press.

Guo, L., Hsu, S.-H., Holton, A., & Jeong, S. H. 2012. A case study of the Foxconn suicides: An international perspective to framing the sweatshop issue. *International Communication Gazette*, 74(5), 484–503. http://gaz.sagepub.com/content/74/5/484, accessed on October 19, 2017.

Gutiérrez, G. 1988. *A Theology of Liberation*. Revised edition. Maryknoll, NY: Orbis Books.

Habermas, J. 2001. *The Postnational Constellation: Political Essays*. Translated by M. Pensky. Cambridge, MA: MIT Press.

Haltiwanger, J. 2018. Here's everything we know about the troubling disappearance and death of the Saudi journalist Jamal Khashoggi. December 10. www.businessinsider.com/who-is-jamal-khashoggi-turkey-accuses-saudi-arabia-of-murdering-reporter-2018-10, accessed on October 27, 2019.

Hamilton, K., & Clemens, M. 1999. Genuine saving rates in developing countries. *World Bank Economic Review*, 13(2), 333–56.

Hamlin, A. P. 2001. Economic systems. In Becker et al. 2001, 1, 439–45.

Hammes, D. L. 2018. Pareto efficiency. In Kolb 2018, 2586–88.

Hardin, G. 1968. The tragedy of the commons. *Science*, 162, 1243–48.

Hargreaves-Heap, S. P., & Hollis, M. 1987. Economic man. In Eatwell et al. 1987, 2, 54–55.

Hartman, L. P., Arnold, D. G., & Wokutch, R. E. (eds.). 2003. *Rising above Sweatshops: Innovative Approaches to Global Labor Challenges*. Westport, CT/London: Praeger.

Heilbroner, R. L. 1987. Capitalism. In Eatwell et al. 1987, 1, 347–53.

Held, D., & McGrew, A. (eds.). 2000. *The Global Transformations Reader*. Cambridge: Polity Press.

   2002. *Governing Globalization: Power, Authority and Global Governance*. Cambridge: Polity Press.

Held, D., McGrew, A., Goldblatt, D., & Perraton, J. 1999. *Global Transformations. Politics, Economics and Culture*. Stanford, CA: Stanford University Press.

Hess, K. M. 2013. "If you tickle us …": How corporations can be moral agents without being persons. *Journal of Value Inquiry*, 47, 319–35.

Hesse, H. 1993. Globalization. In Enderle et al. 1993, 402–10.

Hilb, Martin. 2008. *New Corporate Governance: Successful Board Management Tools*. Berlin: Springer. Other English editions in 2005, 2006, 2015, 2016.

   2016. *Integrierte Corporate Governance: Ein neues Konzept zur wirksamen Führung und Aufsicht von Unternehmen*. 6., überarbeitete Auflage. Berlin: Springer.

Hilb, Michael (ed.). 2017. *Governance of Digitalization. The Role of Boards of Directors and Top Management Teams in Digital Value Creation*. Bern: Haupt.

Hill, A. 2016. Open the Pandora's box of pay and reap the benefits. *Financial Times*, June 21, 10.

Hösle, V. 2019. *Globale Fliehkräfte. Eine geschichtsphilosophische Kartierung der Gegenwart* [*Global Centrifugal Forces. A Mapping of the Present Based on the Philosophy of History*]. Freiburg: Karl Alber.

Hsieh, N. 2017. Business responsibilities for human rights: A commentary on Arnold. *Business and Human Rights Journal*, 2(2), 297–309.

Huang, Y. 2008. *Capitalism with Chinese Characteristics: Entrepreneurship and the State*. New York: Cambridge University Press.

International Integrated Reporting Committee (IIRC). 2013. *The international <IR> framework*. http://integratedreporting.org/wp-content/uploads/ 2015/03/13-12-08-THE-INTERNATIONAL-IR-FRAMEWORK-2-1 .pdf.

IOD. 1994. *King Report on Corporate Governance*. Johannesburg: Institute of Directors (IOD).

2002. *King Report on Corporate Governance for South Africa 2002*. Johannesburg: Institute of Directors.

2009. *King Report on Governance for South Africa 2009*. Johannesburg: Institute of Directors.

2016. *King Report on Corporate Governance for South Africa 2016*. Johannesburg: Institute of Directors.

James, H. S. 2018. Collective choice. In Kolb 2018, 514.

Jennings, P. L., & Velasquez, M. 2015. Towards an ethical wealth of nations: An institutional perspective on the relation between ethical values and national economic prosperity. *Business Ethics Quarterly*, 25(4), 461–88.

Jennings, R. 2017. Vietnam's TTP backup plan, a Free Trade Agreement with Europe, is facing new obstacles. *Forbes*, March 2.

Jensen, M. C., & Meckling, W. M. 1976. Theory of the firm: Managerial behavior, agency costs and ownership structure. *Journal of Financial Economics*, 3, 305–60.

John XXIII. 1963. *Pacem in Terris – Peace on Earth*. Encyclical on April 11, 1963. http://w2.vatican.va/content/john-xxiii/en/encyclicals/documents/ hf_j-xxiii_enc_11041963_pacem.html

Johnson-Cramer, M. E. 2018. Stakeholder theory. In Kolb 2018, 3246–55.

Jonas, H. 1984. *The Imperative of Responsibility: Foundations of an Ethics for the Technological Age*. Chicago: University of Chicago Press. Original version in German in 1979.

Kalkundrikar, A. B., Hiremath, S. G., & Mutkekar, R. R. (eds.). 2009. *Business Ethics and Corporate Social Responsibility: International Conference Proceedings*. Delhi: Macmillan Publishers India.

Karnes, R. 2009. A change in business ethics: The impact on employer-employee relations. *Journal of Business Ethics*, 87, 189–97.

Kates, M. 2015. The ethics of sweatshops and the limits of choice. *Business Ethics Quarterly*, 25(2), 191–212.

Kaufman, S., & Wining, L. 2012. Drilling safety at BP: The Deepwater Horizon accident. *Harvard Business School*.

Kaul, I. (ed.). 2003. *Providing Global Public Goods: Managing Globalization*. New York: Oxford University Press.

Kaul, I., Grunberg, I., & Stern, M. A. 1999a. *Global Public Goods: International Cooperation in the Twenty-First Century*. New York: Oxford University Press.

1999b. Defining global public goods. In Kaul et al. 1999a, 2–19.

1999c. Global public goods: Concepts, policies and strategies. In Kaul et al. 1999a, 450–507.

Kelman, S. 1981. Cost-benefit analysis: An ethical critique. *Regulation: AEI Journal of Government and Society*, January–February, 33–40.

Kerber, W. 1993. Gemeinwohl. In Enderle et al. 1993, 339–42.

Kettner, M. 2002. Moralische Verantwortung als Grundbegriff der Ethik. In M. Niquet, F. J. Herrero, & M. Hanke. 2002. *Diskursethik, Grundlegungen und Anwendungen*. Würzburg: Königshausen und Neumann, 65–94.

Keynes, J. M. 1933/1972. *Collected Writings: Volume X: Essays in Biography*. London: Macmillan.

Kickul, J., & Lyons, T. S. 2012. *Understanding Social Entrepreneurship. The Relentless Pursuit of Mission in an Ever Changing World*. New York: Routledge.

Kim, K. 2012. Mission spirituality. In Betz et al. 2012, 229.

Kim, T. W. 2014. Confucian ethics and labor rights. *Business Ethics Quarterly*, 24(4), 565–94.

King, M. 2016. *The End of Alchemy. Money, Banking and the Future of the Global Economy*. London: Little, Brown.

Kirchgässner, G. 2008. *Homo Oeconomicus: The Economic Model of Individual Behavior and Its Applications in Economics and Other Social Sciences*. New York: Springer.

Kirchschläger, P. G. (ed.). 2017. *Die Verantwortung von nichtstaatlichen Akteuren gegenüber Menschenrechten. [The Responsibility of Non-State Actors for Human Rights.]* Zürich: Theologischer Verlag, 195–215.

Klein, T. 2001. Analogical argument. In Becker & Becker 2001, 59–64.

Knight, G. 2013. Homeland security. *Financial Times*, January 4.

Kolb, R. W. 2012. *Too Much Is Not Enough: Incentives in Executive Compensation*. New York: Oxford University Press.

Kolb, R. W. (ed.). 2018. *The Sage Encyclopedia of Business Ethics and Society*. Second edition, 7 volumes. Thousand Oaks, CA: Sage.

Kolstad, C. D. 2010. *Environmental Economics*. Second edition. New York: Oxford University Press.

Köpf, U. 2012. Spirituality. I. Terminology. II. Church history. In Betz et al. 2012, 224–26.

Korff, W., et al. (Hg.). 1999. *Handbuch der Wirtschaftsethik*. Gütersloh: Gütersloher Verlagshaus.

Krippner, G. R. 2005. The financialization of the American economy. *Socio-Economic Review*, 3, 173–208.

Kromphardt, J. 1991. *Konzeptionen und Analysen des Kapitalismus: von seiner Entstehung bis zur Gegenwart*. 3. Auflage. Göttingen: Vandenhoeck und Ruprecht.

Kropp, R. 2010. Investors ask companies in Sudan to respect human rights: www.socialfunds.com/ news/article.cgi/3076.html.

Krugman, P. 2009. *The Conscience of a Liberal*. New York: Norton.

Kryder, L. G. 2018. Supply chain, sustainable. In Kolb 2018, 3301–03.

Küng, H. 1998. *A Global Ethic for Global Politics and Economics*. London: SCM Press.

1999. A global ethic in an age of globalization. In Enderle 1999, 109–28 (also in *Business Ethics Quarterly*, 1997, 7, 17–31).

Küng, H., Leisinger, K., Wieland, J. 2010. *Manifest Globales Wirtschaftsethos: Konsequenzen und Herausforderungen für die Weltwirtschaft. Manifesto Global Economic Ethic: Consequences and Challenges for Global Businesses*. München: Deutscher Taschenbuch Verlag.

Kuper, S. 2013. Borderlines: Photography special. *Financial Times*, January 4.

Kushnir, K., Mirmulstein, M. L., Ramalho, R. 2010. Micro, small and medium enterprises around the world: How many are there, and what affects the count? Washington, DC: International Finance Corporation, World Bank Group.

Kuznets, S. 1955. Economic growth and income distribution. *American Economic Review*, 45(1), 1–28.

1959. *Six Lectures on Economic Growth*. Glencoe, IL: Free Press..

1966. *Modern Economic Growth*. New Haven, CT: Yale University Press.

Kwon, S. W., & Adler, P. S. 2014. Social capital: Maturation of a field of research. *Academy of Management Review*, 39(4), 412–22.

Labowitz, S., & Baumann-Pauly, D. 2014. Business as usual is not an option: Supply-chains and sourcing after Rana Plaza. New York: New York Leonard N. Stern School of Business – Center of Business and Human Rights.

Laczniak, G. R., & Santos, N. J. C. 2015. The integrated justice model: Fair, ethical and innovative marketing to the poor. In Enderle & Murphy 2015, 261–80.

Ladd, J. 1970. Morality and the ideal of rationality in formal organizations. *The Monist*, 54, 488–516.

Lagarde, C. 2015. Ethics and finance – Aligning financial incentives with societal objectives. Speech at the Event hosted by the Institute for New Economic Thinking: Finance and Society. www.imf.org/en/News/Articles/2015/09/28/04/53/sp050615.

Landes, D. S. 1999. *The Wealth and Poverty of Nations: Why Some Are So Rich and Some Are So Poor*. New York: Norton.

Lange, G. M., Wodon, Q., & Carey, K. (eds.). 2018. *The Changing Wealth of Nations 2018: Building a Sustainable Future*. Washington, DC: World Bank.

Ledgerwood, J. (ed.). 2013. *The New Microfinance Handbook: A Financial Market System Perspective*. Washington, DC: World Bank.

Leo XIII. 1891. *Rerum Novarum – On Capital and Labor*. Encyclical on May 15, 1891. http://w2.vatican.va/content/leo-xiii/en/encyclicals/documents/hf_l-xiii_enc_15051891_rerum-novarum.html.

Levin-Waldman, O. M. 2005. *The Political Economy of the Living Wage: A Study of Four Cities*. Armonk, NY: M. E. Sharpe.

Lin-Hi, N., & Blumberg, I. 2017. The power (lessness) of industry self-regulation to promote responsible labor standards: Insights from the Chinese toy industry. *Journal of Business Ethics*, 143, 789–805.

Lindenberg, S. 2005. Coleman, James. In G. Ritzer (ed.), *Encyclopedia of Social Theory*. Thousand Oaks, CA: Sage, 111–15.

Locke, R. M. 2002. The promise and perils of globalization: The case of Nike. Cambridge, MA: MIT Working Paper IPC-02-007.
    2003. The promise and perils of globalization: The case of Nike, Inc. In T. A. Kochan & R. Schmalensee (eds.), *Management: Inventing and Delivering Its Future*. Cambridge, MA: MIT Press, 39–70.
    2013. *The Promise and Limits of Private Power: Promoting Labor Standards in a Global Economy*. Cambridge: Cambridge University Press.

Locke, R., Amengual, M., & Mangla, A. 2009. Virtue out of necessity? Compliance, commitment, and the improvement of labour conditions in global supply chains. *Politics & Society*, 37(3), 319–51.

Locke, R., Qin, F., & Brause, A. 2006. Does monitoring improve labor standards? Lessons from Nike. Sloan School of Management. MIT, Working Paper No. 24, July.

Locke, R. M., & Romis, M. 2007. Improving working conditions in the global supply chain. *MIT Sloan Management Review*, 48(2), 54–62.

Lu, X., & Enderle, G. (eds.). 2006/2013. *Developing Business Ethics in China*. New York: Palgrave.

Luetge, C. (ed.). 2013. *Handbook of the Philosophical Foundations of Business Ethics*. Dordrecht: Springer.

Luetge, C., & Uhl, M. 2015. Innovative methodology: An experimental approach to ethics. In Enderle & Murphy 2015, 72–92.

Lustgarten, A., & Knutson, R. 2010. Years of internal BP probes warned that neglect could lead to accidents. *Propublica*. www.propublica.org/article/years-of-internal-bp-probes-warned-that-neglect-could-lead-to-accidents, accessed on October 27, 2019.

Lüthi, A. P. 1980. *Messung wirtschaftlicher Ungleichheit*. Berlin: Springer.

Maak, T., & Pless, N. M. (eds.). 2006. *Responsible Leadership*. London: Routledge.

Mandeville, B. 1714. *The Fable of the Bees: Or, Private Vices, Publick Benefits. Containing, Several Discourses, to Demonstrate, That Human Frailties, during the Degeneration of Mankind, May Be Turn'd to the Advantage of the Civil Society, and Made to Supply the Place of Moral Virtues*. London: printed for J. Roberts.

Mansbridge, J. J. (ed.). 1990. *Beyond Self-Interest*. Chicago: University of Chicago Press.

Marques, J., Dhiman, S., & King, R. 2007. *Spirituality in the Workplace: What It Is, Why It Matters, How It Make to Work for You*. Fawnskin, CA: Personhood Press.

Marshall, R., & Lee, L. E. 2016. Are CEOs paid for performance? Evaluating the effectiveness of equity incentives. MSCI ESG Research Inc. July, 1–23.

Martin, J. 2012. *The Jesuit Guide to (Almost) Everything: A Spirituality for Real Life*. New York: HarperOne.

Martin. R. L. 2011. *Fixing the Game: Bubbles, Crashes, and What Capitalism Can Learn from the NFL*. Cambridge, MA: Harvard Business Press.

Matsushita, K. 1984. *Not for Bread Alone: A Business Ethics, a Management Ethic*. Kyoto: PHP Institute.

Mazur, J. 2000. Labor's new internationalism. *Foreign Affairs*, 79(1), 79–93.

McMahon, T. 1985. The contribution of religious traditions to business ethics. *Journal of Business Ethics*, 4, 341–49.

Melden, A. I. 1977. *Rights and Persons*. Oxford: Basil Blackwell.

Mendes-Flohr, P. 2012. IX. Judaism. In Betz et al. 2012, 229–30.

Mezue, B. C., Christensen, C. M., & van Bever, D. 2015. The power of market creation. *Foreign Affairs*, 94(1), 69–76.

Miller, S. 2006. Collective moral responsibility: An individualistic approach. *Midwest Studies in Philosophy*, XXX, 176–93.

Mishan, E. J. 1988. *Cost-Benefit Analysis*. Fourth edition. New York: Praeger.

Miska, C., & Mendenhall, M. E. 2018. Responsible leadership: A mapping of extant research and future directions. *Journal of Business Ethics*, 148, 117–34.

Mitnick, B. M. (guest ed.). 2019. Special issue: Focusing on fields. *Business & Society*, 58(7), 1307–478.

Monks, R. A. G., & Minow, N. 2008. *Corporate Governance*. Chichester: Wiley. Previous editions 1995, 2001, 2004.

Moore, G. 1999. Corporate moral agency: Review and implications. *Journal of Business Ethics*, 21, 329–34.

Moriarty, J. 2005. Do CEOs get paid too much? *Business Ethics Quarterly*, 15(2), 257–81.

  2009. How much compensation can CEOs permissibly accept? *Business Ethics Quarterly*, 19(2), 235–50.

Morris, D., Bogner, L., Daubigeon, L., O'Brien, C. M., & Wronzicki, E. 2018. *National Action Plans on Business and Human Rights: An Analysis of Plans from 2013–2018*. Copenhagen: The Danish Institute for Human Rights.

Morsink, J. 2009. *Inherent Human Rights: Philosophical Roots of the Universal Declaration*. Philadelphia: University of Pennsylvania Press.

Mullainathan, S., & Thaler, R. 2000. *Behavioral Economics*. Cambridge, MA: National Bureau of Economic Research.

Multinational enterprises and human rights (MNEs and HR). 1998. A report by the Dutch Sections of Amnesty International and Pax Christi International. Utrecht: Pax Christi Netherlands. November.

Murphy, P. E., & Enderle, G. 2003. Medtronic: A "best" business practice in the U.S. Manuscript. Mendoza College of Business, University of Notre Dame.

Murphy, P. E., & Murphy, C. E. 2018. Sustainable living: Unilever. In O'Higgins & Zsolnai 2018, 263–86.

Murphy, P. E., & Sherry, J. F. (eds.). 2013. *Marketing and the Common Good. Essays from Notre Dame on Societal Impact*. Abingdon, Oxon: Routledge.

Musgrave, R. A. 1957. A multiple theory of budget determination. *Finanz Archiv*, New Series 17(3), 333–43.

  1958. *The Theory of Public Finance*. New York: McGraw-Hill.

  1969. Cost-benefit analysis and the theory of public finance. *Journal of Economic Literature*, 7(3), 797–806.

  1987. Merit goods. In Eatwell et al. 1987, volume 3, 452–53.

Myrdal, G. 1968. *Asian Drama: An Inquiry into the Poverty of Nations*. New York: Pantheon.

Nagel, T. 2002. Personal rights and public space. In *Concealment and Exposure & Other Essays*. Oxford: Oxford University Press.

Nassauer, S. 2018. Costco to boost its minimum wage to $14 an hour. www
.marketwatch.com/story/costco-to-boost-its-minimum-wage-to-14-an-
hour-2018-05-31, accessed on October 27, 2019.

Neal, J. (ed.). 2013. *Handbook of Faith and Spirituality in the Workplace.
Emerging Research and Practice.* New York: Springer.

Nguyen, T. 2020. Vietnam ratifies EU free trade agreement. What's next?,
The Diplomat, 22 June.

Novak, M. 1993. *The Catholic Ethic and the Spirit of Capitalism.* New
York: Free Press.

North, D. C. 1972. Economic history. In D. L. Sills (ed.),
International Encyclopedia of Social Sciences. New York: Macmillan,
468–74.

Nove, A. 1987. Socialism. In Eatwell et al. 1987, volume 3, 398–407.

Nussbaum, M. C. 2011. *Creating Capabilities: The Human
Development Approach.* Cambridge, MA: Belknap Press of Harvard
University Press.

Nussbaum, M. C., & Sen, A. (eds.). 1993a. *The Quality of Life.* Oxford:
Clarendon Press.

Nussbaum, M. C., & Sen, A. 1993b. Capability and well-being. In
Nussbaum & Sen 1993a, 30–53.

Observatoire de la Finance. 2011. *Manifesto for Finance That Serves the
Common Good.* www.obsfin.ch/founding-texts/manifesto-for-finance-
that-serves-the-common-good.

O'Higgins, E., & Zsolnai, L. (eds.). 2018. *Progressive Business Models:
Creating Sustainable and Pro-Social Enterprise.* New York:
Futurearth. Palgrave Macmillan.

Ohmae, K. 1995. *The End of the Nation State: The Rise of Regional
Economies.* How new engines of prosperity are reshaping global
markets. New York: Free Press.

Oka, C. 2018. Brands as labour rights advocates? Potential and limits of
brand advocacy in global supply chains. *Business Ethics: A European
Review*, 27, 95–107.

On the Media. 2018. A plague of suspicion. December 14. www
.wnycstudios.org/story/on-the-media-2018-12-14

Opio, P. J. 2015. "System D" – Creativity, innovation, and ethics in an
African context: Bridging the gap between the informal and formal
economies. In Enderle & Murphy 2015. 281–306.

Organization for Economic Co-Operation and Development (OECD). 1999.
Principles of Corporate Governance. Paris: OECD.

  2001. *The Well-Being of Nations: The Role of Human and Social Capital.*
  Paris: OECD.

  2004. *OECD Principles of Corporate Governance.* Paris: OECD.

Organisation for Economic Co-Operation and Development (OECD/ Eurostat). 2005. *Oslo Manuel: Guidelines for Collecting and Interpreting Innovation Data*. Paris: OECD.

2012. *Innovation for Development*. A discussion of the issues and an overview of work of the OECD Directorate for Science, Technology and Industry. May. Paris: OECD.

2013a. *How's Life? 2013 Measuring Well-Being*. Paris: OECD.

2013b. *Innovation and Inclusive Development*. Conference discussion report. Cape Town, South Africa, 21 November 2012. February 2013 Revision. Paris: OECD.

2015a. *In It Together: Why Less Inequality Benefits All*. Paris: OECD.

2015b. *Income Inequality: The Gap between the Rich and the Poor*. Paris: OECD.

Orhangazi, Ö. 2008. *Financialization and the US Economy*. Cheltenham: Edward Elgar.

Orts, E. W., & Smith, N. C. (eds.). 2017. *The Moral Responsibility of Firms*. Oxford: Oxford University Press.

Ostrom, E. 1990. *Governing the Commons: The Evolution of Institutions for Collective Action* (29th printing 2011). Cambridge: Cambridge University Press.

2000. Social capital: A fad or a fundamental concept? In Dasgupta & Serageldin 2000, 172–214.

2005. *Understanding Institutional Diversity*. Princeton, NJ: Princeton University Press.

2009. What is social capital? In Bartkus et al. 2009, 17–38.

Ostrom, E., Parks, R. B., & Whitaker, G. P. 1977. Policing metropolitan America. Washington: National Science Foundation. Research Applied to National Needs Program.

Ostrom, V., & Ostrom, E. 1977. Public goods and public choices. In Savas 1977.

Pagel, M., & Mace, R. 2004. The cultural wealth of nations. *Nature*, 428, 275–78. March 18.

Paine, L. S. 2003. *Value Shift: Why Companies Must Merge Social and Financial Imperatives to Achieve Superior Performance*. New York: McGraw-Hill.

Painter-Morland, M., & Ten Bos, R. (eds.). 2011. *Business Ethics and Continental Philosophy*. Cambridge: Cambridge University Press.

Palley, T. I. 2007. Financialization: What it is and why it matters. Political Economy Research Institute Working Paper Series, Number 153, November.

Parfit, D. 1984. *Reasons and Persons*. Oxford: Clarendon.

Pauchant, T. C. (ed.). 2002. *Ethics and Spirituality at Work: Hopes and Pitfalls of the Search for Meaning in Organizations.* Westport, CT: Quorum Books.

Phillips, K. 2002. *Wealth and Democracy: A Political History of the American Rich.* New York: Broadway.

2009. *Bad Money: Reckless Finance, Failed Politics, and the Global Crisis of American Capitalism.* New York: Penguin.

Phipps, K., & Benefiel, M. 2013. Spirituality and religion: Seeking a juxtaposition that supports research in the field of faith and spirituality at work. In Neal 2013, 33–43.

Piketty, T. 2014. *Capital in the Twenty-First Century.* Cambridge, MA: Harvard University Press.

2015. *The Economics of Inequality.* Cambridge, MA: Belknap Press of Harvard University Press.

Pogge, T. W. M. 2002. *World Poverty and Human Rights: Cosmopolitan Responsibilities and Reforms.* Cambridge: Polity Press.

Pogge, T. (ed.). 2007. *Freedom from Poverty as a Human Right: Who Owns What to the Very Poor?* Oxford: Oxford University Press.

Powell, B., & Zwolinski, M. 2012. The ethical and economic case against sweatshop labor: A critical assessment. *Journal of Business Ethics*, 107, 449–72.

Pozen, R. C., & Kothari, S. P. 2017. Decoding CEO pay. *Harvard Business Review*, July-August, 78–84.

Preiss, J. 2014. Global labor justice and the limits of economic analysis. *Business Ethics Quarterly*, 24, 55–83.

Principles for Responsible Investing (PRI). 2018. www.unpri.org.

Prizzia, R. 2007. Sustainable development in an international perspective. In K. V. Thai, D. Rahm, & J. D. Coggburn (eds.), *Handbook of Globalization and the Environment.* Boca Raton, FL: CRC Press, 19–42.

Putnam, R. 1983. *Social Capital: Measurement and Consequences.* Paris: OECD.

Putnam, R. D. 1993. *Making Democracy Work: Civic Traditions in Modern Italy.* With R. Leonardi & R. Y. Nanetti. Princeton, NJ: Princeton University Press.

1995. Bowling alone: America's declining social capital. *Journal of Democracy* 6(1), 65–78.

2000. *Bowling Alone: The Collapse and Revival of American Community.* New York: Simon & Schuster.

Putnam, R. D. (ed.). 2002. *Democracy in Flux: The Evolution of Social Capital in Contemporary Society.* New York: Oxford University Press.

Quinn, F. J. 2017. Supply chain management: Past, present and future: On our 20th anniversary, SCMR asked founding editor Frank Quinn and four industry experts to weigh in on the future of supply chain management. *Supply Chain Management Review*, March–April, 10–12.

Radi, Y. (ed.). 2018. *Research Handbook on Human Rights and Investment*. Cheltenham: Edgar Elgar.

Radin, T. J. 2018. Globalization. In Kolb 2018, 1620–30.

Rand, A. 1957/2005. *Atlas Shrugged* (Original edition 1957, New York: Random House). Centennial edition. New York: Plume.

1964. *The Virtue of Selfishness: A New Concept of Egoism*. With additional articles by Nathaniel Branden. New York: Penguin.

Randels, G. D. 2018a. Other-regardingness. In Kolb 2018, 2568–70.

2018b. Self-regardingness. In Kolb 2018, 3044–45.

Rat der EKD. 2008. *Unternehmerisches Handeln in evangelischer Perspektive*. Gütersloh: Gütersloher Verlaghaus.

Rawls, J. 1971. *A Theory of Justice*. Cambridge, MA: Belknapp Press of Harvard University Press.

1993. *Political Liberalism*. Second edition 1996. New York: Columbia University Press.

Regis, Jr., E. (ed.). 1984. *Gewirth's Ethical Rationalism: Critical Essays with a Reply by Alan Gewirth*. Chicago: University of Chicago Press.

Rego, A., Pina e Cunha, M., & Polónia, D. 2017. Corporate sustainability: A view from the top. *Journal of Business Ethics*, 143, 133–57.

Reich, B. R. 2007. *Supercapitalism: The Transformation of Business, Democracy, and Everyday Life*. New York: Knopf.

Report on the Measurement of Economic Performance and Social Progress (Report). 2009. Under the leadership of J. E. Stiglitz, A. Sen, J.-P. Fitoussi. www.stiglitz-sen-fitoussi.fr.

Rich, A. 2006. *Business and Economic Ethics: The Ethics of Economic Systems*. Leuven: Peeters.

Romer, P. 1990. Endogenous technological change. *Journal of Political Economy*, 98(5), S71–102.

Rönnegard, D. 2015. *The Fallacy of Corporate Moral Agency*. Dordrecht: Springer.

Rosen, S. 1987. Human capital. In Eatwell et al. 1987, volume 2, 681–90.

Rossouw, D., & C. Stückelberger, C. (eds.). 2011. Global survey of business ethics in training, teaching and research (Special issue). *Journal of Business Ethics*, 104(1), Supplement (April).

Rossouw, G. J. 2006. Business ethics and corporate governance in the King II report: Light from the top of a dark continent? In Lu & Enderle 2006, 258–68.

2009a. The ethics of corporate governance: Crucial distinctions for global comparisons. *International Journal of Law and Management*, 51(1), 5–9.

2009b. The ethics of corporate governance: Global convergence or divergence? *International Journal of Law and Management*, 51(1), 43–51.

2009c. The ethics of corporate governance in global perspective. In Kalkundrikar et al. 2009, 3–19.

Rossouw, G. J., & Sison A. J. G. (eds.). 2006. *Global Perspectives on Ethics of Corporate Governance*. New York: Palgrave Macmillan.

Roy, A. 2018a. Supply-side economics. In Kolb 2018, 3304–05.

2018b. Worker Rights Consortium (WRC). In Kolb 2018, 3662–64.

Ruggie, J. G. 2013. *Just Business: Multinational Corporations and Human Rights*. New York: Norton.

Ryan, J. A., 1912. *A Living Wage: Its Ethical and Economic Aspects*. First published in 1906.

Sachs, J. D. 2011. *The Prize of Civilization: Reawakening American Virtue and Prosperity*. New York: Random House.

Sandler, T. 1999. Intergenerational public goods: Strategies, efficiency and institutions. In Kaul et al. 1999a, 20–50.

Samuelson, P. A. 1954. The pure theory of public expenditure. *Review of Economics and Statistics*, 36, 387–89.

1955. Diagrammic exposition of a theory of public expenditure. *Review of Economics and Statistics*, 37, 350–56.

Savas, E. S. (ed.). 1977. *Alternatives for Delivering Public Services: Toward Improved Performance*. Boulder, CO: Westview Press.

Schein, D. D. 2018. Fair Labor Association (FLA). In Kolb 2018, 1333–36.

Scherer, A. G., & Palazzo, G. (eds.). 2008. *Handbook of Research on Global Corporate Citizenship*. Cheltenham: Edward Elgar.

Scherer, A. G., & Palazzo, G. 2011. The new political role of business in a globalized world: A review of a new perspective on CSR and its implications for the firm, governance, and democracy. *Journal of Management Studies*, 48(4), 899–931.

Schmidheiny, S., & Zorraquín, F. 1996. *Financing Change: The Financial Community, Eco-Efficiency, and Sustainable Development*. With the World Business Council for Sustainable Development. Cambridge, MA: MIT Press.

Schrempf-Stirling, J., Palazzo, G., & Phillips, R. A. 2016. Historic corporate social responsibility. *Academy of Management Review*, 41(4), 700–19.

Schulz, W. 1972. *Philosophie der veränderten Welt*. Pfullingen: Neske.

1989. *Grundprobleme der Ethik*. Pfullingen: Neske.

Searcy, C., & Ahi, P. 2014. Reporting supply chain sustainability: A myriad of metrics. *The Guardian*, September 26.

Second Vatican Council. 1965. *Gaudium et Spes*: Pastoral constitution on the church in the modern world. www.vatican.va/archive/hist_councils/ii_vatican_council/documents/vat-ii_const_19651207_gaudium-et-spes_en.html

SEEA. 2003. United Nations, European Commission, International Monetary Fund, Organisation for Economic Co-operation and Development, World Bank (2003): Integrated Environmental and Economic Accounting 2003, Studies in Methods, Handbook on National Accounting, Series F, No. 61, Rev. 1, (ST/ESA/STAT/SER.F/61/Rev.1).

Sen, A. 1981. *Poverty and Famines: An Essay on Entitlement and Deprivation*. Oxford: Clarendon Press.

1982. *Choice, Welfare and Measurement*. Oxford: Blackwell.

1987. *On Ethics and Economics*. New York: Blackwell.

1993. Does business ethics make economic sense? *Business Ethics Quarterly*, 3(1), 47–54.

1996. The concept of wealth. In R. H. Myers (ed.), *The Wealth of Nations in the Twentieth Century*. Stanford: Hoover Institution Press.

1997. Economics, business principles, and moral sentiments. *Business Ethics Quarterly*, 7(3), 5–15. Also in Enderle 1999, 15–29.

1999. *Development as Freedom*. New York: Knopf.

2000. The discipline of cost-benefit analysis. *Journal of Legal Studies*, 29, 931–52.

2002. *Rationality and Freedom*. Cambridge, MA: Belknap Press of Harvard University Press.

2004. Elements of a theory of human rights. *Philosophy & Public Affairs*, 32(4), 315–56.

2005. Human rights and capabilities. *Journal of Human Development*, 6 (2), 151–66.

2008. The economics of happiness and capability. In Bruni et al. 2008, 16–27.

2009. *The Idea of Justice*. Cambridge, MA: Belknap Press of Harvard University Press.

2017a. *Collective Choice and Social Welfare: An Expanded Edition*. Cambridge, MA: Harvard University Press.

2017b. The idea of rights. In Sen 2017a, 420–46.

Shehadeh, R. 2013. A world of false frontiers. *Financial Times*, July 27/28.

Shleifer, A., & Vishny, R. W. 1997. A survey of corporate governance. *The Journal of Finance* LII, 2(6), 737–83.

Shue, H. 1996. *Basic Rights: Subsistence, Affluence, and U.S. Foreign Policy*. Second edition. Princeton, NJ: Princeton University Press. First edition 1980.

Sison, A. G. 2008. *Corporate Governance and Ethics: An Aristotelian Perspective*. Cheltenham: Edgar Elgar.

Smith, A. 1759/1976. *The Theory of Moral Sentiments*. Edited by R. H. Campbell and A. L. Macfie. Oxford: Clarendon Press.

1776/1976. *An Inquiry into the Nature and Cause of the Wealth of Nations.* General editors: R. H. Campbell and A. S. Skinner; Textual editor: W. B. Todd. Volume 1 and 2. Oxford: Clarendon Press.

Smith, L. C., Smith, L. M., & Ashcroft, P. A. 2011. Analysis of environmental and economic damages from British Petroleum's Deepwater Horizon oil spill. *Albany Law Review*, 74(1), 563–85.

Social Philosophy and Policy. 1999. Special issue on responsibility. 16(2), 1–323.

2019. Special issue on responsibility. 36(1), 1–248.

Sorkin, A. R. 2009. *Too Big to Fail: The Inside Story of How Wall Street and Washington Fought to Save the Financial System from Crisis – and Themselves.* New York: Viking.

Stabile, D. R. 1997. Adam Smith and the natural wage: Sympathy, subsistence and social distance. *Review of Social Economy*, 55(3), 292–311.

2008. *The Living Wage: Lessons from the History of Economic Thought.* Cheltenham: Edward Elgar.

Steinmann, H. 2006. Corporate ethics in Germany. In Lu & Enderle. 2006/ 2013, 247–57.

Steinmann, H., & Löhr, A. (Hg.). 1990. *Unternehmensethik.* Zweite, überarbeitete und erweiterte Auflage. Stuttgart: C. E. Poeschel Verlag.

Stiglitz, J. E. 2002. *Globalization and Its Discontent.* New York: Norton.

2006. *Making Globalization Work.* New York: Norton.

2012. *The Price of Inequality.* New York: Norton.

2015. *The Great Divide: Unequal Societies and What We Can Do about Them.* New York: W.W. Norton.

Stiglitz, J., Sen, A., and Fitoussi, J. P. 2009. *Report of the Commission on the Measurement of Economic Performance and Social Progress.* www .stiglitz-sen-fitoussi.fr/documents/ rapport_anglais.pdf.

Stüttgen, M. 2019. *Ethical Investing.* Opportunities and Challenges of Morally Justified Investments. Berlin: Peter Lang. Original version in German in 2017.

Summers, L. 2016. A badly designed stimulus will only hurt the working class. *Financial Times*, November 14.

Sustainable Development Goals (SDGs). 2015. www.undp.org/content/ undp/en/home/sustainable-development-goals.html

Svendsen, G. T., & Haase Svendsen, G. L. (eds.). 2012. *Handbook of Social Capital.* Cheltenham: Edgar Elgar.

Syed, J., Klarsfeld, A., Ngunjiri, F. W., & Härtel, C. E. J. (eds.). 2018. *Religious Diversity in the Workplace.* Cambridge: Cambridge University Press.

Tasioulas, J. 2007. The moral reality of human rights. In Pogge 2007, 75–101.

2010. Taking rights out of human rights. *Ethics*, 120(4), 647–78.

2018. Philosophizing the real world of human rights: A reply to Samuel Moyn. In Etinson 2018, 89–102.

Tavis, L. A., & Tavis, T. M. 2009. *Values-Based Multinational Management: Achieving Enterprise Sustainability through a Human Rights Strategy*. Notre Dame, IN: University of Notre Dame Press.

Thaler, R. 2009. *Improving Decisions about Health, Wealth, and Happiness*. New York: Penguin.

The B Team. 2018. The business case for protecting civic rights. www.bteam .org/announcements/the-business-case-for-protecting-civic-rights.

The Economist. 2005. *The good company: A sceptical look at corporate social responsibility*, January 22–28.

2008. *Just good business: A special report on corporate social responsibility*, January 19.

The Natural Capital Declaration. 2012. www.unepfi.org/fileadmin/docu ments/ncd_booklet.pdf.

Thomas, S. M. 2010. A globalized god: Religions' growing influence in international politics. *Foreign Affairs*, 89(6), 93–101.

Thomas, R. S., & Hill, J. G. (eds.). 2012. *Research Handbook on Executive Pay*. Cheltenham: Edward Elgar.

Topf & Sons. 2011. Builders of the Auschwitz ovens: A historical museum of the city of Erfurt. www.topfundsoehne.de/ts/en/index.html.

Tsui, A. S., Enderle, G., & Jiang, K. 2018. Income inequality in the United States: Reflections on the role of corporations. *Academy of Management Review*, 43(1), 156–68.

2019. On addressing the puzzle of extreme income inequality. A response to Agarwal and Holmes. *Academy of Management Review*, 44(2), 1–4.

Tsui, A. S., Jiang, K., and Enderle, G. 2016. Income inequality in organizations. Paper presented at the "A Global Compact for Sustainable Development Conference," University of Notre Dame, Indiana, April 4, 2016.

Ulrich, P. 2008. *Integrative Economic Ethics: Foundations of a Civilized Market Economy*. Cambridge: Cambridge University Press.

UNECE, OECD and Eurostat. 2008. *Measuring Sustainable Development*. Working Group on Statistics for Sustainable Development. New York: United Nations.

United Nations (UN). 1948. *Universal Declaration of Human Rights*. www .ohchr.org/EN/ UDHR/Pages/Introduction.aspx.

2003. *(Draft Norms) Economic, Social and Cultural Rights. Norms on the Responsibilities of Transnational Corporations and Other Business Enterprises with Regard to Human Rights*. Commission on Human Rights, Sub-Commission on the Promotion and Protection of Human Rights, Fifty-fifth Session. E/CN.4/Sub.2/2003/12/Rev.2.

2005. Millennium ecosystem assessment. www.millenniumassessment .org/en.

2007. *Business and Human Rights: Mapping International Standards of Responsibility and Accountability for Corporate Acts.* Report of the Special Representative of the Secretary-General on the issue of human rights and transnational corporations and other business enterprises, John Ruggie. Human Rights Council. Fourth Session, A/HRC/4/35.

2008a. *Promotion of All Human Rights, Civil, Political, Economic, Social and Cultural Rights, Including the Right to Development. Protect, Respect and Remedy: A Framework for Business and Human Tights.* Report of the Special Representative of the Secretary-General on the issue of human rights and transnational corporations and other business enterprises, John Ruggie. Human Rights Council. Eighth Session, A/ HRC/8/5.

2008b. *Promotion of All Human Rights, Civil, Political, Economic, Social and Cultural Rights, Including the Right to Development: Clarifying the Concepts of "Sphere of Influence" and "Complicity."* Report of the Special Representative of the Secretary-General on the issue of human rights and transnational corporations and other business enterprises, John Ruggie. Human Rights Council. Eighth Session, A/ HRC/8/16.

2009. *Promotion of All Human Rights, Civil, Political, Economic, Social and Cultural Rights, Including the Right to Development. Business and Human Rights: Towards Operationalizing the "Protect, Respect and Remedy" Framework.* Report of the Special Representative of the Secretary-General on the issue of human rights and transnational corporations and other business enterprises. Human Rights Council. Eleventh Session, A/HRC/11/13.

2010. *Promotion and Protection of All Human Rights, Civil, Political, Economic, Social and Cultural Rights, Including the Right to Development. Business and Human Rights: Further Steps toward the Operationalization of the "Protect, Respect and Remedy" Framework.* Report of the Special Representative of the Secretary-General on the issue of human rights and transnational corporations and other business enterprises. Human Rights Council. Fourteenth Session, A/HRC/14/27.

United Nations Human Rights Office of the High Commissioner (UN). 2011. *Guiding Principles on Business and Human Rights: Implementing the United Nations "Protect, Respect and Remedy" Framework.* New York and Geneva: United Nations.

2012a. *The Corporate Responsibility to Respect Human Rights: An Interpretive Guide.* New York and Geneva: United Nations.

2012b. *The Future We Want.* Outcome document of the United Nations Conference on Sustainable Development. Rio de Janeiro, Brazil, June 20–22, 2012. https://sustainabledevelopment.un.org/content/documents/733FutureWeWant.pdf.

2015. *Transforming Our World: The 2030 Agenda for Sustainable Development.* www.un.org/ga/search/view_doc.asp?symbol=A/RES/70/1& Lang=E.

United Nations Development Programme (UNDP). 1990. *Human Development Report 1990.*

2010. *Human Development Report 2010. 20th Anniversary Edition: The Real Wealth of Nations: Pathways to Human Development.* New York: Palgrave Macmillan.

United Nations, European Commission, International Monetary Fund, Organisation for Economic, Co-operation and Development, and World Bank (UN et al.). 2003. *Handbook of National Accounting: Integrated Environmental and Economic Accounting 2003.* New York: United Nations. unstats.un.org/unsd/envaccounting/seea.asp.

United Nations Global Compact (UNGC). 2000. www.unglobalcompact .org

Universal Declaration of Human Rights (UDHR). 1948. www.un.org/en/universal-declaration-human-rights/

Velasquez, M. G. 2003. Debunking corporate moral responsibility. *Business Ethics Quarterly*, 13, 531–62.

2006. *Business Ethics. Concepts and Cases.* Sixth edition. Upper Saddle River, NJ: Pearson Education.

Violini, L., & Rangone, G. 2020. Human dignity, development policies and the EU's human rights conditionality. In Carozza, P. G., & Sedmak, C. (eds.), *The Practice of Human Development and Dignity.* Notre Dame: University of Notre Dame Press.

Virt, G. (ed.). 2002. *Der Globalisierungsprozess. Facetten einer Dynamik aus ethischer und theologischer Perspective.* Freiburg i. Ue.: Universitätsverlag.

Visser, W., Matten, D., Pohl, M., & Tolhurst, N. (eds.). 2010. *The A to Z of Corporate Social Responsibility.* John Wiley & Sons.

Vocation of the Business Leader: A Reflection (Vocation). 2018. Fifth edition. Published by Dicastery for Promoting Integral Human Development, Vatican City. Co-published by John A. Ryan Institute for Catholic Social Thought of the Center for Catholic Studies, University of St. Thomas, Minnesota, USA. First edition 2012.

Vu, K., & Nguyen P. 2019. Vietnam, EU sign landmark free trade deal. www.reuters.com/article/us-eu-vietnam-trade/vietnam-eu-sign-land mark-free-tradedeal-idUSKCN1TV0CJ, accessed on October 27, 2019.

Waldman, D. A., & Galvin, B. M. 2008. Alternative perspectives of responsible leadership. *Organizational Dynamics*, 37(4), 327–41.

Waltman, J. L. 2004. *The Case for the Living Wage*. New York: Algora.

Ward, A. 2018. BP's final bill for Gulf of Mexico spill tops $65bn after latest $1.7bn charge. *Financial Times*, January 17.

Warsh, D. 2006. *Knowledge and the Wealth of Nations. A Story of Economic Discovery*. New York: Norton.

Webb, S., & Webb, B. 1897. *Industrial Democracy*. London: Printed by the authors especially for the Amalgamated Society of Engineers.

Weber, M. 1987. Politics as a vocation. In *Max Weber. Selections in Translation*. Edited by W. G. Runciman; translated by E. Matthews. Cambridge: Cambridge University Press, 212–25.

Wegner, J., & Pascual, U. 2011. Cost-benefit analysis in the context of ecosystem services for human well-being: A multidisciplinary critique. *Global Environmental Change*, 21, 492–504.

Weischedel, W. 1992. *Das Wesen der Verantwortung*. Third edition. Frankfurt am Main: Klostermann. First edition 1933.

Wells Fargo. 2017. Wells Fargo sales practices investigation report. www .wellsfargomedia.com/assets/pdf/about/investor-relations/presentations/ 2017/board-report.pdf?%3Ca%20href=.

Werhane, P. H. 1985. *Persons, Rights, and Corporations*. Englewood Cliffs, NJ: Prentice-Hall.

   2016. Corporate moral agency and the responsibility to respect human rights in the UN guiding principles: Do corporations have moral rights? *Business and Human Rights Journal*, 1(1), 5–20.

Werhane, P. H., & Bevan, D. 2015. Capitalism in the twenty-first century: Tracing Adam Smith in emergent variations of free enterprise. In Enderle & Murphy 2015, 239–60.

Werhane, P. H., & Freeman, R. E. (eds.). 2005. *The Blackwell Encyclopedia of Management. Second Edition: Business Ethics*. Malden, MA: Blackwell.

Werner, A., & Lim, M. 2016. The ethics of the living wage: A review and research agenda. *Journal of Business Ethics*, 137, 433–47.

Wettstein, F. 2009. *Multinational Corporations and Global Justice*. Stanford: Stanford University Press.

   2012. CSR and the debate on business and human rights: Bridging the great divide. *Business Ethics Quarterly*, 22, 739–70.

Whelan, D. J. 2010. *Indivisible Human Rights: A History*. Philadelphia, PA: University of Pennsylvania Press.

Whelan, G., & Muthuri, J. 2017. Chinese state-owned enterprises and human rights: The importance of national and intra-organizational pressures. *Business & Society*, 56(5), 738–81.

Whipp, L., & Fleming, S. 2016. Push for higher wages squeezes US profits. *Financial Times*, July 2/3, 12.

Wicks, A. C., Freeman, R. E., Werhane, P. H., & Martin, K. E. 2010. *Business Ethics: A Managerial Approach*. Upper Saddle River, NJ: Prentice Hall.

Wiedenhöfer, K. 2013. Conflict zones. *Financial Times*, January 4.

Wilkinson, R., & Pickett, K. 2009. *The Spirit Level: Why Equality Is Better for Everyone*. London: Penguin.

Williams, O. F. (ed.). 2008. *Peace through Commerce: Responsible Corporate Citizenship and the Ideals of the United Nations Global Compact*. Notre Dame: University of Notre Dame.

Williamson, O. E. 1975. *Markets and Hierarchies, Analysis Antitrust Implications*. New York: Free Press.

Windsor, D. 2018a. Public goods. In Kolb 2018, 3209–81.

    2018b. Cost-benefit analysis. In Kolb 2018, 773–78.

Witt, A. 2018. Socialism. In Kolb 2018, 3187–91.

Wolf, M. 2014. *The Shifts and the Shocks: What We've Learned – and Still Have to Learn – From the Financial Crisis*. New York: Penguin Press.

Wood, D. J., & Logsdon, J. M. 2002. Business citizenship: From individuals to organizations. In *Ethics and Entrepreneurship*. The Ruffin Series No. 3. A publication of the Society for Business Ethics. Charlottesville: Society for Business Ethics, 59–94.

Worker Participation Committee (WPC). 2015. Review of the freedom of association policy. University of Notre Dame, May.

    2018. Freedom of association policy review. Final report and recommendations by the Worker Participation Committee. University of Notre Dame, September.

Worker Participation Committee: Criteria Subcommittee (CS). 2017. Minutes from May 6, 2016 to August 9, 2017. Available from G. Enderle.

World Bank. 1993. *The East Asian Miracle: Economic Growth and Public Policy*. New York: Oxford University Press.

    2006. *Where Is the Wealth of Nations? Measuring Capital for the 21st Century*. Washington, DC: World Bank.

    2008. *The Growth Report: Strategies for Sustained Growth and Inclusive Development*. Washington, DC: World Bank.

    2011. *The Changing Wealth of Nations? Measuring Sustainable Development in the New Millennium*. Washington, DC: World Bank.

    2017. *Riding the Wave: An East Asian Miracle for the 21st Century*. Washington, DC: World Bank.

    2018. World Development Indicators. http://databank.worldbank.org/data/reports.aspx?source=world-development-indicators

World Bank and Nordic Trust Fund. 2013. *Human Rights Impact Assessment: A Review of the Literature, Differences with Other Forms of Assessments and Relevance for Development.* Washington, DC: World Bank and Nordic Trust Fund.

World Business Council for Sustainable Development (WBCSD). 2016. Action2020 plan. http://action2020.org/business-solutions/operational ize-the-un-guiding-principles-on-business-and-human

World Commission on Environment and Development (WCED). 1987. *Our Common Future.* New York: Oxford University Press, New York.

World Economic Forum. 2015. *Global Risks Report.* Tenth edition. www3 .weforum.org/docs/WEF_Global_Risks_2015_Report15.pdf.

Yawar, S. A., & Seuring, S. 2017. Management of social issues in supply chains: A literature review exploring social issues, actions and performance outcomes. *Journal of Business Ethics*, 141, 621–43.

Yunus, M. 1999. *Banker to the Poor and the Battle against World Poverty.* New York: Public Affairs.

2004. The micro-credit movement: Experiences and perspectives. In Arruda & Enderle 2004, 15–33.

2007. *Creating a World without Poverty: Social Business and the Future of Capitalism.* With K. Weber. New York: Public Affairs.

2018. *A World of Three Zeros: The New Economics of Zero Poverty, Zero Unemployment, and Zero Net Carbon Emissions.* With Karl Weber. New York: Public Affairs.

Zingales, L. 2015. Presidential address: Does finance benefit society? *The Journal of Finance*, 70(4), 1327–63.

Zsolnai, L. (ed.). 2004. *Spirituality and Ethics in Management.* Dordrecht: Kluwer.

Zsolnai, L. 2015. *Post-materialist Business: Spiritual Value-Orientation in Renewing Management.* New York: Palgrave Macmillan.

Zwolinski, M. 2007. Sweatshops, choice, and exploitation. *Business Ethics Quarterly*, 17, 689–727.

Index of Names

Index of Subjects

Printed in the United States
by Baker & Taylor Publisher Services